THE DOME BUILDER'S HANDBOOK

Carey Smoot

·Edited by John Prenis·

RUNNING PRESS

Philadelphia, Pennsylvania

Dedications

This Book Is Dedicated

To Plato, Archimedes, Kepler, Poinsot, and all the other mathematicians who have investigated the fascinating properties of regular and semi-regular solids.

To Buckminster Fuller, who was working out his first ideas of the geodesic dome about the time I was born.

To the unknown kid who brough a soda straw model of a stellated dode-cahedron into my second grade class, awakening in me a lasting fasci-nation for geometric forms.

To the Whole Earth Catalog, through which I became aware of books about domes.

To Lloyd Kahn and his friends for producing Domebooks 1 and 2.

To Tina and Seven, for allowing my dome to usurp the trunk space of their rented LTD on our trip to Canada, and for putting up with both of us when we got there.

To Pat and Bea, who introduced me to Running Press, a small, young and informal enterprise which strives to introduce craftsmanship into the field of craft books.

To Buzz and Larry Teacher of Running Press, for their faith in my ability to somehow produce a dome book.

To our valiant contributors, whose hard work made this book possible.

Copyright © 1973 Running Press
All rights reserved under the Pan-American and International Copyright Conventions

Printed in the United States of America
Distributed in Canada by Van Nostrand Reinhold Ltd., Ontario
Library of Congress Catalog Card Number 7419509
ISBN 0914294032
This book may be ordered directly from the publisher. Please include 25¢ postage.
Try your bookstore first.

Running Press, 38 South Nineteenth Street,
Philadelphia, Pa. 19103

Acknowledgements

Interior Graphics and Layout
Jim Wilson *With Help From Werner Krupp*

Special thanks to Vic Marks for permission to reprint material from *Cloudburst,* copyright (c) 1973 Cloudburst Press

Our thanks also to Edward Popko for the illustration on the rear cover, reproduced from *Geodesics* copyright (c) 1968 University of Detroit Press

Our Contributors

Gary Allen
Fred Barger
Jim Bohlen
Don Butler
Lonny Brown
Russ Chernoff
Morrie Chodeck
Ed Cooley
Stephen Ervin
Pete Hjersman
Doug Lais
Thad Matras
Dave Mielke
Andrew Ralph
Denny Rock
Bob Schuler
D. Scott Sims
Carey Smoot
Stan Vandenbark
Kathe Welles
W. E. Wright

Cover design   **Seymour Chwast/Push Pin Studios**

Premise

This book is for people who want to build their own domes. It's also for those who are interested in domes and want to learn more about them. We've tried to put together a clear explanation of what they are all about, with as gentle an introduction to the technical side as possible. We don't want to offer blueprints, but rather a collection of ideas from which you can choose to plan your own dome. The dome you design yourself will be the best for you.

This book is written by the only real dome experts we have—the people who have been out there building their own domes. They can tell you what works and what doesn't from their own hard-won experience. They have taken the time and trouble to detail those experiences for the rest of us and we owe them all our heart-felt thanks.

One of our aims is to point out the problems as well as the advantages of domes—not that we wish to discourage anyone. We do want to foster a practical and realistic view of domes. There has been a lot of soft-headed enthusiasm about domes. They have been proclaimed as an instant solution to all housing problems. This is misleading, to say the least.

If you want to build a dome because they are cheaper than other forms of construction, you may be disappointed. Domes are still experimental, and when you need special tools or hardware you will have to improvise. The minor hassles and bugs you encounter will probably eat up any cost advantage. And remember that the bare shell is only a fraction of the cost of a finished house.

If you want a dome because you've been dazzled by over-dramatic dome hype, you may tackle a project bigger than you can handle without seeing the practical difficulties. If you have plenty of enthusiasm but aren't sure of your ability, a small play dome or a meditation dome in the back yard will probably satisfy you, and it will provide valuable experience.

If you want to build a full fledged dome house, it should be because you want to live in that kind of space and are willing to go to a little extra trouble to have a house that is unique.

We hope that this book will make you want to get involved with domes, even if you never build one. That's why we've included so many models and model ideas. The beauty and symmetry of dome forms cannot really be described in words or shown in a photograph. It has to be experienced directly, at first hand.

You will find a lot of references to *Domebook 2* in this book, simply because it is the best collection of basic dome know-how available. It's been very convenient to be able to say "see *Domebook 2*, p xx" instead of repeating things that we've had no direct experience with. Of course, *Domebook 2* does not have the last word on domes, nor will any book as long as domes continue to evolve. This book should not be considered as a repeat or a replacement of *Domebook 2*, but as a supplement, building on previous experience and hopefully filling in some of the gaps.

We want to see more people building domes. We'll listen to your ideas, look at your plans. We'd like to hear your comments and suggestions about this book. If you found something wrong or hard to understand, let us know. This book is far from being as complete as we'd like it to be. If you know of books, people, materials, products, or tools that we missed, please tell us. We'd like the second edition of this book to be as big an improvement over the first as *Domebook 2* was over *Domebook 1*. Consider this a beginning.

Table of Contents

The Theory . . . . John Prenis

Why Domes? 1
An Introduction to Domes 2
Models 8
Dome Design 16

The Practice . . . . Our Contributors

My Process 18   **Pete Hjersman**
    discovering relationships through models, a tube frame dome, tensegrities, a
    great circle dome, a tension dome

A Simple 2V Tent Dome 25   **John Prenis**
    a small easy to make portable wood frame dome with a plastic skin

A Tube Frame Dome 31   **Ed Cooley**
    a 4V vinyl-skinned dome; an interesting new vent opening

Spherical Dome Membranes 33   **Carey Smoot**
    tips on the fabrication of dome skins from canvas or plastic

A 3V Canvas Skinned Dome 36   **Steve Ervin**
    a temporary dome of 2 x 2's with strapped plastic hubs

A 3V Plastic-Draped Dome 39   **D. Scott Sims**
    a frame of salvaged lumber covered with a big plastic sheet; building and
    sealing a plywood dome

The 16 Foot Personal Dome 41   **Jim Bohlen Russ Chernoff**
    very complete details of a 4V triacon plywood dome covered with cedar
    shingles

A Three Quarter Sphere 51   **Lonny Brown**
    a 3V 3/4 strapped hub plywood dome with angled support posts and a
    canvas-resin waterproofing system

Our 2V Triacon Dome 57   **Kathe Welles**
    a strapped hub plywood dome; how to install plexiglass windows and use si-
    licone caulk

How to Put Up a Dome Singlehanded 63   **Fred Barger**
    erecting a ply hub dome unassisted; some hassles to avoid

Better Domes and Gardens 67   **Andrew Ralph**
    thoughts on interior design and decoration

Thoughts, Ideas, and Dreams of Domes 70   **W. E. Wright**
    a circus tent dome; ideas for twin domes with a connecting solar collector

Zomes 73

Great Lakes Zome 74   **Dave Mielke**
    an experimental plywood zome

Domes and Zomes 75   **Doug Lais**
    cardboard models, greenhouse domes and zomes; experimental verification
    of Bernoulli's principle

Ferro-Cement "Domes" 77   **Thad Matras**
    low cost ferro-cement structures

Big Foot Foam-Imagination and Reality 80   **Bob Schuler**
    some thoughts on man and nature and technology

Polyurethane Foams and Dome Structures 82   **Gary Allen**
    answers to some commonly asked questions about foam

Dome 7072 85   **Don Butler**
    an experimental cardboard dome

My Building Career 89   **Stan Vandenbark**
    some remarks on the building of several domes and geometric structures;
    building permits; words to the wise

Chord Factors 93

Manufacturer's Page 96

Selected Bibliography 97

Last Word 101

Why Domes?

For the last few million years, most men have lived in round, dome-shaped structures. Even today, many still do. These structures, made of branches, mud, thatch, skins, leaves, stones, or snow use natural materials in an intuitively valid way (there are no straight lines or right angles in nature). These structures also show an appreciation of the fact that convexly curved surfaces are stronger than flat ones, that most materials are stronger in tension than in compression, that pre-stressing members by forming them in a curve adds strength, and that a hemisphere encloses more space with less material than any other shape. In short, "primitive" wigwams, yurts, igloos, etc. show a fine appreciation of some very sophisticated engineering principles! Rather than sneer at our ancestors for living in huts, we should feel proud of their ability to create elegant solutions to complex problems with limited resources.

If the simple and elegant dome home has served so long and so well, how did it come to fall out of use? Why is it that our present buildings are so overwhelmingly rectangular? The answer probably lies in an increasing sophistication of tools and materials. In order to build more ambitious structures like palaces, temples and fortifications, men found it necessary to modify the natural materials available. The building of a small hut could by done by cut-and-try, and what didn't fit in one place would probably fit fine somewhere else. In order to construct larger structures according to prearranged plans, however, materials of uniform dimensions were needed. It soon became clear that simple geometric shapes were the easiest solution. The rectangular solid quickly became standard. It was easy to make and check, and it would always fit properly with another such solid. Thus we have the limestone blocks of the Egyptian pyramids, and the bricks of the Babylonian ziggurats. Can you think of another shape for a brick that still makes sense?

Once the rectangular shape was settled on, it immediately began to exert a strong influence on the structures built with it. It became natural to construct buildings with rectangular plans. Anyone who has ever played with a child's set of blocks will understand this. This was not without advantages. The rectangle has the useful property that it can be subdivided into smaller rectangles or extended to make bigger ones. For most of recorded history, the rectangle was almost unchallenged. The dome was used only for mystical or ceremonial purposes, where a little extra effort was called for to please the gods or the spirits of the dead.

However, there was a price to be paid: dullness, monotony, wasted corners. The rectangular form became so boring that it became necessary to 'dress it up' with non-functional ornament. The world was ready for a change.

In 1951 Buckminister Fuller patented a method for constructing a spherical surface by subdividing it into triangles. The geodesic dome arises naturally from the study of the regular solids. The sphere encloses the greatest amount of space with the least amount of material. The triangle is the only inherently rigid structural configuration. Used in combination, they make the geodesic dome the strongest, lightest, most efficient building system ever devised.

Because it presents the least possible surface to the weather the dome conserves heat better than any other shape. The shape of the dome also encourages natural air circulation, making the dome easy to heat and cool.

Its network of interlocking triangles makes a dome very strong. A load applied at any point is spread over the adjacent members and shared among them. Because of this, flimsy looking materials, when assembled in the form of a dome, can support amazing loads.

The dome provides large volumes of clear space unobstructed by beams or columns. The larger the dome, the more efficient it becomes at enclosing space. Fuller has drawn plans for domes that would enclose whole cities. The dome, acting as a weather shield, would greatly reduce heating and insulation costs. Walls would be necessary only for soundproofing and privacy.

Because of its many identical parts, the geodesic dome is ideally suited to mass production. Because of its basic simplicity, it can be quickly erected by unskilled workers. Because of its lightness, a dome can be delivered by air.

For all these reasons, the dome is growing rapidly in popularity. It has proven its adaptability to all climates. Thousands have been built all over the world, from the radomes of the DEW line in northern Canada, to the new dome enclosed research base in the Antarctic. The dome, an age-old shape, is making a strong comeback in a space age form.

It's very interesting that many people become dome enthusiasts without knowing any of the facts above. I'd like to explore some possible reasons for this.

One reason may be that we are simply bored by conventional cubic geometry. We no longer take joy in the exploration of our personal space because it has become so monotonous. It is worth noting that children take to domes immediately, especially if they can climb on them!

Another reason is the visual appeal of domes. The sphere is a simple, natural, and highly pleasing shape. Domes are highly symmetric. The patterns formed by dome struts have a kaleidoscopic richness. One is continually seeing new designs in them.

I also believe that domes have a strong psychological appeal. A dome encloses you like an eggshell or a pair of cupped hands—gently, tenderly. In a dome, there is an inward focus. You feel that you are at the center of things. There is simply no way that you can be shoved into a corner!

Another interesting thing about domes is that they are so new that no historical associations have yet been attached to them. No president has yet been born in a dome; no dome bears the sign "George Washington slept here." John Wayne never fought off an Indian attack from inside a dome. And how would we feel about domes if the Bastille had been a dome? Or the Winter Palace? Domes thus appeal to many because they have no links with an old life style. They are part of a future yet to be written.

Who really invented the geodesic dome? This centuries-old lion in the Summer Palace, Peking, is holding a clearly recognizable geodesic sphere under its paw.

Denny Rock

An Introduction To Domes

Buzz Teacher

John Prenis

Let's start off as though we had never heard of Buckminster Fuller or domes or even conventional building techniques. Let's start with just some imaginary boards and nails.

One board isn't good for much.

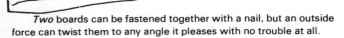

Two boards can be fastened together with a nail, but an outside force can twist them to any angle it pleases with no trouble at all.

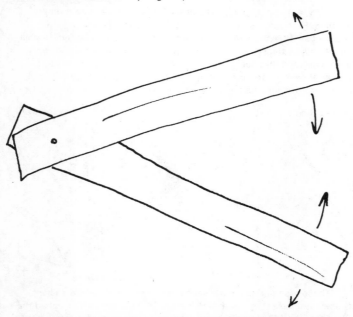

If we try to stabilize the angle by adding a third board across the other two, we make an interesting discovery. Not only is the first angle stabilized, but so are the two new angles formed. The boards have

become perfectly rigid. It is impossible to distort this triangle without bending or breaking the boards or pulling a joint apart.

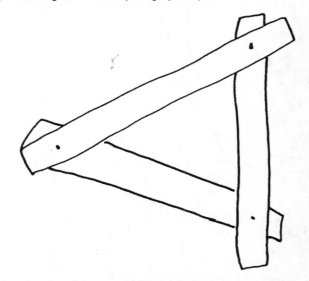

Let's try four boards in a square. Strangely, four are no more rigid than two.

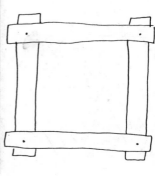 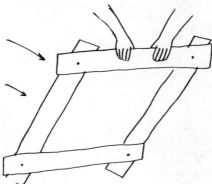

2

If we nail a fifth board across the square diagonally, however, we turn it into two triangles, and it becomes rigid instantly.

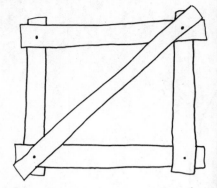

How about five boards? Six?

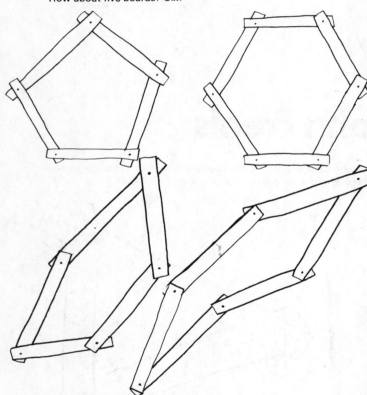

More boards do not help. Not until we divide them up into triangles do they become rigid.

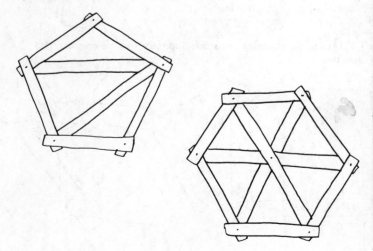

The triangle is the only truly rigid shape. It is the basis for all structures.

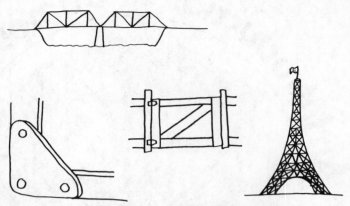

The triangle also shows up where we do not expect it. Going back to our flexible square, we can make it perfectly rigid by nailing a piece of plywood over it. But it's still the triangle that's doing all the work. We can prove this by cutting out some pieces, leaving triangles behind. The square is still rigid—in fact, it is even stronger than before, because we have taken away some dead weight. If, however, we cut away the part of the plywood that provides triangle bracing, we find that the plywood does no good at all! If a structure is rigid it is being braced by triangles somehow, whether you can see them or not.

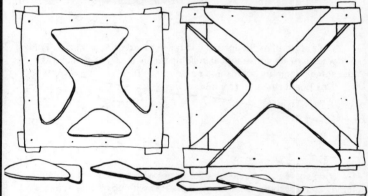

Now, again let us imagine that we have never seen an ordinary building. How many shapes are there that we can use for our structures? We want to keep our work simple, so let us require that all our beams be the same length, that each wall be the same as every other wall, and that each corner joint be the same as every other corner. If we stick to these requirements, there are only five different structures that we can build.

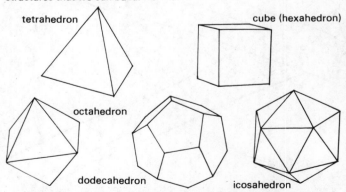

tetrahedron   cube (hexahedron)

octahedron

dodecahedron   icosahedron

These are the five regular solids, first discovered by the ancient Greeks. Because they were described by Plato, they are also called the Platonic solids. Their Greek names tell us how many sides they have. Tetrahedron, four sides; hexahedron, six sides; octahedron, eight sides; dodecahedron, twelve sides; icosahedron, twenty sides. Only the cube has a familiar every-day name, but that is Greek, too. It comes from the Greek word for a gambling die!

Of these five, we see that three are made of triangles. As we might expect, the tetrahedron, octahedron, and icosahedron are rigid, while the cube and the dodecahedron are not.

Let's look more closely at these shapes. To begin with, let's make a count of their sides, edges, and corners.

	sides	corners	edges
tetra	4	4	6
cube	6	8	12
octa	8	6	12
dodeca	12	20	30
icosa	20	12	30

Notice how the solids seem to want to pair up. The cube and the octahedron have the same number of edges. So do the dodecahedron and the icosahedron. The cube has just as many corners as the octahedron has sides, and vice versa. The same goes for the icosahedron and the dodecahedron.

What can we do with this? Suppose we try putting a cube inside an octahedron—one cube corner for each octa face. And we can put an octa inside a cube—one octa corner for each cube face. We can also do this with the dodecahedron and the icosahedron:

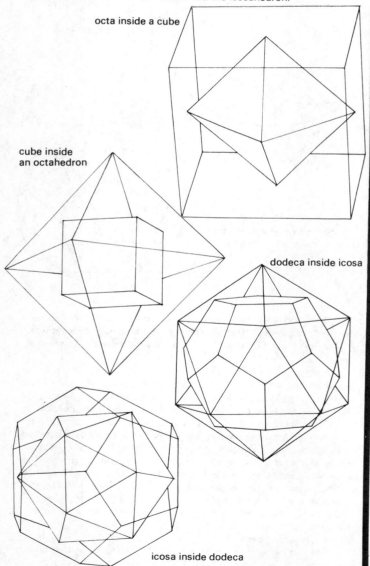

octa inside a cube

cube inside
an octahedron

dodeca inside icosa

icosa inside dodeca

Finally, we can make the inner solid the same size as the outer one. Now each solid is neatly embedded in the other.

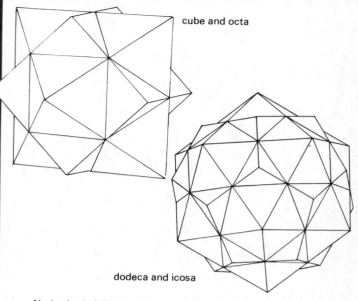

cube and octa

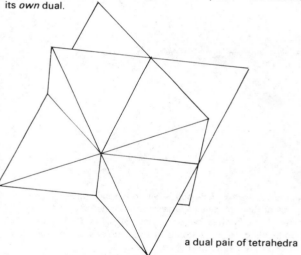

dodeca and icosa

Notice how the respective edges of each pair of solids bisect each other, at 90 degree angles. And notice how each corner of one solid corresponds with a side of another. This relationship is called *duality*.

And what has the tetrahedron been doing all this time? Go back and look at our side-corner-edge table and you will see that the tetra is its *own* dual.

a dual pair of tetrahedra

Together, the pair of tetrahedra have 8 corners and 6 pairs of edges. Do these numbers look familiar? They should—go back to the table and you will see that they are the number of corners and sides of the cube. This means that by connecting the corners of the tetrahedron like a follow-the-dots puzzle, we should get a cube:

two tetrahedra
inside a cube

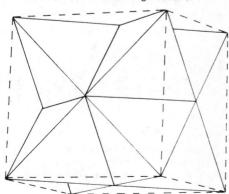

This brings up the question of what we will find if we try connecting the corners of our other dual pairs.

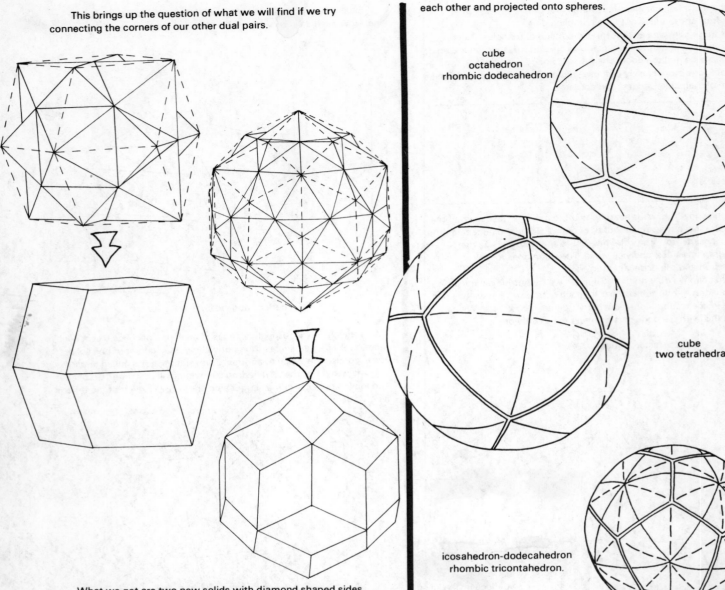

each other and projected onto spheres.

cube
octahedron
rhombic dodecahedron

cube
two tetrahedra

icosahedron-dodecahedron
rhombic tricontahedron.

What we get are two new solids with diamond shaped sides. Looking back at the table, we see that the first must have 14 corners and 12 sides. The other has 32 corners and 30 sides. Their names are rhombic dodecahedron (12 diamond shaped sides) and rhombic triacontahedron (30 diamond shaped sides).

We now have three related families of polyhedra:

cube tetra tetra

cube r. dodeca octa

dodeca triaconta icosa

Let's bring our table up to date:

	sides	corners	edges
tetra	4	4	6
cube	6	8	12
octa	8	6	12
r.dodeca	12	14	24
dodeca	12	20	30
icosa	20	12	30
r.triaconta	30	32	60

You may have noticed that as the solids become more complex, from the tetra to the triaconta, they become less jagged and more spherical. Here are the three families of polyhedra superimposed on

One thing is apparent right away. The interlocked solids form networks of triangles. They also bear a close resemblance to dome frameworks. Actually, they *are* simple dome frameworks, as we shall soon see.

Another thing that becomes evident on close study is that the edges of the linked solids now join to form a set of circles, each one of which cuts the sphere exactly in half, like the equator of the earth. These are called *great circles* because they are the largest possible circles that can be drawn upon a sphere. And just as a straight line is the shortest distance between two points on a flat plane, the shortest distance between two points on a sphere is always part of a great circle. Mathematicians have a special term for curves of this sort. They are called *geodesics*. The word comes from the Greek roots for earth-dividing, and was originally used to describe the surveying of large areas, where the curvature of the earth had to be taken into account. Thus the equator and the circles of longitude are geodesics in both meanings of the word. Now you know how the "geodesic" got into the phrase "geodesic dome."

The fact that domes are derived from geodesics helps to explain their strength. Applied stresses are carried along the most direct possible path. A dome works like a set of interlocking arches, each supporting the others.

Now to the matter of how dome frames are developed. This is really a matter of developing a framework of triangles that will be a close approximation to a sphere. You will recall that the icosahedron was the largest solid we could make with equilateral triangles. It is actually a primitive dome frame. It is not really very spherical, however, and if built in a large scale, the structural members would be very long and cumbersome. The big triangles would sag and require internal bracing. To be most useful, the bracing would have to form smaller triangles. And since it's going to be there anyway, it might as well be used to give the structure a more spherical shape. The subdivision of large triangles into smaller ones is what dome geometry is all about.

You have already seen one way of breaking down the large icosa triangle. This was the set of interwoven great circles we saw a short time ago.

icosa ————
dodeca ═══
r. triaconta – – –

Each icosa triangle is divided into six smaller identical triangles. There are 20 x 6 or 120 of them covering the whole sphere. It turns out that this is the largest number of identical triangles into which sphere can be subdivided. A dome built using this scheme would look like this:

We can continue this scheme of breakdown by drawing additional lines parallel to the original ones.

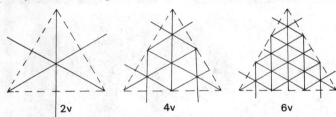

2v   4v   6v

First the side of the original triangle is divided into 2 parts, then 4 parts, then 6. The number of parts into which the icosa side is divided is known as the *frequency* and is a measure of a dome's complexity. Above we have sketched parts of 2, 4 and 6 frequency domes. The higher the breakdown, the more spherical the dome. In the higher breakdowns, the members representing the edges of the original icosa are not really necessary, and are usually left out. This breakdown is called the *triacon* because it was originally

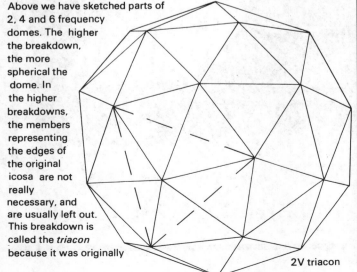

2V triacon

developed from the triacontahedron.

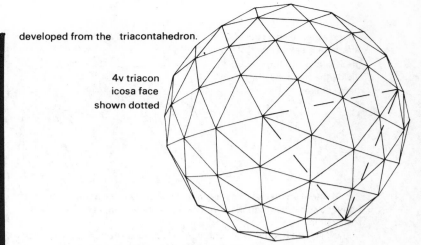

4v triacon
icosa face
shown dotted

There is another type of breakdown, and for this, we must go back to the original icosa triangle. Instead of drawing lines perpendicular to the triangle's sides, we can draw lines parallel to them. In this way, we get what is called the alternate breakdown.

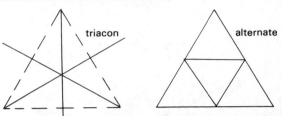

triacon   alternate

In the alternate breakdown, the icosa edges remain part of the dome structure.

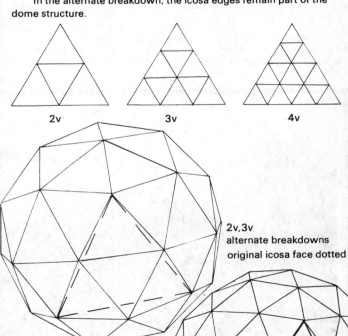

2v   3v   4v

2v,3v
alternate breakdowns
original icosa face dotted

There are some interesting differences between the two breakdowns. Since the triacon breakdown is symmetrical about a line drawn down the center of the icosa triangle, the triacon is possible only in even frequencies. There can be no such thing as an odd frequency triacon. If someone tries to sell you one, run! The alternate, on the other hand, is possible in all frequencies. In even frequency alternate breakdowns (2V, 4V, 6V) great circles are formed which divide the dome neatly into hemispheres.

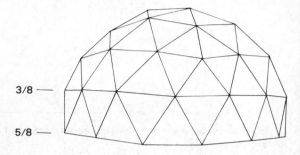

The triacon breakdown does not have this feature in any frequency. In order to make a triacon half-sphere, some triangles have to be cut in half.

While odd frequency alternate breakdowns do not separate neatly into hemispheres, they tend to form bands of triangles which allow them to be separated into domes which are slightly more than a half sphere, or slightly less.

3/8 —

5/8 —

The terms 3/8 and 5/8 do not refer to actual volume, but are simply a way of saying "less than half a sphere" or "more than half a sphere". Notice that the dividing line is not even, but slightly zig-zag.

Another factor in deciding which breakdown to use is the number of different strut lengths involved.

# different lengths needed		
frequency	alternate	triacon
2V	2	2
4V	6	4
6V	10	6

The triacon requires fewer different lengths because of its higher symmetry. On the other hand, the struts vary in length much more than in the alternate breakdown.

The two breakdowns we have been discussing, alternate and triacon, are the two "standard" dome patterns. It may be interesting to see how they got their names.

The original dome breakdown developed by Buckminster Fuller looked something like the triacon. For a while, it was the only one. Then another was developed. So at lectures, when Bucky had finished explaining his breakdown, he would say, "And here we have the *alternate* breakdown." The term stuck and became the common name, even after other breakdowns were developed. The triacon is so called because it was derived from the pattern of the rhombic triacontahedron. Because of its high symmetry, it required fewer different strut lengths than Bucky's original breakdown, which it soon replaced. While other breakdowns have been developed for various special purposes, the alternate and the triacon remain the two most often used.

By now you should find it fairly easy to identify different types of domes. What you do is look for a point where five struts join. Then find another and draw another line between them. If this line is defined by actual struts, the dome is an alternate breakdown. If there are no struts along the line, the dome is a triacon. What you are doing is picking out corners of the original icosa. The line you draw between them is an icosa edge, and counting the number of parts into which it is divided gives you the frequency of the dome.

Carey Smoot

Models

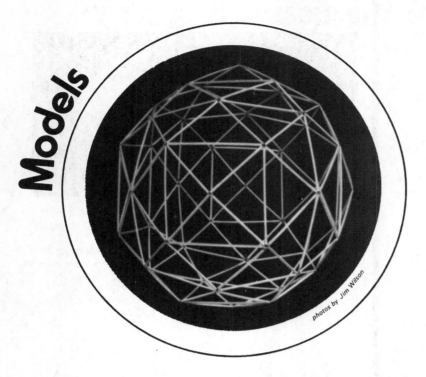

photos by Jim Wilson

NOTE:
Most of the photos in this section
are 3-D stereo.
Instructions for viewing,
and a cut-out stereo viewing aid
can be found in the back
of this book.

Now that you have some idea of what domes are and how they work, it is a good idea to build some models. The best drawings and photos are inferior to the simplest model when it comes to demonstrating three dimensional relationships. There is simply no substitute for the ability to see everything from all angles that a model gives.

Models are invaluable tools for visualizing and conceptualizing, for checking old ideas and generating new ones. Playing with models can lead to the discovery of valuable insights—not to mention the fact that they are fun to make and beautiful as well.

There are several model kits suitable for building dome models on the market, and a list of them is given later. The system I prefer, however, is simple, cheap and easy, and the materials are available at the grocery store or five and ten. For struts, ordinary 3/16″ paper soda straws are used. (The larger 1/4″ plastic straws will not work with this system.) Hub connectors are made from bent pipe cleaner halves. It happens that two pipe cleaners fit neatly and snugly into a soda straw, and this convenient fact is the basis for the system. A diagram explains it far better than words:

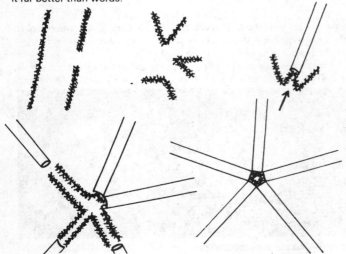

A box or two of straws and four or five packets of pipe cleaners will be enough for several models, and will cost less than a couple of dollars.

I recommend that you start by making models of the five regular solids discussed last chapter. In this way you can see for yourself that the tetrahedron, octahedron, and icosahedron are rigid, and that the cube and the dodecahedron are not.

After you have made the cube, you can stabilize it by tying strings across the diagonals of its faces. If you criss-cross each face with two diagonal strings, you will end up with two tetrahedra inside the cube. (This is easier to see if you use two different colors of string.) This is the dual pair of tetrahedra inside a cube that was discussed earlier.

You can make the other dual pairs this way too. For the cube-octahedron pair, first make an octahedron. Then make a cube with edges 0.71 times the length of the octa edges. (Make your measurements and calculations in millimeters and centimeters— dealing with fractions becomes much easier.) If you make the octa edges 20 cm. long, the cube edges will come out to 14.2 cm. You will find that the octa will just fit inside the cube. Connecting the corners of the two solids with string will give you the rhombic dodecahedron.

For the icosahedron-dodecahedron pair, make the dodeca edges 0.62 times the length of the icosa edges. Connecting the corners with string will give you the rhombic tricontahedron.

We can make some more interesting shapes from our dual pairs. By trimming the corners off them, we get the cuboctahedron and the icosidodecahedron. As you might guess from their names, they combine the faces of the cube and octahedron, and the icosahedron and dodecahedron. They are related to the domes we have discussed in an interesting way. If you look back at the picture of the 2V alternate

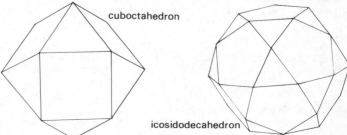

cuboctahedron

icosidodecahedron

dome and imagine the pentagon spokes left out, you will see the icosidodecahedron.

There is another pair of solids that is related to our domes. If we trim the corners off the octahedron and the icosahedron, we get the truncated octahedron and the truncated icosahedron (what else?). Look at the 3V alternate dome, and you will see that the truncated icosa is its skeleton.

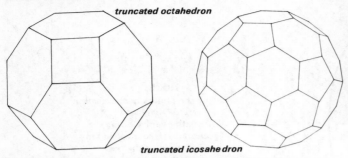

truncated octahedron

truncated icosahedron

These four solids are part of another set of thirteen semi-regular solids called the Archimedean solids (because we know Archimedes studied them, although his original work is lost). Each one has equal edges and identical corners, like the Platonic solids, but the faces may be composed of more than one kind of regular polygon.

There is an interesting way to construct the cubocta and the icosidodeca with just paper and bobby pins.

To make the cubocta, you need four sheets of paper and a dozen bobby pins. Start by drawing a large circle on a sheet of paper with a compass. Without changing the setting, use the compass to mark off 6

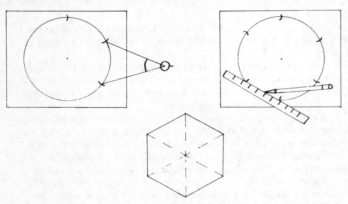

equally spaced points around the circle. Connect the points with a ruler, and you have made a regular hexagon. Cut it out and use it as a pattern to make three more hexagons. Fold all the hexagons corner to corner. Crease each fold twice.

Now take each hexagon and bring two opposite corners together. Clip with a bobby pin. You should have four 'bow tie' shapes like this:

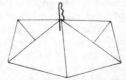

Now take two of them and clip them together at the corners with two more bobby pins.

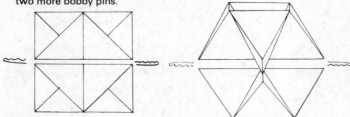

Do the same with the last two 'bow ties'. Now put the two halves of your model together and put clips on the last four corners.

This way of making the cuboctahedron was devised by Buckminster Fuller. It is one of his favorite shapes.

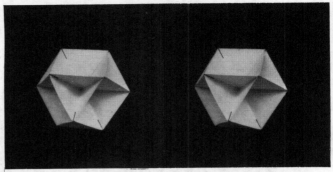

paper and bobby pin cubocta

To make the icosidoseca, you will need thirty bobby pins and six sheets of paper. Use the pattern to trace and cut out six decagons. Crease them as you did the hexagons for the cubocta. Now take each one, bring two opposite corners together, and clip them with a bobby pin. You should have six "dog bone" shapes like this:

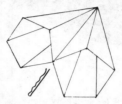

Now take two of them and use a bobby pin to clip them together like this:

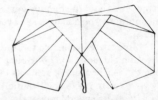

Now put a third one on top and clip it in place with six more bobby pins. This completes half the model. Follow the same steps to

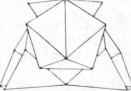

assemble the other half. Now you can put the two halves together and clip them together with the last ten bobby pins. Make sure that the two halves are in proper relation to each other.

Notice that the model is limp until you put in the very last bobby pin. When this happens the model tenses and becomes surprisingly

paper and bobby pin icosidodeca

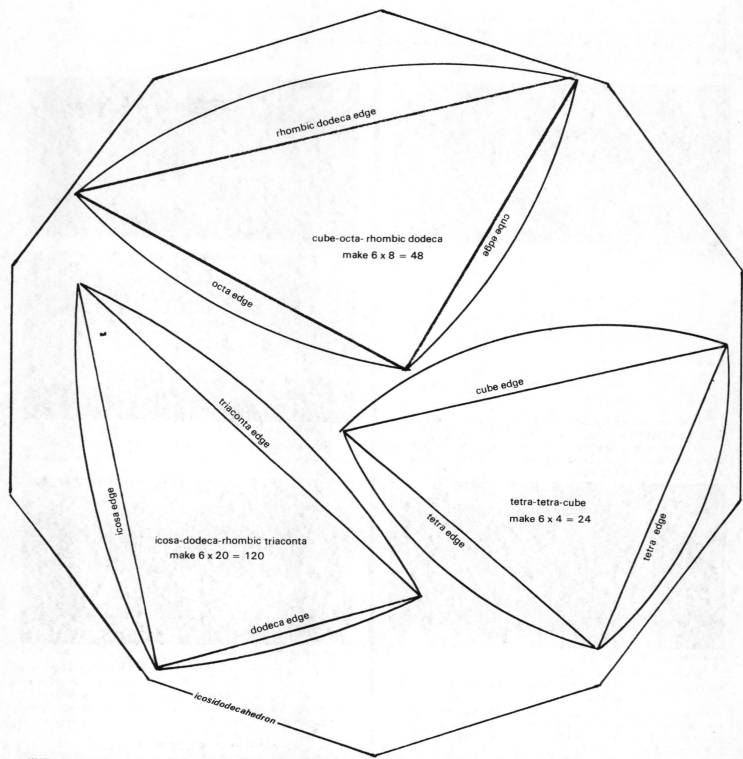

rhombic dodeca edge

cube-octa- rhombic dodeca
make 6 x 8 = 48

cube edge

octa edge

cube edge

triaconta edge

icosa edge

tetra-tetra-cube
make 6 x 4 = 24

tetra edge

tetra edge

icosa-dodeca-rhombic triaconta
make 6 x 20 = 120

dodeca edge

icosidodecahedron

stiff like magic, because the tension of the edges puts the center of the model in compression. If you remove the compressive stress by cutting out the center of the model and making it hollow, the model becomes limp again!

The three dual pairs can also be made as paper models. Use the triangles above to make patterns. Trace and cut out half the required number of pieces, then turn the pattern over and do the rest, so that you will have an equal number of right and left handed pieces.

Use an old ball point pen and a ruler to score each triangle along the straight lines, and bend up the curved tabs. The triangles can then be glued together, tab to tab. The tabs, left on the *outside* of the model, form continuous great circles when the model is finished. You

might like to color the tabs, using a different color for each solid.

The icosa-dodeca-rhombic triaconta combination may give you some difficulty because the tab corresponding to the dodeca edge is so narrow. Tape this edge from the back. That will give you sixty right-left pairs of triangles whose tabs can be glued together to complete the model in the usual fashion.

Now to try some dome models. This becomes a bit more complex, since instead of one or two different strut lengths, you will have three or four or more to deal with. The problem of figuring out the right lengths for all these struts is taken care of through *chord factors*. Chord factors are simply a handy way of expressing the lengths of the struts in terms of the dome's radius. To find the length needed for a particular strut, all you need to do is to multiply the chord factor for that strut by the dome radius. Once you have a set of chord factors for a particular dome, you can calculate strut lengths for any size dome you want. A list of chord factors for various types of domes will be found later in the book.

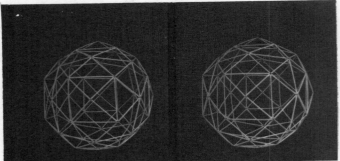

soda straw 4v octa triacon

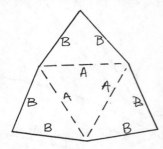

As an example, let's consider the 2V alternate dome. There are two different strut lengths required: A 0.61803, B 0.54643.

Suppose we want to make a 25 cm. diameter model. We multiply all the chord factors by the desired radius (12.5 cm.) and get: strut A 7.7254 cm., strut B 6.8375 cm.

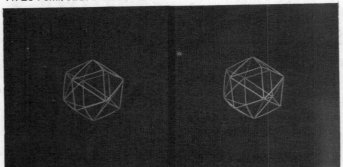

soda straw 2v octa triacon

We can round these off to 7.7 cm. and 6.8 cm. One more thing—the hub joints have a width of .4 cm. This has the effect of making each strut .4 cm. longer than it should be. If we do not take this into account, the dome will be a bit larger than the 25 cm. diameter, and the sides will be slightly out of proportion. We can take care of this by subtracting the width of the joint (.4 cm.) from each strut, getting: A 7.3 cm., B 6.4 cm.

How many straws do we need? We can find this out easily enough if we remember that an icosahedron has 20 faces, 30 edges and 12 corners. Looking again at the icosa triangle subdivided in the 2V pattern, we see that there will be 2 'B' struts for each icosa edge, and 3 'A' struts for each icosa face. 30 x 2 = 60 'B' struts 20 x 3 = 60 'A' struts
How many pipe cleaners will be needed? Looking again at the icosa triangle, we know that there will be a five way hub at each of the icosa vertices. That means 12 five way hubs.

We can also see that there will be a six way hub in the middle of each icosa edge (just imagine another 2V triangle alongside). That

means 30 six way joints. So we need:
5 x 12 = 60
6 x 30 = 180
240 pipe cleaner halves or
120 whole pipe cleaners.

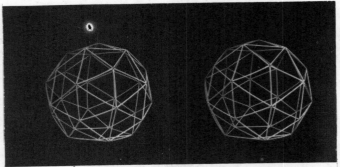

soda straw 2v icosa triacon

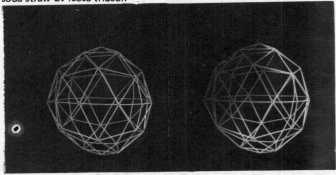

soda straw 3v octa alternate

These numbers are for a whole sphere. If you want to make a hemisphere, you'll only need half the parts, plus a few extra to fill out the bottom edge.

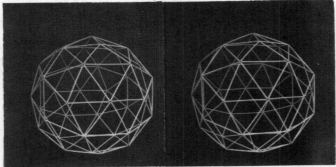

soda straw 2v icosa alternate

In this way you can figure out for yourself just what you'll need to make any given dome. Making models will help you with details you'll have to keep in mind when building a real dome. And the more carefully you model your dream dome, the fewer mistakes you'll make in its construction.

COMPUTER CARD MODELS

Wherever there are keypunches, there are wastebaskets full of mispunched cards. Usually these cards can be had for the asking. They are made of a light cardboard that is very nice to work with, and sometimes you can find colored ones. Computer cards can be used to make very nice models of the Platonic and Archimedean solids. The cards are folded in half lengthwise, overlapped at the proper angle, and stapled with a miniature stapler, like the Tot 50.

Try making a cube to get the idea. Fold 12 cards, put them together, and staple as you go. It takes almost less time to do than it does to tell about it, because the corners of the cards are already cut to the 90° angle needed to make the corners of the cube.

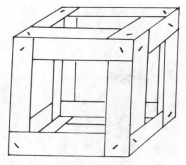

To make shapes involving triangles, the corners of the cards have to be trimmed:

Triangles should be assembled and stapled before the rest of the model is put together if possible, because the openings in the triangles are too small to allow free use of the stapler later.

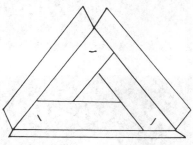

To make pentagons and hexagons, you do not trim the cards. Instead, you judge the angle by eye, or by using a guide set at the required angle.

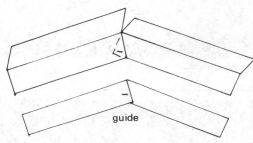

This method is good for building models of the dodecahedron, the cubocta, the icosidodeca, the truncated tetra, the truncated octa, the

small rhombicuboctahedron, and other models of moderate complexity with equal edges. Models more than two or three feet across tend to be flimsy. This method makes very handsome models.

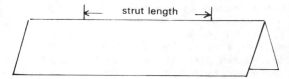

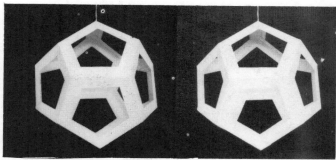

computer card dodeca

computer card rhombic dodeca

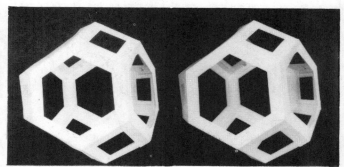

computer card truncated octa

computer card cubocta

computer card small rhombicubocta

12

Computer cards can be used to make dome models too, but this takes a different technique. First fold the cards as usual: Next, mark off the strut length on one card. Use a protractor to measure off *two* axial

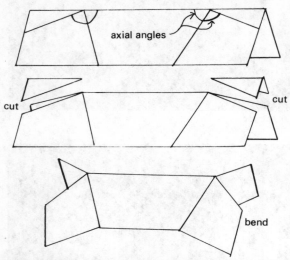

angles for each end. Cut away the corners. This card can now be used as a template to cut all the other cards for that strut length. You'll need to make one template for each strut length. Once all the cards are cut, fold out the end tabs that will hold the model together. When all the pieces are ready, you put them together by slipping the tab of one card into its neighbor, and so on around the vertex, stapling as you go. The trimmed tabs ensure that the angles will be correct.

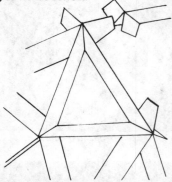

Still another useful way to make models of the Platonic and Archimedean solids is the cardboard and rubber band method. Cardboard polygons are equipped with notched tabs that allow them to be linked together with rubber bands.

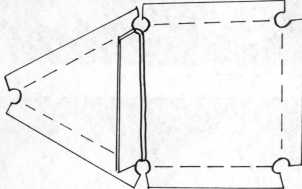

For each different polygon you use, you will need a pattern. Draw the polygon on a piece of light cardboard (a cereal box or shirt cardboard will do). Make the edges three or four inches long. Then draw a 3/8 inch border all around for the tabs. Cut it out, and you are ready to make copies.

cardboard cube inside computer card octa

computer card icosa

computer card 2v icosa triacon

cardboard and rubber band truncated icosa

Place your pattern on another piece of cardboard and trace around it. Then use a push pin to mark the inner corners of the piece by pricking through the corners of the pattern into the cardboard beneath, cut out the copy with scissors, and use a ruler and an old ballpoint pen to score the piece from each pin prick to the next. This makes it much easier to fold the tabs. Now use a paper punch to punch out a 1/4 inch hole centered over each pin hole. Then, with scissors, cut a piece out of each corner to make the notches. Finally, bend up each tab along its scored line.

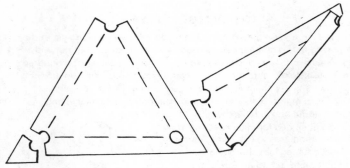

When you have built up a large stock of these pieces, you can make a wide variety of models. Models can be built with the tabs on the inside or on the outside. Leaving the tabs on the outside is easier but putting the tabs on the inside results in a more attractive model. In this case the last couple of rubber bands may have to be maneuvered into place with a knitting needle poked between the edges of the model.

Completed models can be taken apart for storage, or their parts used to build other models.

GIANT MODELS

Perhaps after making some regular models you still aren't sure you understand what a full size dome would *feel* like. The obvious solution is to make a full size model. It needn't cost as much as you might think. The material is ordinary newspaper—cheap, available, and easy to work with. The basic idea is to roll the paper into long tubes, trim to length, punch holes in the ends, and bolt them together. Rolled newspaper isn't as flimsy as it sounds. You can take a tube rolled from six layers of paper and bend it over your knee. With some encouragement, the wrinkles pop right out, leaving it as strong as ever. Used in a dome, the strength of these tubes will suprise you.

Things that you will need are scissors or tin snips, a yardstick, a paper punch, a broomstick, cellophane tape, crayons, some 3/16" stove bolts, nuts and washers, and of course plenty of newspaper. If you already have most of these things around the house, all you will need to buy will be the stove bolts, which are not expensive. I bought enough hardware for a 2V alternate dome for only $1.11.

To start, open out five or six pages of newspaper and pile them together. Start rolling from one corner to the diagonally opposite one.

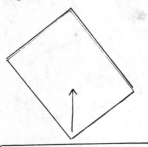 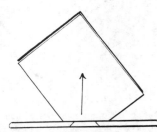

A variation that makes longer tubes uses four staggered stacks of paper. This can make tubes four feet long.

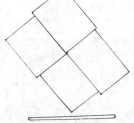

When you are finished you will find that a single piece of tape is enough to keep the tube from unrolling. Another nice thing about this method is that it makes the tube thickest in the center, where the bending stress is greatest.

If you have any trouble removing the broomstick, pull while twisting against the direction in which the tube was rolled.

A finished roll will be about 36" long, but the ends will be rather flimsy. This is taken care of by trimming about four inches off each end, after which the tube can be trimmed to the desired length.

Let's try an example. Suppose you want to make a 2V alternate model. The first step is to find out how large the dome will be. If we restrict the design to short tubes (easiest to make) the longest strut in the dome can be no longer than 26 - 28". Looking up the chord factors for 2V alternate, we find:

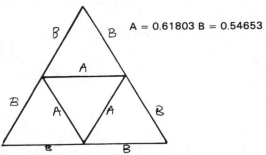

$$A = 0.61803 \quad B = 0.54653$$

The A's are the long struts. We know that:
dome radius x chord factor = strut length or, dome radius x 0.61803 = A = 26" Working backwards with the aid of a little algebra gives us the dome radius.

$$\text{dome radius} = \frac{26''}{0.61803} = 43\ 3/4''$$

The dome will be about 3 1/2 feet high, and about 7 feet across. This is a nice size for an indoor model. To find B we use the radius we have just found: 43 3/4" x 0.54653 = 24"

There must be enough room at the ends of the tubes to punch a hole, so we add an inch to the end of each strut getting:
A = 28" B = 26"

This dome will require 35 A's and 30 B's. When you have all the tubes rolled and trimmed, color code the ends with crayon so that you can tell them apart at a glance. Next, flatten the ends and use the paper punch to punch a hole 1 inch from each end. Make sure that the second hole is in line with the first. The going will be easier if you punch only one wall of the tube at a time.

To fasten this dome together, you'll need 26 one inch stove bolts, plus washers to keep nuts and bolt heads from pulling out. The bigger the washers the better.

Now you are ready to start putting the model together. Count out ten A's and arrange them in a circle.

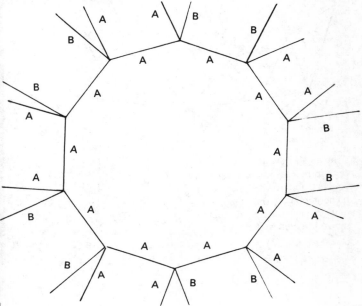

Count out ten more A's and ten B's and bolt them all together so that A's and B's alternate around the circle in pairs as above.

In the next step, you join the A's and B's into triangles and connect them with a row of ten B's. These joints are not complete. To hold the struts in place, you can either bolt the joints temporarily, or clip them together with spring clothespins. Looking around the circle, you should see tall triangles alternating with short triangles, which gives the ring a roller-coaster look.

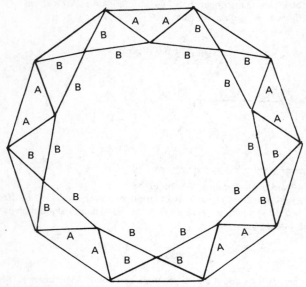

The next step is to add a B to each joint where four B's come together. This completes these joints. Now bolt two A's to each joint where two A's and two B's come together. This completes these joints. Now you have five groups of A's and B's to be clipped together temporarily; each B between two A's.

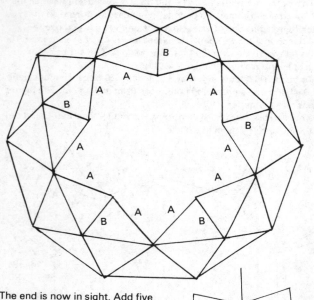

The end is now in sight. Add five A's to form a pentagon at the very top. Last, add five B's as spokes in the pentagon. All the temporary joints can now be bolted together, and your model is finished.

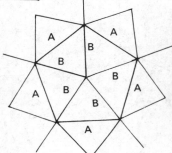

OTHER MODEL IDEAS

The large 1/4" plastic straws that you were warned against at the beginning of this chapter can be used to make models—but not with pipe cleaners. If you have access to a paper cutter, cut several hundred strips of thin cardboard (cereal box cardboard works well) about 5/16" x 3" and use them in place of pipe cleaners. The straws are available in many colors (try a bar or restaurant supply house) and make colorful and durable models.

Another idea for making connectors for giant models is to cut garden hose or plastic tubing into short lengths and bolt them together. Struts are cut from wooden dowel stock that fits snugly inside the tubing. Both struts and connectors can be used to make other models, like a giant tinkertoy set.

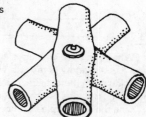

COMMERCIAL MODEL KITS

Ikosa-Kits consist of thin wooden splints that fit into holes punched in slices of vinyl tubing. They're cheaper than other kits, because you do the work of punching the holes. Kits 3 and 4 are recommended for dome builders. 3 has 200 pcs. and costs $2. 4 has 400 pcs. and costs $3.00. *Ikosa-Kits Route 3, Box 480 Eugene, Ore. 97405*

"D Stix" or "Think Stix" from Edmund Scientific are 1/8" colored wooden rods that fit into flexible plastic 5, 6, and 8 way connectors. Nice but expensive. If you buy a set, you'll soon run short of 6 way connectors, and you'll have to cut rods to length since the set is not specifically intended for domes. Best bet is to buy connectors separately and get 1/8" dowel rod at a lumberyard or hobby store. Sets are $4.00, $6.50, and $9.00. 6 way connectors are $3.50 per pack of 50. *Edmund Scientific Co. 614 Edscorp Building Barrington, N.J. 08007* Dome East makes kits of flexible plastic connectors and 3/16" wooden rods. The connectors are very rugged, and rather clumsy for small models. They are best for big models—get long 3/16" dowels from a lumberyard. Dome Kit I—$6.00 6 or 5 way hubs— $2.75 for a pck of 25. *Dome East 325 Duffy Avenue Hicksville, N.Y. 11801*

Dynamic Domes sells kits of colorful plastic tubes and flexible star shaped hubs. The instructions are clear and well written and the models go together smoothly and easily. The finished models are durable and very handsome. Kit 1, which makes the regular solids and a 2V hemisphere costs $7.00 and is highly recommended for beginners. 3V and 4V kits are also available. Extra hubs and struts can be ordered separately.
Dynamic Domes, Box 425, Brampton, Ontario L6/2L4, Canada

Jim Wilson with Dynamic Dome model

Dome Design

There is nothing mysterious or esoteric about the design of a dome. As with any other structure, the main requirements are forethought and common sense.

The first thing you should consider is just why you want to build a dome. Make an honest appraisal of your desires and your abilities. Perhaps some other structure would be better suited to your needs. Domes require painstaking work and attention to detail. They should not be attempted for frivolous reasons.

You should be well acquainted with the site. Ask older residents about such things as prevailing winds, frost line, drainage, local materials, etc. You should know your own needs. Your home should grow out of your living patterns so that it will aid, not thwart them. Finally, you should make a careful inventory of your finances, skills, time and labor available. Building your own home is a big project, and requires very careful planning.

Interior design should be considered well before, not after, the dome is built. Your style of living will determine the interior arrangement of the dome, which will in turn determine many details of the dome itself.

The attempt to partition a dome into rooms usually destroys most of its charm. Try to keep your dome as open as possible. Small domes are usually completely open, with perhaps an upper level sleeping loft. A good plan for medium size domes is to give half the space to the living room and half to enclosed kitchen, bath, and private bedroom, with a sleeping loft on top. This arrangement preserves the open, spacious feeling of the dome, while providing enclosed areas for functions requiring them. Many variations are possible.

Try to work with, not against, the curves of the dome. Try to think in terms of functional areas, not square rooms divided by walls that somehow have to be forced into a round plan. Some things are uncompromisingly rectangular. Try to put refrigerators, cabinets, etc. against vertical interior walls, where they will fit without trouble.

You have a lot of choices when deciding what kind of dome to build—triacon or alternate, 3V, 4V, 5V, pent vertex or hex vertex uppermost, 3/8, 1/2 or 5/8 level truncation. The breakdown and frequency you choose will be affected by the materials available and the size you want. Higher frequencies will mean more parts to make and keep track of, but they will be smaller and easier to handle. The

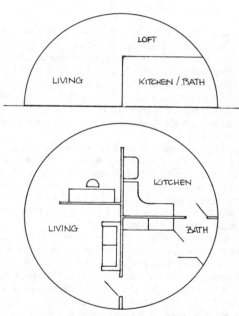

orientation of your dome will affect placing of windows and ventilators. A 5/8 truncation gives a tall dome with more vertical walls and perhaps space for an upper level. Consider all the alternatives; make *lots* of models.

How big should your dome be? You should already have some idea of the space you will need. Dome size is usually limited at any particular frequency by the materials used. For instance, the largest a 3V plywood dome can be is 24 feet in diameter, because of the limit imposed by the size of a 4' x 8' sheet. A larger dome would require panels to be spliced together. A smaller dome would waste material. If several materials are involved, pick the plan which makes most efficient use of the most expensive material, and accept the fact that you will have to waste some of the cheaper material. Better yet, plan to use the waste somewhere else. If you are in doubt about the size of your dome, make it larger than you think necessary. Extra space can always be put to use, and domes are hard to add on to.

What frequency should your dome be? 3V is the most popular for moderate sized domes, so try it as a starting point. Use the chord factors and your intended radius to figure out the dimensions of your triangles. Then make scale patterns of them and try fitting them together on graph paper to find the most efficient way to cut out your skin material. If the largest dome you can make without undue waste is too small, try a higher frequency or a different breakdown.

A dome can be positioned in one of three different ways. It can sit with a vertex, a face, or an edge of the basic icosa facing up. Most domes are built vertex up, but investigate the other possibilities. They make a great difference in how the dome is cut off to meet the floor line. This is something that can only be decided with the help of a model.

Leakage is one of the big dome problems and should be carefully considered in your planning. Think about where water will go when it hits the dome. If your plan requires spliced panels, use them on the lower part of the dome, where the slope is steepest, and water will have little time to get into the joints. Skylights and windows should present sloping surfaces to water runoff.

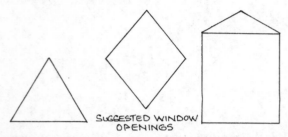

SUGGESTED WINDOW OPENINGS

If you give water a place to collect and pool, it will eventually work its way in. Give special attention to the relatively flat top of the dome.

The only certain solution to the leak problem seems to be the use of asphalt shingles, fibreglass, or some other type of whole-dome covering. Next best seems to be caulk combined with something else, like tape or roofing compound. Don't expect caulk alone to do the whole job and don't expect it to make up for poor work. Even expensive wonder caulks are often defeated by sloppy workmanship and poor joint preparation.

In your calculations, your struts will be mathematical lines. In practice, your struts will have physical thickness. Decide whether you are measuring from the inside of your struts or the outside, then stick to that decision. Otherwise you will be lost in confusion. Don't forget to allow for the width of your hubs also. It helps to make scale drawings of the hub to see just how everything fits together there. Such drawings can prevent many blunders.

Figures in the tables of chord factors are given to six places. It may seem silly to calculate dimensions to the tenth of a millimeter when you know that expansion and contraction will cause changes many times as great. Finish your calculations, though, before you do any rounding off. Any sloppiness here will be magnified later on, and that goes double for mistakes. Make sure all calculations are checked and double checked, preferably by someone else.

When cutting parts, make extensive use of jigs and templates so that parts will be as uniform as possible. Careful workmanship is essential. A 'funky' dome is bound to be a leaky one.

Take your time. The strangest dome story I've ever heard concerns a dome that was being put up during a rock festival. Everybody was pitching in and having a great time. When the dome was about half-way up, however, someone said, "This isn't going to work—it's not curving inward. It's going to be a big cylinder, not a dome." "Pipe down, man—we're having too much fun to stop now." And when they finally got it up, it *was* a big cylinder. It seems that in the rush of making the parts, all the struts had been left the same length. So that evening they took it down and trimmed the struts to the proper lengths. Next morning, they put it up again, this time as a proper dome.

Always think twice before doing anything irrevocable. I was told of a group in Maine who built a platform and trimmed it to the calculated diameter of their dome. When they started putting up the dome frame, however, they discovered that the dome was just a *little* larger than they had thought it would be. They had to go back and bolt extensions to their platform for the dome to rest on, and it never was as solid as it could have been.

Mark everything clearly. There are many similar parts in a dome and a little care will prevent confusion later.

Plan the erection sequence carefully and in insulting detail, as though the dome were going to be put up by a crew of idiots. Overconfidence can really do you in. Things can get very complicated when several people are working at once. Color code all parts and use a color coded model as a guide. Otherwise, you're sure to make some very dumb mistakes.

Leaving out color coding is asking for trouble. Of course you, the dome designer, know exactly where everything goes without the color coding. Do it anyway. The third time I put up my portable dome, the temporary color coding had worn off. It had been a few months since I had put the dome up last, but I went ahead anyway, full of fool-confidence in my ability as a self-taught dome expert. The dome went up beautifully, until I got to the last five struts. They just wouldn't fit. Too long. I sat down and thought it out, and finally realized that I had used ten short struts for the base ring instead of ten long ones. There was no way out of it but to take it all down, with a couple dozen people looking on, and begin all over. Very embarassing.

Another time, my helpers and I had the dome about three quarters complete when it became obvious that something was badly wrong. Struts refused to stay in place, hubs pushed outwards, while others pressed inwards. I pushed and pulled at base hubs, and shifted leveling blocks from one spot to another, to no avail. Naturally this was just the time when a crowd of curious bystanders gathered to ask foolish questions about the dome and why it wasn't working. Finally we found the trouble—someone had put a short strut where a long one should have been. When that was corrected, the distortion disappeared, and so did all our problems. With proper color coding, the mistake would have been obvious at once or, more likely, would not have happened at all.

Be sure tools and materials will be available when needed, and don't skimp on things like ladders and scaffolding. Trying to make do with makeshifts can get somebody hurt.

The idea behind these horror stories is not to frighten you, but to help keep you from making similar mistakes. *Your* dome should go together like a charm.

My Process

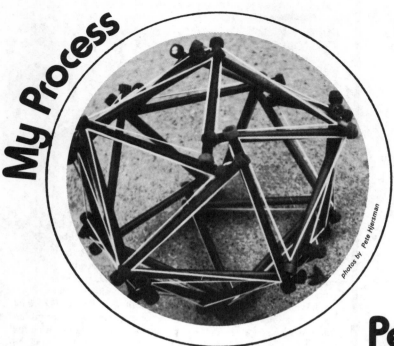

photos by Pete Hjersman

My exploration of domes has been a constant process—making models, discovering new ideas and interrelationships, building domes, re-doing models, etc. Through this process I have discovered many relationships between various domes and geometric shapes.

I first started with the 5 regular polyhedra, of course. The tetrahedron, cube, octahedron, dodecahedron, and the icosahedron. The icosa can be made a dome shape just by removing one pent cap (remove any 5 struts that join at one hub). I learned that only the tetra, octa, and icosa are stable. They have triangular faces. The first dodeca I made had 3' struts. I kept waiting for it to take shape . . . Maybe when I get this strut in, nope, well, maybe this one . . . I finally ended up with a big pile of spaghetti on my floor, just lying there in a heap. Yep, that triangulation sure helps!

Ah—what happens if I triangulate the faces of the dodeca with 5 triangles each? Well, I came out with a stable structure, but what is it? It's definitely not a 2V alternate. We will come back to this.

Meanwhile, back to the tetra. If I put 4 triangles in each face of a tetra what happens? An octahedron is formed! This form looks very organic—it hung in my room for a long time. I didn't have any particular luck in further triangulation of the octa or dodeca, so on to the icosa.

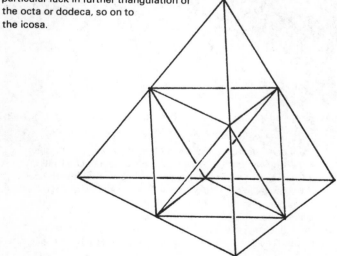

Pete Hjersman

The first dome I ever saw and went inside was a conduit dome that Don and Paul built in Davis. When I saw it, a nondescript parachute covered it—it was anything but flashy. It didn't make much of an impression on me, but then I started thinking about it, went back to Davis and got plans to copy it. My brother and I went in on it—a 2V alternate breakdown (class 1, method 1) conduit hemisphere. We followed the fabrication directions given in *Domebook* for tube frame domes, so I'll skip all the standard stuff and relate new things we learned.

Squishing tubes in a vise can easily result in a broken vise. We used a pneumatic press in a high school auto shop. This gave much cleaner, flatter ends. We squished them flat across but if I did this again I would use a curved line like rear view mirror brackets on trucks: I'm sure this would be stronger.

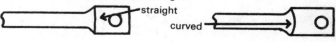

straight

curved

One of the biggest problems with a bolted hub is that several struts are invariably flying around loose for a while. They tend to bend very easily on the crimp line. This is a plus for a hub system where the struts fasten to a plate or something independent of the other struts.

Since conduit comes in 10' lengths and this dome has only two strut lengths, it is easy to calculate the lengths so the pipe can be cut without waste:

A chord—.618(chord factor) x $\frac{1.000}{.618}$ = 1.000 (ratio)

B chord—.547(chord factor) x $\frac{1.000}{.618}$ = .884 (ratio)

Now, add the two lengths together: 1.000 + .884 = 1.884
The holes will be drilled 3/4" from each end. There will be 4 ends, so 3" is subtracted from the 10' (120") to become 117" and the equation becomes 1.884x = 117"

$$x = 62.1" = A$$
$$.884x = 54.9" = B$$

Cut the pipe according to these dimensions:

62.1" + 1.5"		54.9" + 1.5"
63.6" = 5.3'		56.4" = 4.7'

Drill the holes 3/4" from each end. The dome will be about 16' 9" in diameter.

We have used this dome many times. My brother toured the local high schools and gave discussion/demonstrations with it. It was used as an emergency first aid shelter at a whole earth festival in Davis. I used it at Quick City last spring. (As you can see from the photograph, I had a parachute tensed inside the frame. This made it very strong in the wind. The domes that were covered on the outside had trouble in the wind.) Right now it is sitting in a client's backyard so they can try out the space before they buy it—a rather new approach for architecture! Next, it will be on our roof—a place to relax and . . . uh . . . watch the stars!?!

TENSEGRITY

The next thing I delved into was tensegrities. Boy, did I struggle with that first icosa—whew! The easiest way I've found for making quick tensegrity models is with tinker-toy struts (or cut slots in lengths of dowels), rubber bands and surgical tubing: slip a band over each strut, using the slots in each end. These strut-bands are then linked together in whatever configuration desired, from tetras to spheres. With the larger shapes, the struts tend to slip off the bands they are linked to, so cut a 1/4" ring of surgical tubing and slip it over the end.

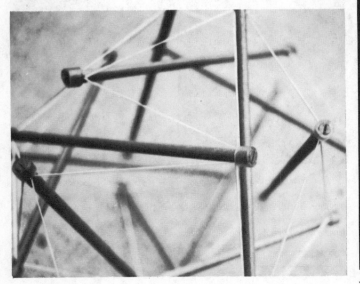

Tensegrities are incredible for gaining an understanding of relationships of polyhedra and great circles and Archimedean solids and truncations and duals. Let me start with an example:

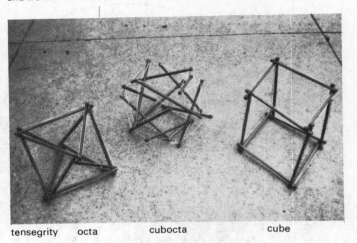

tensegrity   octa   cubocta   cube

To build a tensegrity octahedron you need 12 struts   12 rubber   bands 24 rings of tubing (essential for this process) You will notice that each vertex has 4 struts coming together. Slip each strut end half-way along the neighboring strut until they are all separated—now what do you see? A tensegrity cuboctahedron! (an Archimedean solid). The cubocta can be developed by truncating the octa. If you look closely at the cubocta, you will notice that three struts lie in a plane—they describe a great circle.

Now, if you slide the struts the rest of the way—that is, enlarge the squares that were formed at the vertices of the octa and shrink the octa triangles—you will form a cube. The cube is the mathematical dual of the octa!

This same sequence can be done with the dodeca—icosadodecahedron—icosa.

tensegrity dodeca   30 struts   30 bands   60 tubing rings

The icosadodeca is also formed of great circles. If all the short struts are removed from a 2V alternate, an icosadodeca results.

If I start this sequence with the tetra, I go through the truncated tetra (Archimedean solid) to an icosa. This icosa differs from the other in that the compression members (struts) are separated from the tension members (bands). This type of tensegrity is termed discontinuous compression—the compression members are not continuous. The sequence will end back at another tetra, since it is its own dual.

icosadodecahedron

tetra — truncated tetra — icosa

Another type of tensegrity can be developed by connecting the vertices to the centroid of the figure by struts. A stable cube is developed and an unstable tetra. The tetra cannot be made with rubber bands—I used string.

A large tensegrity sphere is a lot of fun—it can be dropped, rolled about, worn over your head . . .

Fuller points out that some molecular geometries are identical to tensegrity structures. (See *World Design Science Decade*, "Document 2")

90 struts   90 bands   180 tubing rings

TRIACON

Along about this time, I finally made a model of a 2V triacon (class II, method 3). As I was absorbing the differences between this and the 2V alternate I suddenly knew the triacon looked familiar: It's the same as the triangulated dodeca! Ah—another connection.

PLYDOMES

My next adventure was plydomes—domes made of 4' x 8' sheets of plywood bolted together and bent into a geodesic pattern.

Some openings are triangles and some are pentagons. If you enlarge the triangles, you will get an icosa; from the pentagons, you will get a dodeca! Another example of duals and their usefulness in understanding geodesic geometry.

The openings have edges that form complex curves— waterproofing would be difficult at best. It seems to me this dome has very limited usefulness.

SKIN PATTERN

I now had my conduit dome up for a while, and decided to cover it with polyethylene sheeting. I wanted to find a way to make the skin with as little joining as necessary; that is, to reduce the linear footage of seams. By dividing the dome into 5 equal nets (of 8 triangles each) one pattern can be used to cut all 5 sections. These sections can be cut from a 14' roll of plastic, available at hardware stores. For this first net, I used tape for the seams, which sort of lasted 3 months. I did find out about an adhesive, produced by Uniroyal, which can be used for polyethylene. I did a test with it—outside in the weather, with a load straining the seam for six months—and it was still a strong bond. It is applied just like contact cement, a little on each edge, allowed to get tacky, and pressed together. Very simple. It is reasonably inexpensive, but is not easy to obtain because it is an industrial adhesive. I had to get mine direct from the factory. It has a snappy name—"M 6405"—and is available from UNIROYAL 407 N. Main Street Mishawaka, Indiana 46544

I'm sure that other companies make a comparable adhesive, I have just not found them.

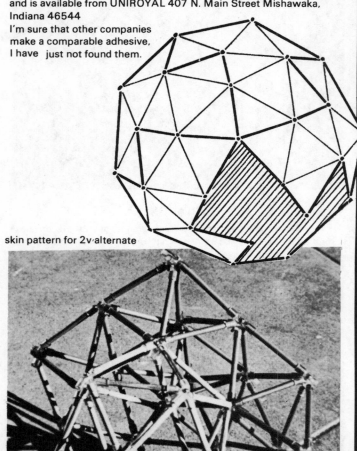

skin pattern for 2v alternate

OCTET-TRUSS

The ways that tetras and octas fit together seem endless. As I already mentioned, a 2V tetra forms an octa inside. The four spaces left over form congruent tetras. They can be packed to fill space; no room will be left over. An easy way to visualize this is with cubes. We're all familiar with the way cubes can be packed—look at almost any skyscraper or apartment building. An empty box can be completely filled with cubes and no room will be left over. This is filling space or close packing.

If the octet-truss is packed spherically it appears to form a complete sphere with an icosa inside. Actually, it will not close, for the same reason that regular tetras will not pack to form an icosa—the edge to radius ratio of an icosa is 1.0515. If it was 1.000, then tetras would pack. It's close.

It is more practical if the truss is packed in a plane. Then it can be used as a truss system in building.

I was showing a photo of one octet-truss building to a friend and he said, "Isn't that the same one that used to be located a couple of hours south of where it is now?" Sure 'nuff! They just moved the whole structure to a new location.

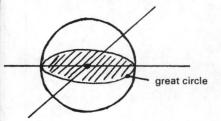

great circle

GREAT CIRCLES

From the octet-truss I moved into great circles. A great circle is like the hemisphere line on a world globe. It is the largest diameter circle that can be drawn on a regular sphere. The plane it forms cuts the sphere in half—it passes through the center of the sphere.

Everything I investigate in theory and with models I try to relate to actual structures. So what use are great circles? Aside from being important in understanding geodesics (a great circle is a geodesic line), domes can actually be built using only great circles. Every line in an icosadodecahedron forms an arc of a great circle. These lines can be made circular—drawn on the surface of a sphere. This is the basis for another dome I did.

GREAT CIRCLE DOME

Materials   24 10' pieces of PVC   PVC solvent   16 couplings   18 bolts/nuts

Joints—pipes bolted together where they cross   Circumference = 60'

Diameter = 19.1'   height = 9.5'

Most of the PVC was 3/4" class 200, but some was schedule 80 and it worked just as well. This is a simple dome to make—all the arcs are great circles and they are all of equal length. A half circumference, such as A-F, will have 5 equal segments. Add about an inch to each end (for the end bolt) of the overhead arcs, and drill 4 equally spaced holes. The distance between any two holes or joints will be 10 (circumference of the complete circle divided by 10 equal segments). The bottom ring, a complete circumference, will have 10 holes. If you use 10' lengths of PVC, the 30' arcs will each require 2 couplings (a special piece used for connecting lengths of PVC). The bottom ring will require 6 couplings. Try to locate the holes in the pipe and not the couplings.

To assemble, we first coupled the length of pipe into 5—30' lengths and 1—60' length. Do a neat job with the solvent—there will be a lot of stress at these points. Also, the solvent dries quickly, so it must be done rapidly. Then drill the holes (we used 3/16'' bolts). Finish coupling the bottom ring.

We bolted the pipe together starting with the top pentagon and worked our way down. As we continued to bolt, I became increasingly worried that something was wrong—I had never tried this type of structure before, nor had anyone else I knew. It was an experiment—would it work? So we kept on bolting and it *still* just lay flat. To help matters, a couple of kids were running around screaming, "It won't work. It won't work." Great for my jangled nerves. Well, finally it began to take shape, to rise slowly off the ground, and—whew! to assume its proper shape. I cannot express the immense, deep relief I felt when we finished and it worked!

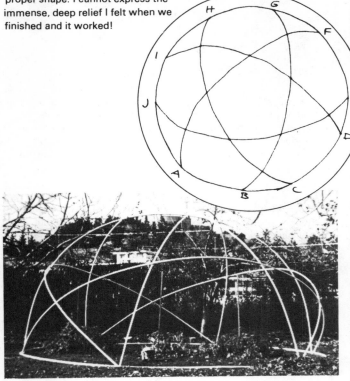

With scraps, I built a 4' copy and set it outside my window. One day it occurred to me that the dome could be much stronger if the pents were triangulated. If I used wires it would not add very much weight. The next idea was to have 2 sets of 5 wires in each pentagon and separate them with a spacer. So I collected 12 orange juice can lids and some wire. The lids were of consistent size and strength and almost exactly the right diameter. The PVC spacer was held in by the lip on the lid. I just used baling wire for this model, but it still could almost support my weight!

Shortly after this, an opportunity came up to build another portable, inexpensive dome, so I suggested a tension dome, using the concepts I developed with the 4' model.

TENSION DOME

The main advantages of this dome are savings in weight and cost. The conduit costs about 13 cents a foot, the cable less than one cent a foot. The cable also weighs much less and is easier to transport and to store. Here is how I did the dome: Materials:

Struts—3/4'' thinwall conduit; cut to 5' 0'', flatten ends, drill holes 4'—10 1/2'' apart (3/4'' from each end), bend ends (same as conduit dome), amd make 35.

Cable—6 strand, #20 TV guy wire; center-to-center length of cables is 4' 2 3/8''. When cutting the cable, add about 2'' on each end to form loops. On each cable make the first loop, then place in jig (board with two nails or bolts 4' 2 3/8'' apart) to make the second

loop. This must be done very accurately—there is no way to adjust the cable lengths in the dome. Turnbuckles would double the cost of the dome. Wrap the wire carefully; braze or solder to keep from slipping. Make 60.

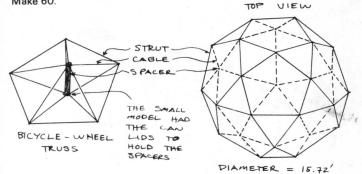

Spacers—conduit, 18'', make 6.
Bolts—3/8'' x 2'', need 32 with nuts and washers.
This dome is assembled differently from most domes. This procedure seems to be the easiest:

(1)   Bolt together 12 groups of 5 cables each.

(2)   Lay out struts and bolt together, loosely putting cables between struts.

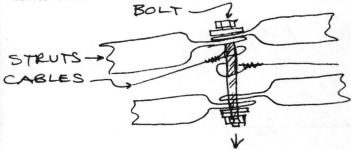

(3)   Tighten bolts holding struts.
(4)   Pop in spacers—this is the tricky part. It's easier if the spacer in the top pent is put in before the whole dome is bolted together. The best way to put in the spacers (since they will be a very tight fit) is to loosen one bolt that connects five cables. This way the spacer need only be slipped over a short length. Put the spacer over the opposite bolt, then get about six strong people to stretch the cables apart, and slip in the spacer. Tighten the loose bolt and the dome is finished.

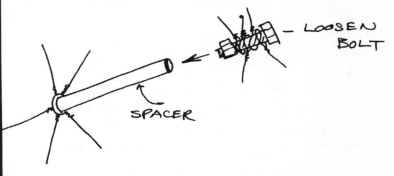

Here's the way I found the cable lengths, in case you want to do a different size dome. The strut length will be the 4' 10 1/2'' center-to-center dimension, not the 5' 0'' (remember to subtract 3/4'' from each end before doing the calculations). The spacer length of 18'' was arbitrary; perhaps a different length would make a stronger dome.

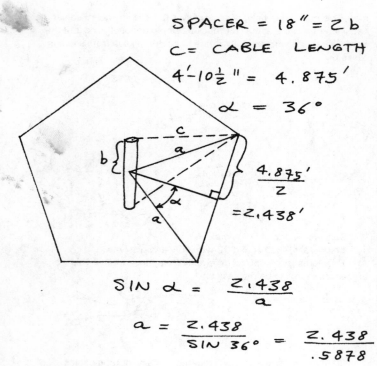

$$\text{SPACER} = 18'' = 2b$$

$$c = \text{CABLE LENGTH}$$

$$4'\text{-}10\tfrac{1}{2}'' = 4.875'$$

$$\alpha = 36°$$

$$\frac{4.875'}{2} = 2.438'$$

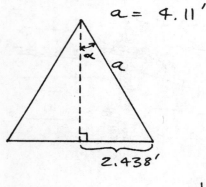

$$\text{SIN } \alpha = \frac{2.438}{a}$$

$$a = \frac{2.438}{\text{SIN } 36°} = \frac{2.438}{.5878}$$

$$a = 4.11'$$

2.438'

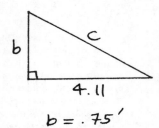

4.11

$$b = .75'$$

NOTE: —If tension is too much in the pents, shorten the spacer length; if there is too little tension, make longer struts.
—Shorter spacers will give more room inside. With the 18″ spacers a lot of interior space is taken up.

If you look at the geometry of this dome, many things can be seen. It can be developed from the Archimedean solid the icosadodecahedron, from great circles, or from a 2V alternate. Look at the struts on the drawing. If you take out the cable and flatten all the pentagons, the solid which results is the icosadodeca. If you follow any 5 struts from one side to the other, across the dome, you have traversed a great circle arc (same as in the great circle dome). Now look at the diagram with the cables—what does it form? A 2V alternate.

If you try to develop tension domes from higher frequencies, you will discover more Archimedean solids—the truncated icosahedron from the 3V alternate, for instance.

ICOSA DOME

I did a small icosa for a school play-yard, 2 x 4's with strap hubs (see Pacific dome, in *Domebook 2)*. The bottom struts do not lie flat, but angle towards the center of the icosa. If the bottom angles are recalculated, then it would lie flat. If the bottom pent is to lie flat, the angle will be 36° instead of 32°, for the pieces on the bottom. For the bottom end of the 10 side struts, the bottom will be 36°, the top end 32°. The problem here is that there are three types of struts instead of one:

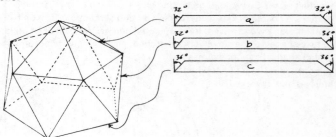

The strapping is very strong and will easily support anyone climbing on the icosa. However, as an environment for little people, the strapping could be hazardous. The outside was partially covered with plywood and carefully painted with inspiration direct from the hearts of the little people. Such eloquence! Why can't the art of little people be considered as valid as the art of big people?

DIAMONDS

I have often been interested in the diamond configuration possible with domes. The diamond is established when any two adjacent triangles have their opposite vertices connected and the center strut removed. Instead of being a convex figure, the dome becomes convex-concave—a very interesting surface.

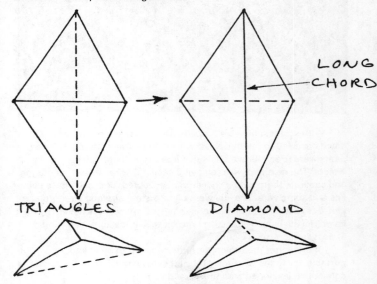

LONG CHORD

TRIANGLES   DIAMOND

This basic configuration is used for large domes—up to almost 400' diameter. Fuller's laminar dome also uses diamonds, in conjunction with regular triangles (see patent #3,203,144).

The triacon breakdowns are easier to generate diamonds from than the alternate. For example, the 2V triacon is based on the rhombic triacontahedron (the dual of the icosadodecahedron).

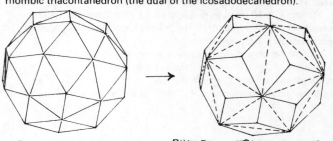

2V, TRIACON   RHOMBIC TRIACONTAHEDRON WITH DIAMONDS

The dotted lines form an icosa, so the chord factors become 0.6180 for the solid lines, 1.0515 for the dotted lines.

The 4V triacon makes a very attractive dome with diamonds. If the geometry is studied, 5 different configurations can be seen: icosahedron, icosadodecahedron, dodecahedron, 2V alternate, great dodecadodecahedron.

Diamond 1   Diamond 2

 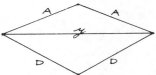

Hemisphere—make 30   Hemisphere—25 + 10 halves
Sphere—make 60   Sphere—make 60

Member	Chord Factor
A	.336
D	.363
X	.546
Y	.616

These are of sufficient accuracy for models, but more places are necessary for a full size dome. A and D are in the *Domebook*, X and Y would have to be calculated.

The hassle with this dome is the vertices—some join three struts, some 10 struts, some twelve.

MODEL MAKING

A fast and cheap way to make reasonably good looking models is with applicator sticks (available at pharmacies) and vinyl or surgical tubing. Cut the tubing in rings and punch holes with an ice-pick or nail—5 or 6 evenly spaced holes. Push the sticks into the holes. A lot of models can be built very quickly this way.

Well, that's it. I've tried to share some of my knowledge and experiences. I hope you benefit. If by chance you try something I've suggested and learn something from it—let me know. Feedback is a valuable part of my process. Thanks—have a pleasant journey.

Peter Hjersman
691 Fairview
Oakland, Ca. 94609

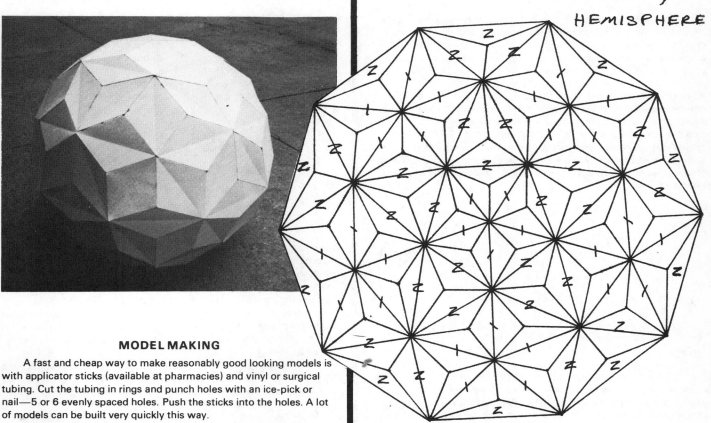

4v, TRIACON WITH DIAMONDS LABELED, HEMISPHERE

A Simple 2V Tent Dome

Morrie Chodeck

John Prenis

This chapter is about a small simple tent dome that I made for a camping trip in Canada. Its portability makes it handy for part-time domers, who can take it apart and store it in the basement when necessary. It's not expensive, demands no fancy wood working, and can be built with hand tools if need be. It's small enough to transport on top of a car, but large enough to stand and walk around in. It sleeps four or five people comfortably. The one-piece suspended skin rules out the possibility of leaks. Because the skin is separate from the frame, construction is non-critical, and small errors are not as troublesome as in other forms of dome construction. To me, this proves that you do not need fancy tools or a lot of money to have fun with your own dome. I think it's a good idea for every dome builder to start with a simple dome like this one. Mine has taught me a lot, and been a lot of fun.

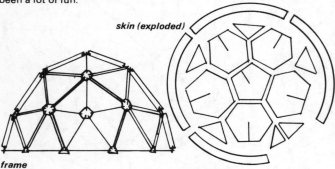

skin (exploded)

frame

The original version of the dome is 14 feet in diameter and consists of a plastic skin suspended from a wooden frame. The geometry is 2V alternate and has two different types of triangles. The skin is made out of 6 mil clear polyethylene and the frame out of 1 x 3 furring strip (actual measurement 3/4'' x 2-5/8''). The dome has a groundsheet which overlaps a groundskirt attached to the inside edge of the skin, making it quite waterproof. There are seven screened vents, and the top two are protected by a large pentagon of plastic stretched over the top of the wooden frame.

Furring strip is cheap and available in a variety of lengths. Despite the many flaws in the wood, it is far stronger than necessary for a

dome of this size. My design called for 30 short struts and 35 long ones. I bought 40 eight foot lengths of furring strip and made my struts 51 and 45 inches long so I could get one long and one short strut from each piece of wood. With a choice of two places to cut each strip, I was able to avoid knots. Badly flawed strips yielded only one strut. By careful planning. I was able to leave the worst of the knots and splits in the scrap pile. For joints, I decided on a simple plan of

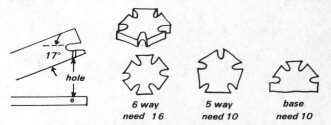

17°

hole

6 way
need 16

5 way
need 10

base
need 10

interlocking slots. The ends of the struts were slotted so as to fit into slots cut in hubs of 3/4'' plywood. This system appealed to me because it required no bevels or compound angles. The slots were made by first drilling a 3/4'' hole, then finishing the slot with a saw and a wood rasp. Later, the ends of the struts were drilled to take wood screws. A 1/2'' screw eye was put in each hub and then opened slightly with pliers. Working alone, it took me about a week to finish the struts and hubs. Helpers and a power saw would have speeded things up greatly.

The first erection of the frame taught me that the base struts must be in a perfect circle and the base hubs leveled, or the struts will refuse to stay in place. This is very frustrating—push a stubborn strut into its hub, and another pops out on the other side of the dome. A spontaneous demonstration of the dome's omni-directional stress-sharing characteristics.

When I began to put up the second course of triangles, I learned something else. The horizontal struts form a ring which is in tension due to the weight of the struts above. This tension pulls the joints apart. Somehow this elementary insight had escaped me. After some abortive experiments with clothesline, I decided to put a wood screw into each joint and settle that problem once and for all.

With the frame more or less ready, I began work on the skin. I had decided earlier to use 6 mil polyethylene because it is cheap, easily heat sealed, and readily available. Polyethylene is supposed to have only a year of useful life in direct sun, but I did not expect to be using the dome that long.

Several phone calls failed to locate a ready source of colored poly in the Philadelphia area, so I was forced to make the skin entirely out of clear poly. I've heard since that cement supply houses sell white poly to put over curing concrete. The 8 x 100 foot roll of clear poly that I bought turned out to be more milky than clear. It had been folded before rolling to make it more compact.

It took about 2 days to cut out the plastic. This I did with the aid of two triangular cardboard templates, one 49-1/2″ x 49-1/2″ x 49-1/2″ and one 49-1/2″ x 43-1/2″ x 43-1/2″. A one inch margin was left on the edges for heat sealing. The lack of a large clear area for handling the plastic was a great inconvenience.

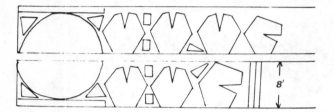

The pattern I developed called for the skin to be made up of 5 hexagons, 1 pentagon, and 5 triangles. Breaking up the pattern in this way allowed me to eliminate about half the seams and thus cut down on the heat sealing necessary. The pattern below was designed to make good use of the plastic and also to make sure than no more than three pieces of plastic come together at any one point. This helps eliminate hassles when heat sealing. I goofed this part and had some four way seams to deal with. Vent openings were cut out and flexible fiberglass screening taped into them. I had originally intended to heat seal the screening between two layers of plastic, but this did not work. Again, I goofed by not checking my work closely enough and ended up with a vent in an odd place.

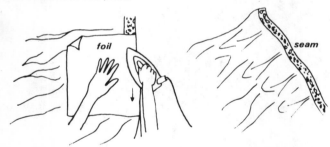

Heat sealing of the seams was done on an ironing board with an ordinary electric iron set at "rayon." The seam was sandwiched between two sheets of aluminum foil; then the iron was run slowly down the edge. This takes practice to do properly, but it is really no harder than sealing a plastic bag. The finished seam will look bubbly and patchy, but if properly done it will be strong and absolutely waterproof. If overheated, the plastic shrinks slightly along the seam, causing wrinkles. If these wrinkles are allowed to fuse together, they will tear apart and cause leaks when the plastic is opened out.

The central seams of the hexagons and pentagons were sealed first. Then the hexagons were sealed to the top pentagon one by one. Then the base triangles and the door were added. The door was cut from scrap plastic with a generous overlap along the edge so that it would hang closed by itself. The groundskirt went on last. By this time I was thoroughly sick of heat sealing and glad to see the last of it.

I've learned since that there are other ways to heat seal. I've heard

that a Teflon-surfaced iron works, though I haven't tried it. Another thing that sounds worth trying is to take a 100 watt soldering iron, grind the tip flat on one side, drill a hole in it, and bolt on a ball bearing so that it spins freely. When the bearing is hot, it can seal a long seam in one pass. An occasional spray of silicone lubricant keeps it from sticking. A solid-state light dimmer of appropriate wattage can be used to regulate the temperature. With a little practice, an excellent seam should be possible.

Poly can also be glued (write to adhesives manufacturers) or sewn.

With the heat sealing finished, I cut oversize vent flaps from scraps and taped them in place so that the vents could be closed in case of rain. Lastly I added the ties by which the skin hangs from the frame. A simple way to do this is to place a marble or pebble inside the plastic, fold the plastic around it, and tie a string around the resulting neck.

 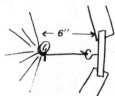

A worthwhile variation is to substitute a washer or wooden bead with a length of cord tied through it for the marble. This gives you a length of cord hanging down inside the dome, handy for hanging a second skin, sunshades, insulation, etc.; while preserving the watertight integrity of the skin.

While the cord is out, use some to outline the triangle that will be the door. This takes the strain off the plastic and keeps it from tearing.

With the skin finished and lying in a great heap on the kitchen floor, I was faced with the task of folding it into a manageable package. I figured out a folding plan with the help of a model, and after an hour of wrestling, the skin was folded into a compact bundle.

Erection of the dome is straightforward. A string tied to a peg in the ground is used to lay the base struts and hubs out in a circle, after which they are screwed together. Then the base hubs are leveled with flat stones or wood scraps. After this is done, the successive courses of triangles are assembled and screwed together. When the frame is complete, the large 'rain hat' pentagon is pulled over the top of the frame and tied down. Hanging the skin inside the frame takes only minutes. Next, the groundskirt is pulled flat and straightened from the inside. Then the groudsheet is carried in and laid down, overlapping the groundskirt to make a weathertight seal. Now the finishing touches are added, sunshades are hung, and the proud dome builder can admire his handiwork.

Original Bill of Materials (1971 prices)

Qty	Item	Price
40	8 ft. lengths of 1 x 3 furring strip	$15.00
1	8 x 100 ft. roll of clear 6 mil poly	10.00
130	1″ no. 8 wood screws	1.20
	scraps of 3/4″ plywood for hubs	——
	twine for ties	——
26	steel washers	.25
26	1/2″ screweyes	.75
2 yds.	26″ fiberglass screening	2.20
100 ft.	2″ polyethylene tape	2.80
1 roll	2 sided aluminum foil vapor barrier (for sun shade)	6.40
	Total	$38.60

photos by Buzz Teacher

A SIMPLE 2V TENT DOME
John Prenis

I was quite pleased with the dome in Canada. We had three good rainy days during the month we were there, and the dome held up well, with no leaks. A clear dome is nice to be in on a rainy day. You have lots of room and all of the light there is. It was fun to lie back and watch the raindrops tracing paths-of-fastest-descent over the dome skin. Turning over, I could see a film of condensed moisture on the underside of the ground sheet. Suddenly it was like being in a submarine. Water, water, everywhere, but none inside the dome!

At night, I lit the dome with candles, and there was a pattering sound like rain as all the bugs within a quarter-mile gathered to bash their heads against the plastic. From the outside, the dome glowed, softly luminous, like an enormous pineapple gumdrop.

I awoke every morning at sunrise. In a clear plastic dome, the dawn comes up like thunder, and you get up with the sun, like it or not. In the light of the sun, the dome warmed up very quickly. A big drawback of the clear plastic was the heat build-up inside. The dome was shaded for only part of the day, and once in the open sun, the inside temperature would go up to 100°, while outside it would be 80°. Hanging triangular sunshades cut from aluminized vapor barrier inside helped a lot, but temperatures inside the dome were usually ten degrees above those outside. I was very sorry that I had not been able to get any white poly. I had wanted to make 3/5 of the skin from white poly and 2/5 from clear poly. When setting up the dome I would have put the clear poly facing north, for light, and the white poly facing south, to temper the heat of the sun.

At night the dome lost heat very quickly. Plastic has almost no insulating value, and I was grateful for a warm sleeping bag.

The experience in Canada taught me a number of things. First, the tape usually sold with plastic film is not very permanent. After some exposure to the weather, the adhesive dries out and gives up. The tape holding the screens will eventually have to be replaced—sewn-in screens would have been much better.

The view from the dome is rather murky. The plastic blends everything into a soft blur. To get a clear view of the outside, we had to bend down and peer through one of the vents. Some small windows of clear vinyl taped or sewn into the skin would have been nice.

Another little problem was the lack of a positive door closure. If I had had the time, I would have liked to put in a zipper or snap fasteners. It makes no sense to screen the windows and leave the door hanging open. I ended up taping the door shut with masking tape each night to keep the mosquitoes out.

The biggest problem with the dome was that the rigid joint system made it too delicate to stand mishandling during erection. With about four feet of leverage working against the joint, it was all too easy to split a strut or break a hub. The dome had to be very carefully

handled, which means that I had to put it up all by myself—I simply couldn't trust unskilled helpers not to bust something. Putting in all those screws was a real pain. Any unevenness in the ground would cause struts to pull out. It was always a chore to get the dome settled "just right" and usually the dome would not "settle down" until it was almost entirely up. And when it was up, I didn't dare let anyone climb on the frame.

I decided to design a new version that would overcome these disadvantages. It would have to be rugged, simple to make, and inexpensive. Also, it would have to utilize as many parts from the previous version as possible. I finally settled on a hub made of furring strip and plywood that the struts would bolt onto, giving both flexibility and strength.

This system may be rather crude and lacking in elegance, but it is simple, easy, and anyone ought to be able to do it.

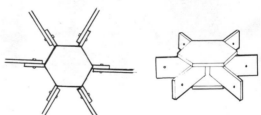

The first step was to get some new lumber. Buying the new furring strips was a bit of a shock. Inflation had almost doubled the price I paid two years ago. And the new strips were only 2-1/4" wide as opposed to 2-5/8" for the old ones. I began to wonder if perhaps conduit or PVC pipe would now be a cheaper way to build a dome.

(Fuller says that if we were to pay a fair price for the time and energy Nature uses to make petroleum, a gallon of crude oil would cost a million dollars. I wonder what a tree is really worth?)

New Bill of Materials

130 2" X 3/16" stove bolts	$ 4.50
1/2 lb. 1 1/2" nails	.50
4 oz. wood glue	.50
1 sheet 3/8" exterior plywood, sheathing grade	6.50
12 8' lengths of 1 x 3 furring strip	8.00
	$20.00

The best lumber, free of large knots and splits, was saved for the hub arms. The rest was made into struts. I turned all my old struts into new struts by drilling holes in the ends, ignoring the old notches. Holes were also drilled in the ends of the hub arms. The hexagons and pentagons for the hubs were cut out of 3/8" exterior plywood with a saber saw attachment on my 3/8" electric drill. About half a sheet of plywood was used.

I developed a special procedure for putting the hubs together. First, I drew lines in pencil to indicate where the nails would go, then I "started" the nails part way into each hex so that they would be where I wanted them later. Next, I set the hub arms into a special jig. This consisted of six (or five) triangles of corrugated cardboard nailed to the old door I was using for a workbench.

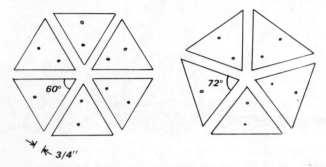

The idea is to hold the hub arms in place while the plywood is being nailed on. It worked fine. First the arms were set in place, then a generous amount of glue was applied. A hex (or pent) was laid on top, and centered, and then only a few hammer blows were needed to sink the nails. Then the hub could be lifted out, flipped over, more glue applied, and the remaining hex (or pent) nailed on. I'm sure I used more nails than were necessary. The only remaining step was to screw in an eyehook, and the hub was finished.

Morrie Chodeck

My hubs are strong, but very bulky. They take up almost as much space as the struts, and they add about 45 lbs. to the weight of the dome. I'm not too happy about that. However, this system has the interesting advantage that it is not limited to one type of dome. If I want to, someday I can use my present hubs and struts as part of a larger dome—like a giant Tinkertoy.

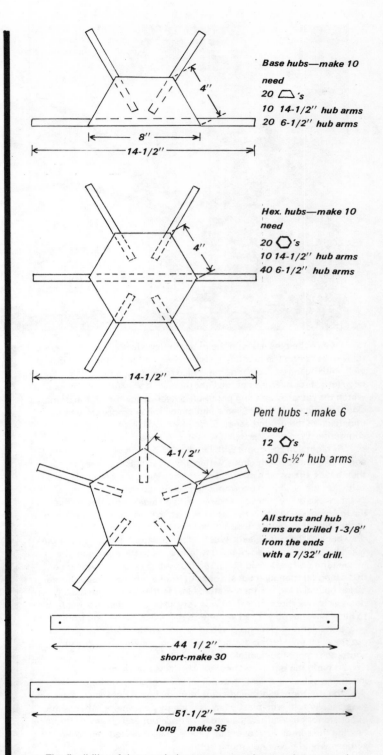

Base hubs—make 10
need
20 ⬡'s
10 14-1/2" hub arms
20 6-1/2" hub arms

4"
8"
14-1/2"

Hex. hubs—make 10
need
20 ⬡'s
10 14-1/2" hub arms
40 6-1/2" hub arms

4"
14-1/2"

Pent hubs - make 6
need
12 ⬠'s
30 6-½" hub arms

4-1/2"

All struts and hub arms are drilled 1-3/8" from the ends with a 7/32" drill.

44 1/2"
short-make 30

51-1/2"
long   make 35

The flexibility of the new hub system caused some phenomena I hadn't anticipated. I've come to realize that dome hubs are of two types. Rigid hubs always maintain a fixed angle. It's easy to put up a dome with them, because the half-completed structure holds its shape due to the rigidity of the hubs. Also, the angle established by the hubs helps you make sure that the struts are going into the correct positions. However, you have to be careful not to strain a rigid hub. With the full leverage of a strut working against it, it is easy to break something. Flexible hubs, on the other hand, cannot be broken by any mishandling. They will accept any angle you shove them into without protest. However, their flexibility means that any strut structure put up with them needs constant support until it is finished. Also the hubs themselves do not predetermine the shape of the structure.

My new version of the dome was color coded like this: R = red
B = blue

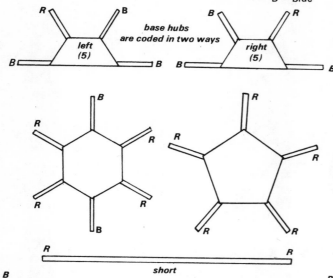

base hubs are coded in two ways

left (5)   right (5)

short

long

Erection goes as follows: First, a stake is driven where the center of the dome is to be. Then a 15-1/2 foot string and some flour are used to mark out a circle. Ten long struts (not 9, or 11!) are counted out and distributed around the circle. Next the base hubs are placed around the circle, right and left alternating. Then the nuts and bolts are poured onto a large sheet of plastic, and the bolting together begins. Four people is a good number. First the base ring is bolted together. The nuts should be as tight as you can get them with your fingers. If you can afford wingnuts, get them. When the base ring is complete, it is pulled into a better circle if necessary—the dome becomes cranky if the base is not reasonably circular. Next the triangles of the first row are bolted together. If there is any trouble in getting hub and strut to meet flatly, the hub can usually be wiggled into a better position. As each triangle is completed, it is propped up with a strut until it can be connected to its neighbors. When the first ring is completed, it will be self-supporting, although wiggly.

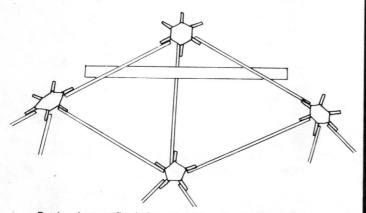

Putting the next five hubs up is tricky. They have to be put up one at a time and well supported or they will suddenly flop inward and

conk you when you least expect it. When one is up, brace it like this with an extra strut to keep it from falling inwards. When the ring of struts outlining the upper pentagon is finished, everyone can breathe easy.

The five spokes of the upper pentagon get special treatment. They are bolted to the last hub while on the ground. Then one person holds the hub over his head while the others bolt the ends of the struts in place. This method eliminates the need to stand on something to get the last hub in place.

With the frame done, the skin goes up as before. Because the wider hubs add 1-1/2 feet to the diameter of the dome, I had to lengthen the ties on my old skin from 5'' to about 12''. *You* can make a bigger skin and have more room inside.

The new version of the dome disappointed me in a couple of respects. (I guess there never will be a completely satisfactory dome.) There's some slop in the joints because I drilled the holes larger than

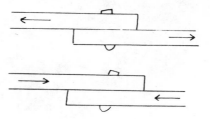

necessary. I still can't bring myself to trust anyone's weight on the frame. (I tried to chin myself from the top, but stopped when I heard ominous creaking noises.) The dome is also heavier and bulkier than before. (170 lbs. vs. 125 lbs.) However, it is flexible enough to tolerate assembly by inexperienced helpers, and it isn't bothered by uneven ground. With help, it goes up in about an hour. It's already been the star attraction at a crafts fair and a kiddie carnival, and now that I don't have to treat it so gently, I expect to have it out a lot more often.

I remember the first time my dome was erected for a public occasion. After it was over, about a dozen young people gathered in the dome. We had a lively conversation going when suddenly a plump, elderly woman crawled in through the door, grasped someone's hand, and began shaking it, saying, "God bless you! You will walk strong in the service of the Lord. Hallelujah!" She began going around the circle, asking our names, giving each of us a big smile, a handshake, an off-the-cuff fortune, and a blessing. A couple frowned, but she radiated such warmth and sincerity that most of us smiled and gave it right back. The dome seemed to contain and concentrate the smiles, the good feelings, the exuberance, the pure wackiness of it all. For a moment I wondered in the back of my mind if the dome were in danger of floating away.

John Prenis
161 W. Penn Street
Philadelphia, Pa. 19144

A Tube Frame Dome

Carey Smoot

Ed Cooley

Our approach to the idea of dome-as-house was to achieve an enclosure as light as the dome of heat and light cast by a campfire in the woods. We used a steel tube frame with a one-piece 20 mil vinyl skin, and it feels quite separate from the interior, which is post and beam (gravity-oriented) and mostly wood and soft materials. The actual space makers (loft, furniture, etc.) are very fluid—we find ourselves moving the furniture constantly.

The site is on a riverbank among fir, cedar and maple trees, so the clear shell is perfect for taking it all in.

The doorway is sunken so the continuity of the dome is unbroken.

Some basic information—Our dome is a 4 frequency alternate 26′ diameter icosahedron. The foundation is 11 concrete footings poured in the ground. We used aluminum lawn edging sewn together with wire for forms above the ground.

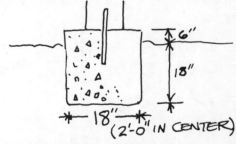

There's a bar in each post and footing as an anchor. The floor is all 2 x 8 joists, 10 doubled, and 10 single with 2 x 6, 8, and 10 tongue and groove decking.

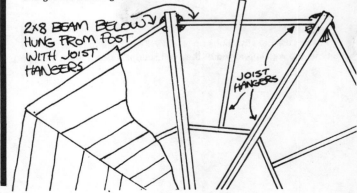

The frame is galvanized steel tubing, .049'' thick, bolted together through squashed ends. It cost about $100 wholesale from an irrigation equipment co. It's strong enough to hold a person in the middle of a strut without bending.

Our skin is 20 mil vinyl, made into one piece on an electrostatic sealer at the Ant Farm. It took 2-1/2 weeks of hard work on a machine that's hard to come by. It's got an 18'' bar that zaps the seam, but getting a straight seam across a vertex that's less than 360° is no fun. You have to wrestle and fight with a mountain of plastic. We discovered that we made a big mistake and had two 11 foot repairs to make. Cleaning the skin is a hassle—5 months of smoke from a wood cookstove and pot-bellied heater make it dirty enough that it's hard to make out stars at night. Running water or a hard, steady rain and lots of soap does the job though.

Insulation—our plan is to use panels of polyurethane foam cut into triangles which could be moved around as weather and whim suggest. They could attach at the hub bolts. Costs will be about $200 for 120 triangles. We made it through the coldest days in the area's history (-10°F) without insulation, but when the fire died at night, everything froze solid. The condensation 'snowed' inside.

Ventiliation—We had condensation 'rain' when there was only one vent at the door. (It stopped when we opened another one opposite.) The dome needs one at the top to let the smoke out.

In another dome we're building now, we're using cold air ducts from the edges to the center to eliminate drafty floors. In our present dome, there's a 5°-15° difference between the floor and the level of the fire.

Also in this new dome, we're using a window/vent designed by Jerry Kernoshak of Eugene. It opens in all three directions and doesn't depend on hinges or sealants.

Foundation		$50	20 man hours
Sand & Gravel	$30		
Rental Equip.	$20		
Floor		$210	200 man hours
Joints	$60		
Flooring	$120		
Stairway	$30		
Frame		$130	20 man hours fabrication
			30 man hours erection
Skin		$200	130 man hours fabrication
			30 man hours erection
Chimney		$36	5 man hours
Rentals		$80	
Digging (foundation and stairwell)			100 man hours

All together we spent about $750 and 500-600 man-hours on the dome itself, not counting the whole septic tank, pump and building inspector trips, or the days of struggling with the skin before discovering it was put together wrong, necessitating patches. It also doesn't include the insulation ($150), vent/hardware ($25-50), front and deck doors ($60-120), a bathroom ($75-150) or any other finish work. It also doesn't include incalculable weeks hanging out with the dome, admiring, fantasizing, waiting.

What all this adds up to is the most beautiful place I've lived in. There's nothing better than a round clear house for feeling one's part in the environment and its cycles. You don't have to go to a window to see the sky or the river—it's just all right here.

I hope all this rambling is useful to someone.

Ed Cooley
Star Route
Marcola, Ore. 97454

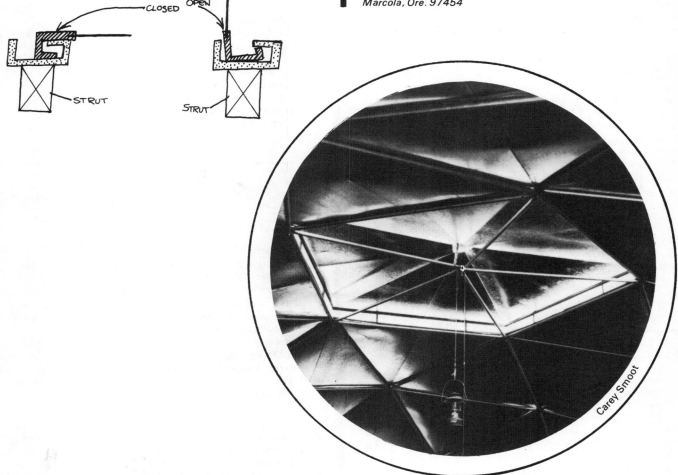

Carey Smoot

Spherical Dome Membranes

Carey Smoot

Carey Smoot

1. First calculate the square footage of your skin area.
2. Calculate gores by determining first the width of cloth you are to use (this determines the widest part of the gore or panel). 2 panels (l & r) make up 1 gore. Add skirt (depends on tie down technique). See details.

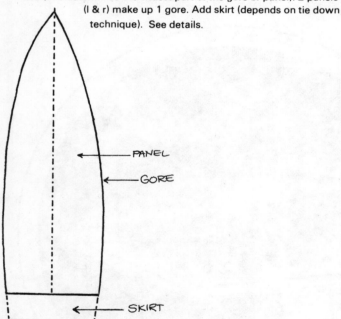

3. I usually use fire and water proof canvas that only comes in 30'' and 31'' widths. So these are a panel. For a hemispherical skin, the widest point is at the base. As an example we will start with 29'' widths at base.
4. Allot 1'' for double seams. Another allocation or consideration at this step is the shrinkage rate of the cloth used. All organic cloths have some shrinkage (usually 2%-5%) and vinyls, glasses and nylons do not. They do, however, "stretch", so probably should be given no tolerances.

5. The math for spherical skins is much easier than those of elliptical profiles. See the section on calculations.
6. After calculations a template should be made. I suggest using a large floor area and a 20' flexible wood batten. Loft and plot the points but use the wood batten to get a "natural" curve from point to point. Add your seam allowance to the template.
7. At this point recheck all calculations and the template.
8. Cutting should be done on a table. Alternate the template to conserve cloth. Mark and roll-up or fold and store in a dry *inside* environment.

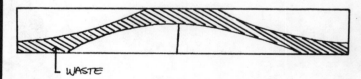

9. Fabrication: Sew from top to bottom as any slippage will cause spiraling of the total membrane. If using organic materials use polyester dacron thread (silicone treated) as it does not shrink and the cloth will close around needle holes to give a waterproof seal. If using nylons, dacrons, or vinyl laminates, a polyester thread is advisable but a waterproof seam design (French felt, over-lap and top stitch, etc.) should be used.
10. Sewing machines: A home model (domestic) machine can be used for light nylon, or cotton canvas, but nothing over 3 oz. For heavier cloth an industrial machine can be rented (Yellow Pages under Industrial Sewing Machines). For large membranes (3000 sq. ft. and over) a puller is recommended on the machine.

Thread Size and Needles

For lightweight cloth, use a #24 dacron thread, 12 to 14 needle.
For 3 to 8 oz., use a #16 thread with 16 or 18 needle.
For 10 oz. and above, use #12 thread. Use 20 to 22 needle.
Usually cloth, threads, webbings, clear vinyls, etc., can all be bought at one place.

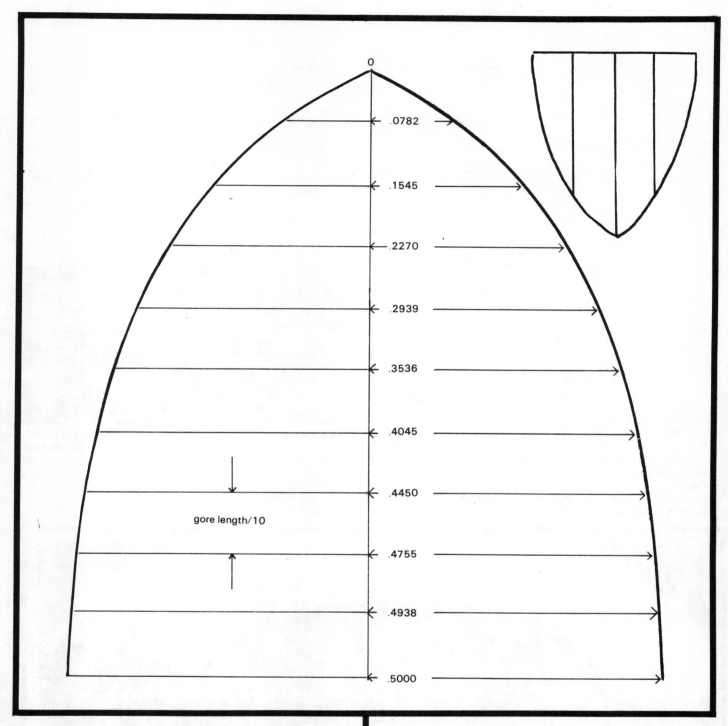

0

.0782

.1545

.2270

.2939

.3536

.4045

.4450

gore length/10

.4755

.4938

.5000

How to calculate the shape of the gores for a hemispherical skin:
1. Decide on the necessary diameter.
2. Find the circumference. Circumference = 3.14 x diameter.
3. Determine the width of the gores. To do this, decide on the number of gores and divide into the circumference to find out how wide the gores will be.

Gore width = $\dfrac{\text{circumference}}{\text{number of gores}}$

If the result is wider than your material, try a smaller number. (Remember that a gore can be made up of two or more strips of material.) The greater the number of gores, the smoother the skin will be (and the more work you'll have putting it together.) Multiples of 5 are good for skins made to be hung inside domes. Many of the tie points can be made to fall on seams, and the tie points can be sewn right into the seams.

4. Determine the length of the gores. Gore length = $\dfrac{\text{circumference}}{4}$

5. To make a template having the exact shape of the gores, tape together several large sheets of paper until you have a piece the length and width of one gore. Draw a line down the center and divide it into 10 equal sections. Determine the width of each of these divisions by multiplying the numbers below by the maximum gore width. Carry your results out to four places. Mark off these lengths from both sides of the center line, and then draw a smooth curve through the points. Take care in laying out your template, because any error will be multiplied by the number of gores.

Details and Miscellaneous Notes

For fastening the membrane to the structure
(a) use a batten fastened to the base struts or the deck.

(b) use an attached skirt with a catenary curves.

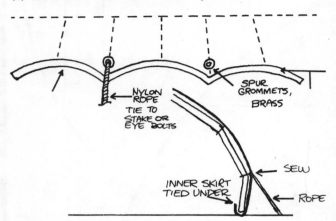

NYLON ROPE TIE TO STAKE OR EYE BOLTS

SPUR GROMMETS, BRASS

SEW

INNER SKIRT TIED UNDER

ROPE

Windows, vents, doors
Metal frame: use p.v.c. pipe with sheet metal screws as described by Jay Baldwin in *Domebook 2*, p. 43.

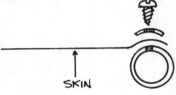

SKIN

Wood frame: use battens to fasten skin around openings. With a little ingenuity, openable flaps can be devised. The top vent can be oversized.

A whole lot hasn't been done in detailing membranes. Experiment. Stop chafing at hubs by putting some coffee can lids over them.

For nomadic skins a one-piece membrane with minimal openings is suggested.

The Inter-Galactic Tool Co. in San Francisco has a nice "hung" membrane dome that folds up.

Resources in California

United Textile & Supply Co., LA.
Envirotecture, P.O. Box 307,
Newhall, CA 91321
Canvas Specialty, L.A.
Jim Sparks, S.F.
Inter-Galactic Tool Co., S.F.

Insulation of canvas membrane framed structures:
John Nolan said we could spray 1" of foam on the first skin and then put on an outer skin. This could be used for any type of structure.
For nomadics: use 1" styrofoam cut into triangles and inserted inside between struts. Would look good and be well insulated.
Notes on minimal surface tension membrane structure:
I have built several—One hyperbolic saddle, 2500 sq. ft. One pentagonal over a geodesic frame.

Carey Smoot

New reinforced poly and vinyl is available from Grifolyn, Texas. Extra strong, clear colors, can be heat-sealed, sewn, taped. Good price.
Carey Smoot
Envirotecture
Box 307
Newhall, CA 91321
(805) 255 0446

Carey Smoot

A 3V Canvas Skinned Dome

Steve Ervin

It all started in the Portland (Oregon) Public Library. We were looking for books about Japanese houses, and on the same shelf there was *Domebook 1*. We took it home and got pretty turned on by the idea of building a dome. We spent a month with plastic straws and cardboard models, and by the time we moved to the country we felt we were pretty ready to build a real dome. We decided to start out with a life size model—that was one of the best decisions we made. We got a load of 1 x 2's, and ripped them up into struts for a 13' diameter dome. We were going to simply wire the hubs together by twisting wire through holes in the ends of the struts, then staple on clear polyethylene and use it as a garden shed/greenhouse/compost cover. We had a lot of friends over one day and started putting it up. Well, by the time we had two courses up we began to wonder. It was clear that the thing was going to be too heavy to hold itself up with our wire hubs, and it was going to take some intricate scaffolding to get the top course on, and besides, it sure didn't look like 13 feet across. On further consideration, it became clear that we were building a 26' dome, having put r = 13 (instead of d = 13) into the chord calculations. Two days later, we had *two* complete sets of struts, this time for 13' domes. Second time around it went up a lot easier, and even though the wire hubs were not really strong enough for anything other than a model, by the end of the day I was hanging securely in a hammock strung across the middle of the dome.

By this time, *Domebook 2* was out and we felt really confident of our ability to handle the equations, and familiar enough with the strut patterns to get it on with the full sized dome. We decided not to go too big—just be enough for a waterbed and two people to be comfortable. We settled on a 16' diameter, 3 frequency vertex zenith, alternate breakdown dome. We were living in Molalla, Oregon, on 40 acres of Douglas fir, at the foot of the Cascades and in the heart of Crown Zellerbach, Weyerhauser, etc. The only time we even *began* to appreciate them was when we rented a 17' truck and went down to the local mill. They had a big pile of odds and ends, all the way from 1 x 4's to 2 x 12's and everything in between. We got one whole truckload of selected odds and ends and another truckload of rough cut 2 x 2's for $40—more than enough lumber for the dome and all our other building needs.

We found our site on the crest of a hill looking out over the Willamette Valley with the sunset on one side and the sun rising out of the Cascades on the other. We cleared some brush (not to mention the poison oak), got high up there a couple of times, and got to work.

First we built a platform for the dome to sit on. As we were on a hill, the ground dropped about 3' across the site, so the platform was almost touching the ground at one side, and 3' up on the other. We decided on an octagonal platform, 17' across (because that was big enough for the dome, and also the length of our longest floorboard.) The platform was constructed quite easily in two days with the help of several friends. First we sank the corner posts (4 x 4's) and the center post (8 x 10), all coated with creosote and levelled across the top. Then we put on the side and radiating girders (2 x 10's), then parallel 2 x 4 joists 18'' on center. Finally we laid down the floor of alternating 1 x 4's and 1 x 6's, with a layer of 15# roofing felt underneath to keep out drafts. We nailed the floor down with cement coated flooring nails, so we didn't have any problem with warping boards or popping nails. But we did have a little drying problem—we put the boards down so green that in a month there were 1/4'' cracks between them. Thanks to the roofing felt it wasn't much of a problem, but one would be well advised to use dry, seasoned lumber on the floor.

For the skeleton of the dome we decided on 2 x 2 struts connected (as in the Pacific Domes) with steel strapping and sections of pipe. We used plastic A.B.S. waterpipe, which conveniently came in the two diameters we needed, 2-1/2'' and 3'' o.d. The struts we ripped and drilled in a day, and the strapper we rented with 3/8'' steel strapping for a week. The skeleton went up fast—we constructed some hexes and pents on the ground and lifted them up in place; other struts went in one by one on the upper courses. It took us two days, but we went swimming in between. We left out one complete hex for our door, and framed up a tall rectangle inside it. The biggest problem we had here was when we woke up one morning and found the whole dome had slid off the platform and tipped onto the ground in a high wind overnight. We tipped it back up into place, repaired a few broken hubs and immediately took the sensible step of bolting it to the platform. The skeleton was extremely solid then, and we spent some time just climbing around on it.

We gave a lot of consideration to the material we were going to use for the skin of the dome, and ultimately our decision had a lot to do with our conception of what the dome was to be. While it was intended as a real shelter, we didn't know how long we were going to

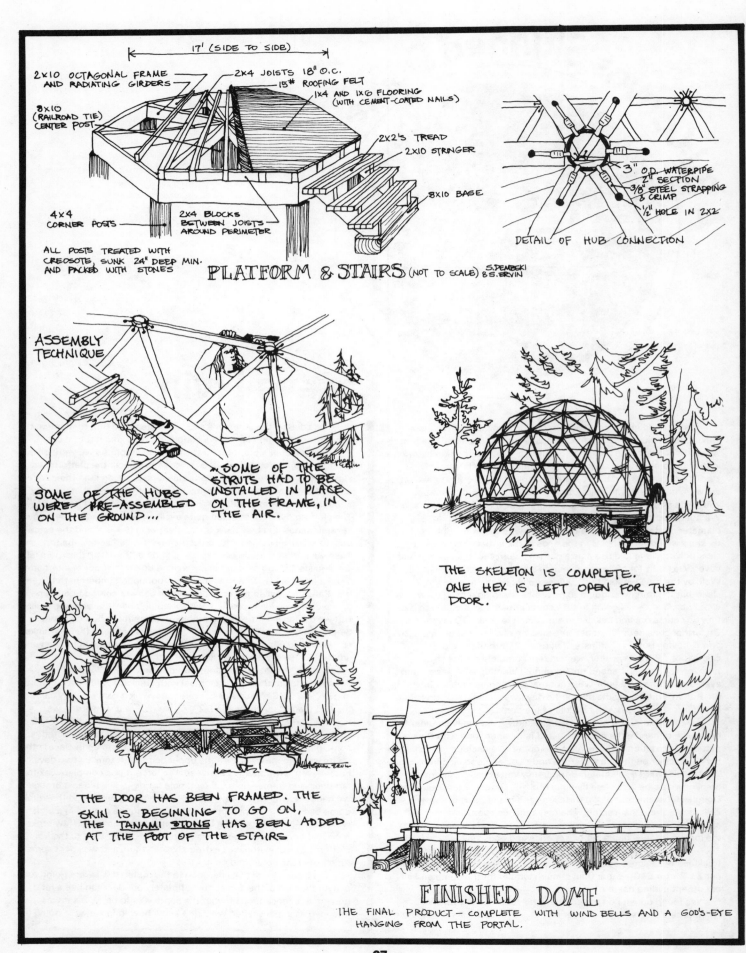

17' (SIDE TO SIDE)

2×10 OCTAGONAL FRAME AND RADIATING GIRDERS

2×4 JOISTS 18" O.C.

15# ROOFING FELT

1×4 AND 1×6 FLOORING (WITH CEMENT-COATED NAILS)

8×10 (RAILROAD TIE) CENTER POST

2×2's TREAD

2×10 STRINGER

8×10 BASE

4×4 CORNER POSTS

2×4 BLOCKS BETWEEN JOISTS AROUND PERIMETER

ALL POSTS TREATED WITH CREOSOTE, SUNK 24" DEEP MIN. AND PACKED WITH STONES

PLATFORM & STAIRS (NOT TO SCALE) S.DEMBSKI & S.ERVIN

3" O.D. WATERPIPE 2" SECTION
3/8" STEEL STRAPPING & CRIMP
1/2" HOLE IN 2×2

DETAIL OF HUB CONNECTION

ASSEMBLY TECHNIQUE

SOME OF THE HUBS WERE PRE-ASSEMBLED ON THE GROUND...

SOME OF THE STRUTS HAD TO BE INSTALLED IN PLACE ON THE FRAME, IN THE AIR.

THE SKELETON IS COMPLETE. ONE HEX IS LEFT OPEN FOR THE DOOR.

THE DOOR HAS BEEN FRAMED. THE SKIN IS BEGINNING TO GO ON. THE 'TANAMI STONE' HAS BEEN ADDED AT THE FOOT OF THE STAIRS

FINISHED DOME

THE FINAL PRODUCT — COMPLETE WITH WIND BELLS AND A GOD'S-EYE HANGING FROM THE PORTAL.

be in Oregon, but we knew it wasn't going to be too long. We wanted to use some 'organic' material that would fit in with the surroundings and would also be comfortable and aesthetic to be inside. We had visited a fellow in Portland who had built a small dome in his backyard and skinned it with patchwork canvas scraps which had been really nice and homey, and we liked the concept of a lightweight skin as in a tipi. There is in fact a small company on the Oregon Coast which makes tipis to order, and so when a friend of ours was going to the coast, we sent him to find out what material they used for their tipis, and where to get it, and so on.

Apparently they were friendly and helpful there, and our friend came back with a handful of samples. They use both synthetic and natural duck (basically canvas, duck just refers to the weave) in a variety of weights, from about 10 oz. to 16 oz. (per square yard). The tipi makers recommended the synthetic, primarily because of its longer life expectancy. What we decided on was 12 oz. cotton canvas duck, 'marine treated' which means it's waterproof and rot-resistant. Besides being more organic and having a nicer feel to it, it was about half as expensive as the synthetic, coming out to about $1 a yard, on a roll 36'' wide. We ordered two rolls, or about 100 yards, from the company in Oakland, California, and it arrived about 3 days later.

We put it on the skeleton with galvanized roofing nails. Our method was to wrap the canvas around as many triangles as it would completely cover, then cut it off, reposition it, and keep going. Where we had vertical seams we put in a ''French seam'' (doubly folded, like on blue jean legs), and on horizontal seams we just let it overlap to let the water run off. We left two side hexes open for windows, and the top vertex pentagon for a skylight. It rains a lot in Oregon, and so we also built a little pointed overhang over the door and covered it with canvas. That addition really made the dome look inviting, and broke up the symmetry of the form just enough to make it interesting. Where the canvas met the platform at the base of the dome we folded it under and glopped on some emulsified asphalt base. After the first rain, most of the asphalt washed away, and so we got some tubes of butyl rubber caulk and did it again. That worked much better.

With the skin in place, all we had left were the windows. On the sides we just stapled some clear poly in place, thinking that we would eventually glaze in some glass. We decided to glaze in the skylight overhead, using plexiglass instead of glass for safety. All I can really say is that was by far the biggest hassle we had on the entire dome. First of all, we cut the plexi with out circular saw, which was ridiculous. It should just be scribed and broken, like glass. Second, our glazing technique was a little primitive: we nailed in a quarter round frame, then some glazing compound, then the plexi, then another quarter round frame, in each of the five triangles. It leaked. It kept leaking for several weeks, while we kept trying different ruses. More butyl caulk, more strips of wood, more canvas; we tried everything. I didn't know about rubber extrusions then, and our whole design was

pretty poor. Anyway, we finally got it to where the leak was slow enough so that we could just hang a can under it and sleep in peace. The matter of skylights must be carefully thought out. After that battle, we just decided to leave the poly in place on the windows, as it was doing quite well.

We moved into our dome about March, with the skin and windows and door pretty well settled. We had no insulation in the skin, and we were considering what to do for that we when we moved in. The canvas we used was natural finish, sort of off-white, and translucent. Being inside the dome when the sun was shining was an incredible experience, as the walls (roof?) all glowed with a warm, beautiful light. We decided not to put in any insulation at all. Had we lived in the dome in January, our decision might have been tempered by the cold. I think we probably would have decided on styrofoam triangles pressed into place, as they would be somewhat translucent still.

Well, our stay in Oregon came to an end in the middle of June, so we only enjoyed the finished dome for a few months. But we really enjoyed it for that time, and I think living in it caused a re-evaluation of our (at least my) concept of shelter, away from the notion of a cave, to a much more open, spacious, light, celestial idea. I've just been reading Frank Lloyd Wright, and it seems that's what he was discovering too. So I guess that says something about the evolution of ideas.

Building the dome was just as much of an experience as living in it—we learned a lot. In retrospect, it was a good decision to decide to build lightweight and temporary in nature, as that way we didn't have to invest so much and were able to leave it in June with no real material hangups. I guess it's still standing there, though I imagine the polyethylene in the windows has probably blown out unless someone has been taking care of it.

The house we build this summer in Maine probably won't be a dome, but we sure had a good time with our dome, and it was a good way to get into housebuilding and clear away a lot of established preconceptions and misconceptions. Breakdown of cost:

Lumber	+$17 truck rental	$ 40
Canvas	(though we only needed about $70 worth)	100
Strapper	(including rental and materials)	25
Plexiglass	(it is expensive)	20
Miscellaneous	(nails, caulk, etc.)	30
Total		$215

Stephen and Suze Ervin
19 Day Street
Box 29
Cambridge, Mass. 02140

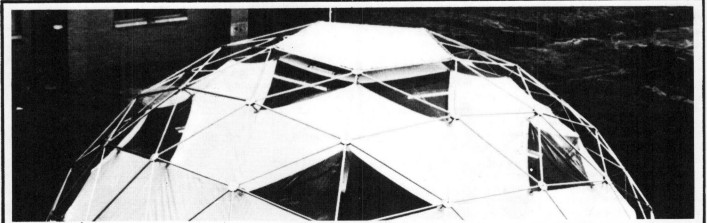

Dome East

A 3V Plastic-draped Dome

D. Scott Sims

D. Scott Sims

This three frequency icosahedron was built in the fall of 1970 near the Ettersberg Road between Briceland and Honeydew in the King's Peak area of northern California on the Pepperwood Flats Commune. It is a 30' diameter 5/8 sphere with the longest strut 6' long. I was building a 50' diameter Dyna Dome for the owner of 160 choice forest acres, leveling land, developing springs, and putting in a sewage system. We built this dome to live and work in while we were developing the land and building the big permanent dome. We made the struts from the 2 x 6's we used for the Dyna Dome foundation forms. First we ripped them into 2 x 3's, and then we ripped them again at a 7° bevel into 1-1/2 x 2's. Next we cut the tip angles, assembled the struts into triangles, and drilled bolt holes. When that was done, we invited all our neighbors and put it up that Saturday. All the chicks who lived on our land cooked quantities of food and we feasted on roast venison that night, with the triangles in the sky around us. The framework fit together like a dream. Each tier of triangles is flimsy until completed, and then it becomes super stable. Always start from the bottom and work up with this kind of dome. Don't put the top triangles together and then try to lift them up—that is impractical and breaks many struts and is extra work. Build the bottom tier first.

Three frequency icosahedron structures have 15 sided bases as both 5/8 and 3/8 spheres. We put in 15 equidistant Douglas fir posts in a circle and one in the center. Then we put in radial floor joists and sheeted them with plywood. We built a trapdoor down into the 3 foot dry crawl space under the floor which we filled with oak and madrone firewood for the winter. We sheeted the dome framework with 6 mil polyethylene film (trade name Visqueen). It comes in rolls of 100' x 20'. We taped three of these rolls together with 4''-wide Arno sheet metal tape, fed it up through one of the triangles in the top pentagon, and let it roll down the sides of the dome.

We held the plastic firmly to the framework with a network of manila rope from the top to the pier posts. The excess plastic and wrinkles were taken out by rolling the plastic at the bottom around the ropes. We dug a 2 foot trench around the perimeter of the dome and buried the edges of the plastic, thereby holding the plastic secure and preventing water from running under our dome home when it rained. I put an airflow vent in the top triangle of the dome for an air exit and five evenly placed wall vents around the base in the plywood floor for equal ventilation. On a hunting excursion I found a righteous old wood cook stove in good shape on an abandoned ranch and moved it into our dome, cutting a stovepipe hole in one of the top triangles. The total cost was $326.76.

When the winter rains came, all of the city hippies living in muslin teepees on our land moved into the dry cozy dome. We put the candle factory workshop area along one edge and sleeping and eating areas on the remaining floor space.

I had helped build plastic covered domes before when we had cut individual triangles out of plastic and then tacked them to the struts with strips of lath and plywood batting, but everywhere there was a hole, there would eventually be a leak. As the wood got wet and dried it would swell and shrink, pushing the nail out farther and farther, making larger leaks as the winter went on. By making the skin one continuous piece, we eliminated this problem, but created others. The flapping of the plastic during wind and rain storms eventually wore microscopic holes in the poly film as it rubbed against the wooden surface. Plastic is waterproof, but will not breathe. Water cannot get in, but it cannot get out, either. As the coffee pot steams and people track water inside, moisture condenses on the inside walls, runs down, and creates miniature storms inside. I often tripped on the storm clouds forming near the top of the dome. The dome had a total atmosphere of its own, like a miniature earth system.

Our thin plastic skinned dome made it through the winter, but 180 inches of rain made living in the dome quite like living on a ship. Once when we had 90 mile per hour winds, the plastic ripped loose where it was taped together, and we had to make immediate repairs in the middle of the night. The most severe test came in mid-December when we woke up to a foot of wet snow covering our whole dome. I was used to looking out on forest green and blue sky and the pure white was really a surprise. I got up and built a fire and lay on my back. Plastic has very little insulation value and as the dome air warmed, the snow began to melt against the plastic and fall off in triangles—the bottom tier first, then the second, and then the triangles around the top, one by one—like a gigantic bee opening its many faceted eye until the sun shone in on the domers. Really amazing—the dome shape distributed the heavy snow load so evenly that the thin plastic film did not even leak.

Polyethylene film is not clear but is somewhat milky—a little visually distorted. Objects outside are easily recognizable. We have been able to watch deer graze early in the morning from inside our bubble, watch hawks fly over, follow the patterns and motions of the moon and stars at night—but plastic domes are definitely for summer living and warm weather climates. Plastic is a poor insulator and only a few degrees difference separates the inside and the outside—almost total heat loss. Not the ideal covering for the Rocky Mountain weather, although another layer of plastic on the inside of the struts would provide a dead air space between for insulation.

Living in a dome is mind expanding with all that space around your head. The acoustics of a dome provides many sharp clear sounds, even magnifying notes to some extent. Learn about domes by living in one, be aware, watch incense flow, feel, hear, and see what it does to your mind and body and soul.

During the spring and summer of 1970 my partners, Gary Abbott and Dean Haney and I built a 26' diameter dome with 530 sq. ft. of floor space on our Synapse Ranch 10 miles south of Lander, Wyoming. We poured a slab on grade foundation and floor and used Dyna Dome patented connectors to put up a 2 x 4 framework with fiberglass resin laminated plywood covering. We failed to use enough fiberglass gauze and matting when we applied the resin and in cold weather since, hairline cracks have formed, allowing moisture to delaminate the plywood. We bought some Huskylite, which sealed up most of the leaks. Huskylite is a rubberized asphalt with aluminum flakes, a material similar to steep roofing tar. It's a product of the Husky Oil Co. and seems to work well for sealing domes. It expands and contracts with the rest of the dome during temperature changes.

We built a second story sleeping loft over one half of our dome. From the living room side all of the dome symmetry is visible and from the loft you can look all around and below. The twelve sided octahedral geometry provides for equal proportioning of space. We have four fiberglass skylights in the top, windows facing the four winds, and a pot-bellied wood stove in the center providing excellent even heating and air circulation as well as lighting.

From Highway 267, a half mile away, our silver dome looks like a huge diamond crystal sitting on top of the hill, sparkling in the sun. Domes hold up well in the severe Wyoming weather—winds flow evenly around as there are no large flat surfaces, snow loads are shed evenly, the shape blends with and complements the rugged mountain environment.

We have recently developed eight sizes of domes which may be purchased in kits of bolt-together panels for the owner who wants to build a dome but is too busy to make the components himself. Synapse domes have been designed with FHA building code minimums in mind. Write to:

Synapse, Inc.
Box 554
Lander, Wyoming 82520

D. Scott Sims

The 16 Foot Personal Dome

Jim Bohlen& Russ Chernoff

The Personal Dome was designed to offer privacy and flexibility for internal arrangements of space. Its structure allows for interconnection with other domes. (fig. 1)

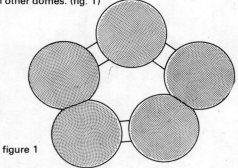

figure 1

The Personal Dome geometry was derived from the dodecahedron which consists of 12 pentagons (fig. 2a). This polygon was chosen as it yields strut locations which allow access to the interior with minimum disturbance of the structural elements. The Personal Dome is 6/10ths of a spherical dodecahedron or a "6/10 sphere" (fig. 2b) which is a 'natural' division and requires only one odd length strut to deal with. A rather large number of subdivisions of the

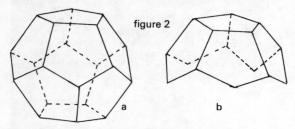

figure 2

triangles was selected as it facilitates installation of such things as doors, windows, sheathing, insulation, and affords geometric similarity. The side struts arising from the foundation are essentially vertical, and provide generous standup room along the dome perimeter on the inside. The geometric similarity permits five evenly

spaced access portals which are important to have when considering the community assembly of domes. Individuality of design will derive from solutions to localized environmental problems. For instance, consider a community of personal domes, joined with passage ways. The form and shape of the passages will be determined by the terrain and the unique social aspects of each community.

The Dodecahedron

Before proceeding further, we should define the elementary geodesic terms. *Frequency* denotes how each pentagon is broken down. The Personal Dome is a two frequency dome.* A spherical 1

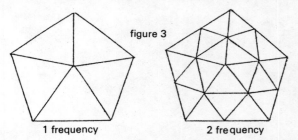

figure 3

1 frequency   2 frequency

freq. dodecahedron consists of 12 pentagons or 60 equal triangles—each pentagon containing 5 of the 60 triangles (fig. 4a and 4b). In a two frequency dodecahedron each of these triangles breaks down into 4 smaller triangles, making 40 triangles total. To visualize this, start with one of the 60 triangles in the 1 frequency dodecahedron. It has

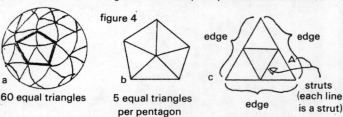

figure 4

a
60 equal triangles

b
5 equal triangles
per pentagon

c
edge   edge

edge   struts
(each line
is a strut)

each equal triangle is subdivided for strength into four triangles

*(Editor's note: The Personal Dome can also be considered as a 4v icosa triacon dome.)

three edges (fig. 4c) and it is subdivided into 4 smaller triangles by dividing each edge in two (this is done in such a way that the edges will begin to curve outward—fig. 5). Dividing each edge in two gives you more strength. As you increase the frequency you get closer to a sphere (and increase the stand-up floor area as well).

figure 5

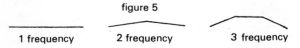

| 1 frequency | 2 frequency | 3 frequency |

The *struts* are the pieces of material out of which the geometric framework is constructed; in fig. 4c for example, each line is a strut and there are 9 struts altogether.

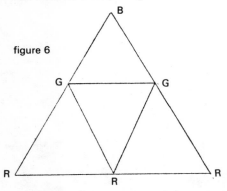

figure 6

The *strut length* is determined by deducting a uniform dimension from each hub-to-hub distance. This dimension is determined from the specific hub design (figs. 8, 9, and 10).

For the 2 frequency dodecahedron there are 4 strut lengths (fig. 6 and table 1). Multiply the chord factor (column 3 - table 1) by the radius in inches; then deduct 6 1/4 inches from that number; this will be the strut length for the hub design which is included. In this same manner, any size dome may be calculated.

The struts are connected to each other by *hubs*. These connecting hubs are made of 3/4-inch exterior-grade plywood; e.g., used concrete forms. The connectors are made of hardwood dowels which are shaped into 3/4-inch diameter pegs. The hubs are inserted into the sawn slots at the ends of the struts, and the pegs are pushed into place. (fig. 7) The holes are all pre-drilled to give the necessary precision and assure ease of assembly and structural integrity.

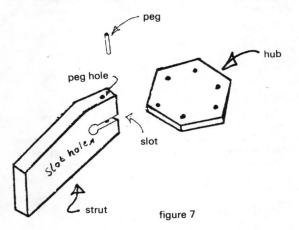

figure 7

Strut Construction

The struts are made from 2 x 4's cut to the exact strut length (table 1). Code the ends B, G, or R, as the case may be. Try to cut the material so that knots in the wood are avoided at the ends where the slots, the slot holes, and the peg holes will be cut (fig. 7). After making a few of the complete struts, place them on the plan (fig. 12) to conform with the outline of the strut end as shown to check your workmanship. Inaccuracies in the beginning will be paid for later when

assembling the dome frame in the field.

If dowels cannot be purchased they can be made by driving a stick of hardwood through a block of steel which has the proper size holes drilled in it. Another feature of the hub design is that poles may be substituted for dimensioned lumber. This alternative can be important in the bush.

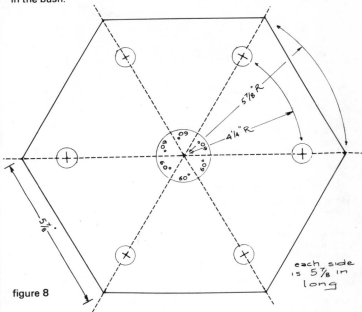

figure 8

each side is 5 7/8 in long

Making the Hubs

Cut plywood hubs according to the plans (figs. 8, 9, and 10). Make three master templates from the plans and then transfer the

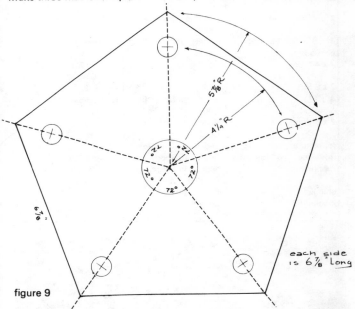

figure 9

each side is 6 7/8 long

outlines of the hubs and hole centres to the plywood panels. Two 3/4-inch 4-ft. by 8-ft. panels are sufficient to make enough hubs for one dome. The G hub is to be installed directionally, meaning that the part of hub on which the holes are drilled more closely together, must point towards the blue (B) hub. The R hub holes are evenly spaced and therefore have no specific directionality. The same for the Blue hub (B).

The hub, strut, and peg system (Peg-A-Strut*) have been tested to failure at five times the design load by the *B.C. Technology Centre* in Vancouver, B.C.

* Registered T.M.

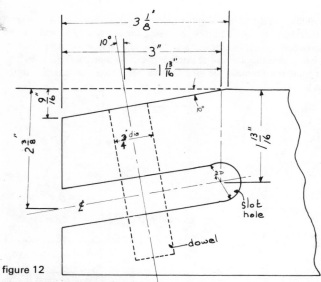

figure 12

table 2 - hub specifications

For the 16-ft. diameter dome only

Color Code	Type	Number Required	Interior Angles
blue	B	5	all 72°
green	G	33	55° 14'
			61° 33'
			63° 13'
red	R	34	all 60°

materials list

Material	Type	Quantity
2' x 4' fir, spruce or cedar	economy grade or better	550 lineal feet
4' x 8' x 3/4'' exterior plywood	waterproof sheathing grade	2 panels
2 x 4 fir for T-beams or 2 x 6 fir	no. 3 grade	20 pcs., 7'10'' to 8' and 50' random length
4' x 8' x 3/8'' exterior plywood	waterproof sheathing grade	18 panels
2 x 4 fir or cedar	economy grade or better	100' random length
foundation posts (11)	cedar, 6'' diameter	
doweling, 3/4'' diameter	fir or hardwood	40 lineal feet
roofing paper	asphalt impregnated breather-type	5 - 100' rolls
shingles	refer to tables	
insulation	as required	

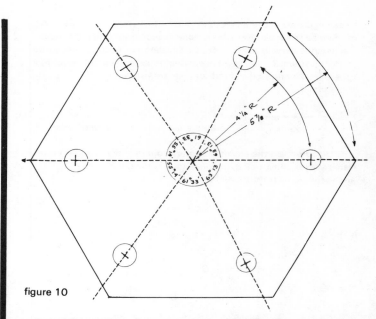

figure 10

Table 1 - strut specifications

Type	Number Required	Chord Factor	Hub Centre to Hub Centre	Strut Length
BG	25	.297781R	28 9/16''	22 3/8''
GG	28	.346155R	33 1/4''	27''
GR	103	.351623R	33 3/4''	27 1/2''
RR	38	.362842R	34 13/16''	28 5/8''
RY	10	.187601R	18 1/8''	14 7/8''

note: RY is the odd or 'truncated' strut

The Foundation

One of the basic reasons for using domes is their light weight and the fact that loads on the shell bear evenly along the whole perimeter of the dome. Consequently, very small design loads are imposed on the floor framing and the foundation. To minimize foundation cost a

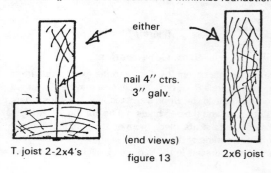

either

nail 4'' ctrs.
3'' galv.

(end views)

T. joist 2-2x4's   figure 13   2x6 joist

raised platform supported on posts is recommended. Here, the small dome philosophy of design demonstrates economy. Since the floor spans are short, very light weight joists may be used. To support a 40 lbs./ft.² live load, 2″ x 6″ joists are adequate. Or, if 2 x 4-inch studs are more commonly available an inverted 'T' beam may be fabricated from them (fig. 13).

The joists connect to ten six-inch diameter posts which are buried in the ground. A centre-post serves to divide the floor span so that 8-foot joists may be used. All joists are installed radially, like the spokes of a wheel, and intermediate nailing joists are installed on 2-foot centres, which give the finished floor frame the appearance of a spider web (fig. 15).

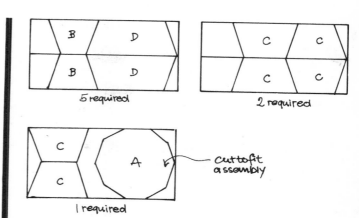

5 required

2 required

1 required

cut to fit assembly

figure 17

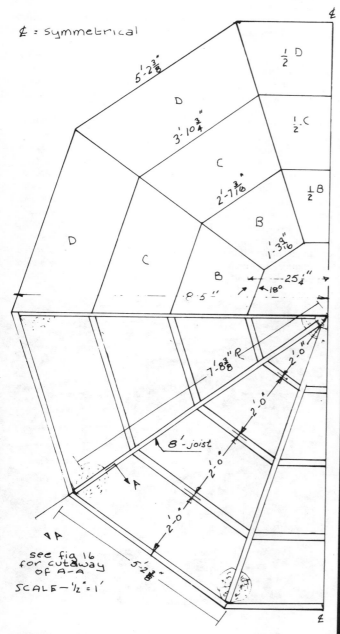

£ = symmetrical

SCALE — ½″ = 1′

see fig 16 for cutaway of A-A

After the foundation and floor framework have been erected, the bottom of the floor joists may be sheathed with insulating board, by nailing to the bottom of the joists. Where inverted 'T' beams are used, the insulating board is fitted between the radial joist and is supported by the 'T' flanges. The tops of the joist are covered with conventional flooring materials. This floor system may enable the space between the joist to be utilized as a return air plenum for a space-heating system.

44

The plywood hubs are fastened on top of the foundation floor (fig. 16).

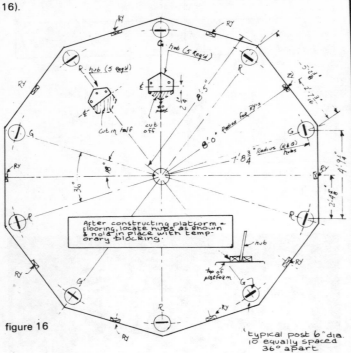

figure 16

The dome can be assembled using the partially assembled framework itself as the scaffold. After assembly and alignment of the completed frame the bottom hubs are securely nailed to the foundation posts. (fig. 14).

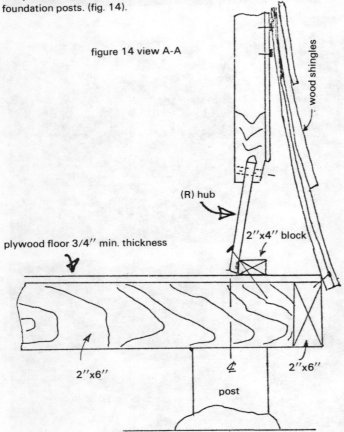

figure 14 view A-A

plywood floor 3/4'' min. thickness

(R) hub

2''x4'' block

2''x6''   2''x6''

post

The plywood sheathing should be cut from 4' x 8' sheets in a pattern similar to that illustrated in figure 17. Refer to figure 15 for the exact sizes.

The Assembly

The struts have been color coded (you did, didn't you?) so that they are merely put in place from the bottom hubs up. No scaffolding is needed, because the dome can be assembled with the structure itself used as the scaffold. Install the struts in a sequence with the bottom row and working upward in sort of a spiral direction. Use the folded paper model (fig. 11) as your assembly guide. To make an easy job of peg insertion dry them out thoroughly by suspending them over the coals of a wood fire or warm them at 200° F. in an oven for 8 hours. This will shrink the pegs and allow them to be easily inserted. After they are in, moisture pickup from the air will cause the dowel to expand and lock into place. Don't plan on removing the pegs at some future date because it won't happen. Have a picnic on top of the dome frame after driving the last peg into place. This will be your structural test. Upon completing the assembly you may notice some hubs appear twisted. This will be due to the dome not sitting level on the foundation or you may have put some struts in the wrong place. Check this out, and if everything looks OK twist the hubs to their correct position. This will level the dome. To check for level, place a 4 ft. carpenter's level on a straight 2 x 4 or piece of evenly cut plywood and align the level edge of the wood with the centres of any two hubs in the row immediately above the base hub row. When certain that the frame is level, fasten it to the posts with dowels or drive spikes through the platform, the base hubs and into the posts. Domes are light and you don't want yours floating away some windy night.

Sheathing (plywood or shiplap) is applied to the struts after the door and window are framed. Breather type building paper covers the sheathing over which is applied the finish material. Flashing is used where required. The smoke pipe and toilet vent are installed and flashed. The sheathing should be at least 5/16-in. or preferably 3/8-in. plywood. Flashing may be obtained by cutting up old auto bodies, gallon oil cans, or thin rust-proof metal. Galvanized iron or aluminum flashing may be purchased at any building supply store. The windows are then inserted and puttied or caulked to keep out the weather.

Framing in the Door

Part of the geometry is removed from the dome to facilitate placement of a door. The structural integrity is maintained by the method of framing the door. Columns are installed from the floor to the two topmost hubs. These columns take the load down to the floor which in turn transmits the weight to the posts. This framing allows the use of an ordinary rectangular door. An old recycled door could be cut to size and installed in a frame that is also modified.

Framing the Windows

A window detail has been worked out that's been tested which *does* keep the rain out. (fig. 18)

The structural strength of the dome does not depend upon the plywood sheathing or any other skin material for structural support. Therefore you may install glass anywhere you prefer. However, do not remove any struts, unless you are prepared to substitute proper bracing, such as is done for the door opening. The importance of attending to detail while installing window glass cannot be over-emphasized in view of the lack of conventional overhanging eaves. Use sealing compounds liberally.

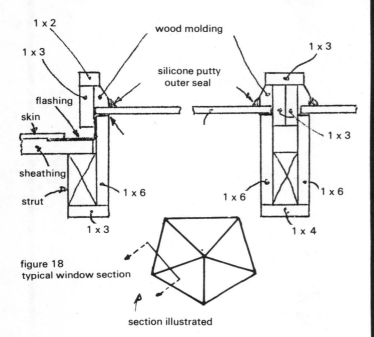

figure 18
typical window section

section illustrated

The Sheathing Skin

As shown earlier, each pentagon is divided into 5 identical triangles, which are subdivided into 4 triangles, two of which are identical (fig. 19). Triangles a, b, and c represent the areas to be

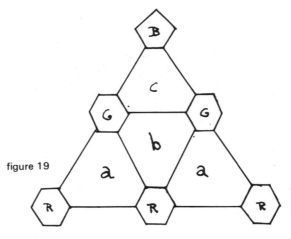

figure 19

covered by the sheathing. The templates to be made are as follows:

figure 20

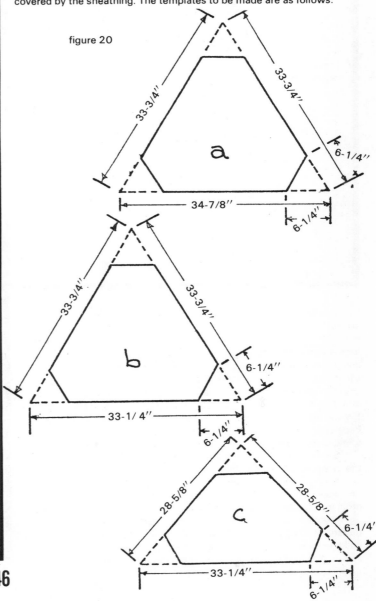

46

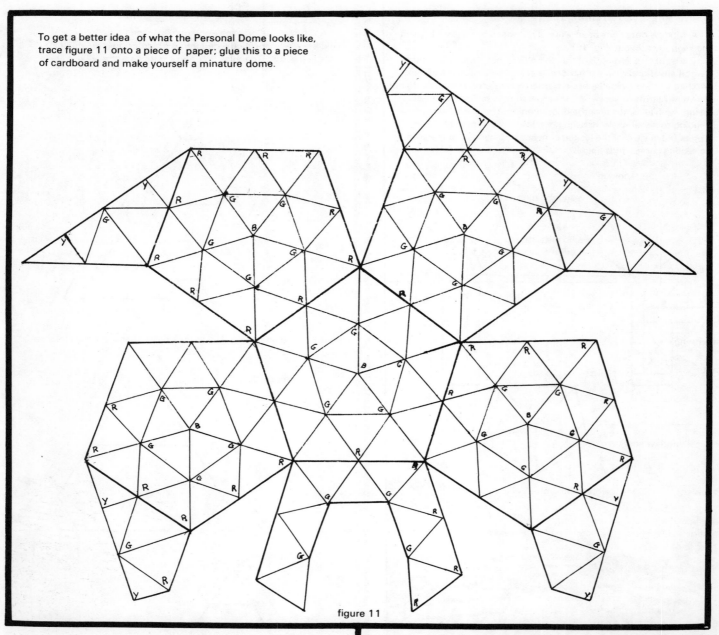

To get a better idea of what the Personal Dome looks like, trace figure 11 onto a piece of paper; glue this to a piece of cardboard and make yourself a minature dome.

figure 11

One of the reasons that we chose the 16 foot dome with this breakdown (2 frequency dodecahedron) was because it could very efficiently utilize 4 by 8 foot sheets of plywood (1/2 inch thick or more) for the skin sheathing. A cutting plan (fig. 21) has been worked out. Just for fun cut a few triangles of different sizes out of your stock of plywood to see how everything fits . . . you'll feel more confident.

The alternation of A panels and B panels (fig. 21) is necessary for only seven 4-foot by 8-foot panels. This situation arises because 28 B's and 68 A's are required. The number of C's would be 25 or less, depending on how many windows are to be included. Along the foundation, partial panels are necessary: 10 half B's and 8 half A's.

Sheath the dome from the top down. This will allow you to use the frame as scaffolding. Sheath in a spiral pattern. The reason for this is to keep the plates as straight as possible. The plates (hubs) have a tendency to twist when stood upon, so the sheathing eliminates this problem. Maintain a constant surveillance to ensure that the hubs are not twisting. If a hub is twisted, it must be straighted or the covering material will not fit properly. Cover the sheathing with *breather type* building paper, installing it with either staples or roofing nails. Make certain that no gaps are left and that the top section laps (by at least 8

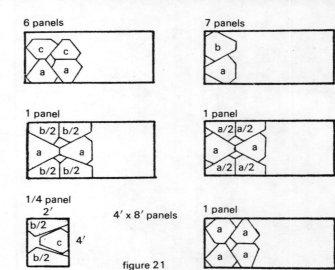

figure 21

in.) over the bottom sections. Avoid laps which end on seams in the plywood.

Cedar Shingle Skins

Skin designs would hopefully be of materials that are close at hand and/or are inexpensive, at the same time being waterproof and resistant to the elements. The framework is able to take the entire design load, so the skin has only to keep out the undesirable elements.

Red cedar shingles are a good solution: (a) they provide a certain degree of insulation as a result of their cell structure; (b) they are durable because of their resistance to rot; (c) they add strength to the structure and aren't too difficult to install if you follow directions.

Shingles are sold in *bundles,* four bundles making a square. A square covers approximately 100 sq. ft. Red cedar shingles come in three lengths (16, 18 and 24 inches) and three grades (1, 2 and 3).

Exposure is the amount of shingle that is exposed to the weather. It's really important to have the right exposure or you're chancing leaking problems. The amount of exposure required is determined by the *pitch* of a roof, the pitch being the slope of a given surface. Shingles should never be less than three layers thick on a roof, and the exposure should never exceed 1/3 the length of the shingle (see table 3 for recommended exposures).

Pitch	Shingle Length (in.)	Exposure (in.)
5 inches in 12 inches or steeper	16	5.0
	18	5.5
	24	7.5
greater than 3 inches in 12 inches and less than 5 inches in 12 inches	16	3.75
	18	4.25
	24	5.75
less than 3 inches in 12 inches	cedar shingles are not recommended	
vertical surface 60 degrees	exposure should not be greater than half the shingle minus one-half inch (single course). Double course up to three-quarters exposure	

table 3

Shingles provide a nice, warm watertight surface if you take the time and effort to use them correctly. Before use, keep them covered, if not inside. They should never be laid when they are wet. A table (table 4) of exposure and coverage for the dome has been compiled so that you can make the best use of a given situation. The table is for use with the 16-foot two-frequency dodecahedron *only*. The 16-in. no. 3 grade shingle is the best shingle for covering this dome in terms of cost as well as in terms of covering a curved surface. The shorter length means that there will be smaller gaps under the butts of the shingles as a result of the angles created on the curved surface.

Surface Segment	Area (ft.²)	Grade	Length	Exposure (in.)	Coverage (ft.²/sq.)	Quantity Shingles (squares)
(a)	285	no. 1	16	7	140.0	1.32
			18	8	145.5	1.27
			24	11	146.5	1.26
		no. 2	16	7	140.0	1.32
			18	8	145.5	1.27
			24	11	146.5	1.26
		no. 3	16	6	120.0	1.54
			28	6	109.0	1.85
			24	10	133.0	1.39
(b)	85	no. 1, 2	16	5	100.0	.85
		or 3	18	5.5	90.5	.94
			24	7.5	100.0	.85
(c)	87	no. 1, 2	16	3.75	75.0	1.16
		or 3	18	4.25	77.0	1.13
			24	5.75	77.8	1.12

table 4

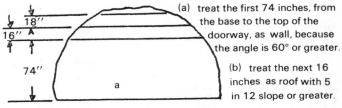

(a) treat the first 74 inches, from the base to the top of the doorway, as wall, because the angle is 60° or greater.

(b) treat the next 16 inches as roof with 5 in 12 slope or greater.

(c) treat the following 18 inches as roof with less than 5 in 12 pitch.

Note: we suggest that 5d hot-dip galvanized nails be used for the entire dome to ensure adequate nail holding for the shingles

Before starting shingling, make sure that you've got *breather type* building paper over the plywood sheathing. The bottom shingle layer should be *double* (fig. 22). Shingle from the bottom up . . . if you're unsure about the methods, ask any old-timer in the area, because they've likely covered many a roof in their time. It's helpful to use a board tacked to the surface as a straight-edge to line up shingles, or a chalked line could do the same thing.

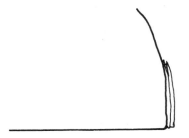

figure 22

If there is a flat grain in the shingle, it is advisable to place it so that the bark side (side nearest the bark) is exposed. The shingles will then be less likely to become waterlogged or to turn up at the butt. Only two nails should be used per shingle.

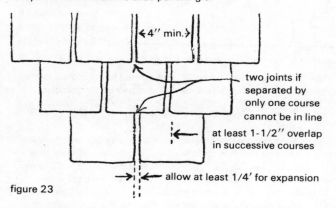

two joints if separated by only one course cannot be in line

at least 1-1/2'' overlap in successive courses

allow at least 1/4' for expansion

figure 23

These are nailed no more than 3/4 in. from the edges, and above the butt line of the next course (row) they should be nailed no more than 2 in. (1 1/2 in., preferably) and no less than 3/4 in. (fig. 24).

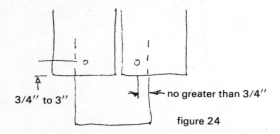

3/4'' to 3''

no greater than 3/4''

figure 24

Nails should be driven flush with the surface of the shingle but should not crush the wood (fig. 25).

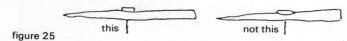

this   not this

figure 25

A study done on old shingled farm structures (in the central U.S.) found that:
(a) exposures greater than 5.5 inches contributed greatly to the number of leaks . . . so be conservative on your exposures.
(b) edge grain shingles significantly reduced the percentage of roofs with warped and loose shingles.
(c) more leaks occured with 16 inch shingles as opposed to 18 inch shingles.
(d) six inches to eight inches in width appeared to be the best as shingles greater than eight inches showed more warpage, breakage, and a slight increase in leaks.

Handsplit Cedar Shakes

Handsplit shakes can be made as well as installed by you do-it-yourselfers. All that is needed is a saw to cut the logs the proper length, a heavy steel blade called a 'froe' and a wooden mallet of some sort.

Shakes are great looking and have the same good qualities as shingles; that being to keep the weather where it's supposed to be. The overlapping technique of covering seems to be the best way of covering a curved surface such as the Personal Dome. Table 5 shows the most optimal usage possibilities for this sixteen foot diameter dome *only*. The 18 inch shake is the best of the commercial shakes for this dome because the shorter length will provide for smaller gaps at the butts on the curved surface. Commercial shakes come in three lengths: 18 inch, 24 inch and 32 inch. Table 6 indicates the correct exposures as recommended by the *Red Cedar Shingle and Handsplit Shake Bureau.*

Surface Segment	Area (ft.²)	Grade (in.)	Length	Exposure (in.)	Coverage (ft.²/sq.)	Quantity Shakes (squares)
(a)	285	m	18	7.5	80	3.6
		n	24	10.0	100	2.9
(b) (c)	172	m	18	5.0	55	3.1
		n	24	7.0	70	2.5

table 5

Note: 6d nails should be adequate.

m- 18'' handsplit and resawn
n- 24'' handsplit and resawn

	For roofs Maximum Exposure (in.)	For walls Maximum Exposure (in.)	Best 3-ply Roof (in.)
18 in shakes	8.5	8.5	5.5
24 inch shakes	10.0	11.5	7.5
32 inch shakes	13.0	15.0	10.0

table 6

Other possibilities for the skin are asphalt shingles, wire mesh and stucco or perhaps ferro-cement. With the ferro-cement it might even be possible to omit the plywood sheathing.

Ventilation

Ventilation can very nicely be obtained by means other than installing opening windows. This is one advantage with domes, in that one can regulate the flow of air to a fine tolerance, unlike conventional dwellings. However, this is not a pure science, and one cannot provide a universal solution to ventilation problems.

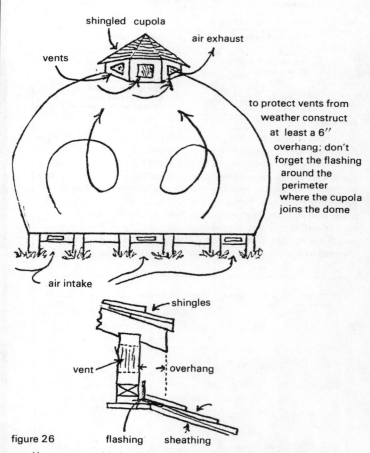

shingled cupola

air exhaust

vents

to protect vents from weather construct at least a 6'' overhang; don't forget the flashing around the perimeter where the cupola joins the dome

air intake

shingles

vent   overhang

figure 26   flashing   sheathing

You must provide for air entering the dwelling and for used air to leave the dwelling. We may be way off base on this concept, but it appears good theory to us. Cut 5 vent slots about 6 inches by 18 inches in the floor, equally spaced around the perimeter. Make the slot openings adjustable by installing a sliding cover operating on a simple wooden track. These floor vents are for air intake. To provide for exhaust, or through *ventilation*, erect a cupola on top of the dome beginning from the hubs surrounding the center pentagonal hub. Do not remove any struts or the dome will be substantially weakened. Install 5 vents of equal area to those in the floor. The top of the cupola may either be shingled or domed with clear plastic or glass and used for penta-star gazing. Whatever you do, be liberal with the caulking compound. The cupola serves the purpose of shedding rain which might work under shingles which would normally lie almost parallel to the ground, thus inviting sister rain to enter. Screen all vents, both intake and exhaust. We hope that necessity will enable you to arrive at simpler solutions which we have not imagined.

Heating and Insulation

Any kind of wood burning stove is OK. You can insulate between the struts with fibreglass batting which comes equipped with aluminum foil pasted to one side. Cut the insulation, which comes in 24-inch rolls, into triangles which are slightly larger than the dome triangles. Then, when you push the cut insulation into the opening between struts, (with the aluminum side towards the inside of the dome) friction will hold the insulation in place.

Two inches of fibreglass will suit the requirement for heating in areas where up to 8000 degree-days* are encountered. For up to 12,000 degree-days, 3 in. of fibreglass is required.

When installing the chimney for the stove remember that the chimney pipe can get red hot. If you don't insulate the pipe from the dome structure you stand a good chance of having your hard-earned labors go up in smoke. Any hardware store should have the insulating 'thimble' and roof-flashing which is required to afford protection and assure a watertight seal around the pipe.

To avoid downdrafts the chimney pipe should extend 3 feet above the roof surface or structure within a horizontal distance of 10 feet from the chimney. This means that you should make the chimney so that it extends 2 feet above the highest point of the dome, which includes the cupola, should you have one.

Lining the Inside of the Dome

Gyprock (drywall) 3/8 inch thick is cheap and easy to work with. It is also fire resistent. Natural material can be used as well: cedar planks, burlap, used weathered planks, drift wood, woven reeds and bullrushes. Just keep the combustible areas away from the stove by at least four feet.

Bibliography

The Canadian Architect
May, 1969

Geodesics
Edward Popko
University of Detroit Press

Standard Roof Construction
Consolidated Red Cedar Shingle Assoc. of British Columbia

Certi-split Manual of Handsplit Red Cedar Shakes
Donald H. Clark
Red Cedar and Handsplit Shake Bureau
Vancouver, B.C.

Peg-A-Strut Dome Plans
B.C. Technology Centre
3504 W. 14th Ave.
Vancouver, B.C.

Profitable Tips about the Application of Red Cedar and Handsplit Shakes
R.C. and H.S. Shake bureau
Vancouver, B.C.

Red Cedar Shingles, Handsplit Shakes and Grooved Sidewall Shakes
Brochure No. 17
R.C. and H.S. Shake Bureau
Vancouver, B.C.

Jim Bohlen
3504 West 19th Ave.
Vancouver 8 B.C.
Canada

Each degree that the mean daily temperature is below 65° F. is a degree day. A chart (Thermal Insulation Bulletin BCI 5.13) stipulating degree-days for different regions of Canada is available for free from the Canadian Wood Council, 77 Metcalfe Street, Ottawa, Ontario.

A Three Quarter Sphere

Lonny Brown

Lonny Brown

Listen you dome-heads and you shall hear
how to support a three-quarter sphere
with posts in the ground, and how to be sure
they meet the angles of a pentagonal floor.

Here's a system that's simple, but unique,
that's bound to impress the smartest dome-freak.
It eliminates problems with disconnected decks
by supporting the sphere direct at the vertex:

It joins the floor to the shell with ease
and supports them both at the five vertices
which the lower pentagon-centers define
where the sphere is cut off at the three-quarter line.

Your dome's radius is what's used to start
to determine exactly how far apart
the five support posts will have to be,
and it's done by pretending it's one-frequency!

'Cause the Icosa points are always the same
no matter what frequency breaks up the frame.
In other words domes of equal radii
have pentagon centers that must coincide,
no matter the class: It's one of the tricks
used to figure out geodesics!

So use the chord factor and this law to discover
the one-frequency side-length: It's really none other
then the distance in straight-line separation
between the pent centers (the post locations!)

Now the unique feature of this design
is: the posts meet the hubs at an incline.
Of course they stand straight - (it's not *that* new fangled!)
It's just that their top ends are angled.

This is so that there'll be a good fit
on the points at which the dome must sit.
Examine your model and you'll soon see,
the base hubs slanting at some degrees

'Cause since it's three-quarter and not hemisphere
no perpendicular hub meets here.
So get out your tables and I'll give you the key:
of course it involves trigonometry!

But first, (and I'm begging your pardon here)
I must switch to prose, since it's getting quite clear
that while it's not too hard just to show'em,
It's impossible to fit these formulas
into a poem!

Whew!

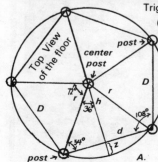

Trigonometry of the Pentagon
(or how to figure out where to place support posts to meet the lower pent vertices of a 3/4 dome)

D radius of dome x 1.051 (the chord factor for a one frequency icosa)
d = D/2
r = d/sin 36° h = r(cos 36°)
z = r-h

Note Diagram A. As explained above, distance D (between support posts) can be determined using the radius of the dome and the one-frequency chord factor. "h" is a perpendicular from D to the center of the floor, bisecting D into d + d. Then a right triangle is formed with "r", the radius of the pent-floor as the hypotenuse (i.e. the distance from the center support post to any outside one). All the angles of this triangle are known since it is 1/5 of a pentagon. For example, the angle at the center (a) must be half of one-fifth of 360°, or 36°. The other angle (b) must then be 54° since a + b + 90° - 180°. (It is also possible to determine b using the formula for the sum of the angles of a regular polygon.) With all this info, you are then in a position to determine r using the laws of trig: Just remember the magic words - SOH CAH TOA, or

Sine - Opposite over Hypotenuse
Cosine - Adjacent over Hypotenuse
Tanget - Opposite over Adjacent

Once you've found r, you're well on your way to discovering the angle (O) at which to cut the post tops (diagram B).

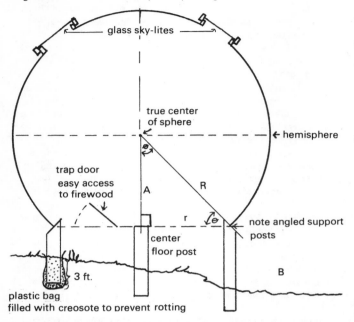

Trigonometry of the 3/4 Sphere and Support Posts
R = radius of dome
r = the length of the side of a simple icosahedron of equal radius divided by twice the sine of 36°

$\cos \Theta° = R/r$

$A = \sqrt{(R^2-r^2)}$

$\sin \Theta° = A/r$ = the angle of the top of the support posts

$\phi° = 90° - \Theta°$

    The hubs of this dome are made from 2-7/8" O.D. electrical conduit pipe cut into 80 3" sections. It was purchased at an electricians and plumbers supply. The cost was $20 plus $10 to have the pipe cut on a power hack-saw. The burred edges were smoothed off on a small grinding wheel, to prevent cutting of the strapping. Plastic plumbing pipe was considered (polyvinyl-chloride) but it seemed too squashable. Note: it is important to subtract the hub diameter from the "ideal" strut lengths (vertex to vertex) computed from the chord factors, to arrive at the actual strut length.

    For securing struts to hubs we used 5/8" crate banding of the type used by freight shippers (described in *Domebook 2*). The two necessary tools were rented at $4.00 per day from a rental place. They also supplied the metal strapping on a wheel, from which I paid only for what I used at 4¢ / ft. The buckles were free.

Carey Smoot

	80	vertices (hubs)
x	6	straps per hub
=	480	straps at
x	2.5	ft/ strap
=	1200	ft of strapping in dome
x	$.04	at $.04 per ft.
= $	48.00	worth of strapping
+$	20.00	for 5 days rental of tools
= $	68.00	total cost of hub-to-strut strapping system

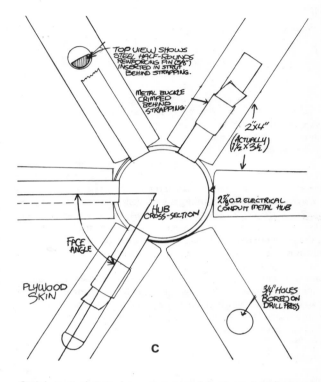

C

    Stainless steel strapping was not used due to cost and non-availablity, so Rust-Oleum was sprayed over the metal strappings after it was in place. I have also seen plastic (nylon?) banding used in packing crates, but I don't know about its applicability to domes (stretch factors? costs?). It certainly wouldn't rust.

    Enough 1/2" diameter half-round steel rods were purchased from a machine shop to place a 3" section behind each strap where it goes through the strut. The purpose of these is to prevent crushing of the wood fibres when the strapping is tightened, and to prevent sagging with time from the weight of the dome itself. The face of the half-round pin meets the strap surface, while the round side fits the drilled hole wall. The half-round cost $15.

    We cut the pins from 20 ft. rods with large bolt-cutters, leaving a very sharp pinched edge on both sides of every pin, which required hours of grinding on an electric bench grinder to insure a rounded-off surface against which the strapping would bend at a smooth 90° angle.

    The struts were made from kiln-dried Canadian spruce 2x4's (actually "dressed" to 1-1/2" x 3-1/2"). Green lumber is too risky to use due to shrinkage. The 2x4's cost $108.

    Three different strut sizes are needed for a 3-freq. geodesic. A 3/4 sphere calls for 50 short struts, 70 mediums, and 90 long ones. Actual lengths were determined by multiplying the chord factors by the radius of the dome (in this case, 12 ft.), and subtracting the diameter of the hub.

    Lumber should be ordered and cut in such a way as to create minimum waste. With this hub system, only axial angles need cutting.

I decided it was not necessary to either bevel rip the struts at the dihedral angles for receiving the plywood skin, or to round off the ends to fit up against the hubs. (see diagram E and the "over-engineered"

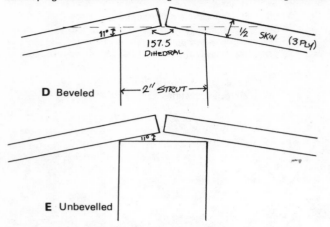

D Beveled

E Unbevelled

3/4 dome in *Domebook 2*, p. 51.) I used a radial arm saw and a jig. A jig was also made for the drill press to drill holes in the struts. The distance from the end was determined by how the strapping tools worked. I strongly advise dome-builders to make a life-size mock-up of the hub junction before proceeding to tear into their actual building materials. Check measurements often while cutting. Remember that some struts have different angles at different ends. Don't compromise or approximate on measurements! Cut all struts of one size at one time. Stack and color-code them by spray-painting the ends, preferably the same colors as in your model. Stack the struts flat and even to prevent warping. Protect them from exposure to rain and direct sunlight.

For the skin, I used 1/2'', "shop-grade" (cheapo) plywood triangles covered with canvas saturated with boat deck latex polymer. I figured the canvas would allow me to get by using the junkiest plywood available, which it did, but working with it was a drag because a lot of the ends were not square, and often the plys had big gaps. Also, after they were up, some of the panels started to peel and buckle before I had a chance to protect them from rain, which made for a couple of extra days work. The plywood cost $220.

I made scale templates of the triangular areas I needed to cover (a three frequency geodesic is made up of two different triangles) and also of the 4x8 ft. plywood sheets. Maneuvering these little templates about, I came up with the arrangement below, which enabled me to cut three triangular panels' worth of skin (2 wholes and 2 halves) from each sheet of plywood.

I made a jig on a barn floor, similar to the ones described in the

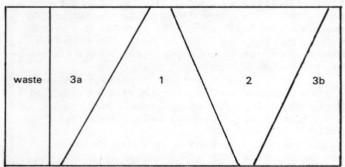

| waste | 3a | 1 | 2 | 3b |

Note: larger size doesn't quite make it. Points were cut and installed separately.

Domebooks, and cut all the panels in one day with a skill saw. The half-pieces were reserved for the bottom first course of the dome, saving the whole ones for higher areas where more strength was desirable. I decided that no extra backing strut was needed where the half-panels met, but joined them with corrugated joint fasteners.

The first step in placing the support posts is to mark where the

center of dome will be. I staked out the post holes distance r from the center with a string, and distance D from each other with another string. If you have some kind of protractor with which you can take on-site readings, you can determine post-hole locations by angles (diagram C) or double check one measurement system against the other. We dug the post holes oversize to allow shifting for final check and placement. Measurements are made from *center to center*. The posts should be deep enough to reach below your frost point (ask the natives), and tall enough to describe a level plane *after* they are angle cut on top. Obviously, if you are building on a slope the posts will be varying lengths.

I saturated the buried parts of my posts with anti-rot creosote and wrapped the bottoms in plastic bags. If you're not using concrete footings, jam large rocks in between the posts and the hole wall. I took the extra precaution of leaving the posts slightly loose until the entire shell was up, just in case they needed some shifting.

I cut the post tops with a chain saw at angle θ, facing up and in towards where the center of the dome was to be. Remember that all 5 perimeter post tops must end exactly in the same plane (use a line level). The center post was cut later, at a height determined by the floor beams.

By now you have probably realized that, unlike most domes, this one was erected before the floor was constructed. I had several reasons for doing it this way. First of all I was still toying with the idea of using a suspended floor (supported by the shell, rather than the other way around). Secondly, as was just mentioned, I wanted to leave the dome as flexible as possible in case some margin of error required it to be "pulled into shape". As it turned out, this was not necessary.

But actually my main reason for not building the floor first was that I was anxious to see the geodesic take shape! Everybody said I was crazy but it worked out just fine by building the floor under the shell which it joined at the bottom horizontal struts. The first step in building the shell was to tie a hub onto a post with a heavy duty 2'' metal band of crate-strapping salvaged from a lumber company. The band goes through the hub and wraps down over the top of the post. It was too thick to drive nails through so holes were drilled to allow me to spike the whole assembly to the post. For easier positioning of dome members, the hub was allowed its back and forth play until the whole structure was up. Then cross-straps were nailed in front and back of each support hub, fixing its position.

To start the dome, the bottom rim of struts was set up around the 5 posts (photo). Even at this early stage they began to assume their proper positions. When the first ring of struts was completed, I experienced that gratifying on-site confirmation that my calculations were correct.

Various shapes and sizes of strut sets were prefabbed on the ground and brought up to the first perimeter to compose the first course of triangles. At first they had to be held up with ropes, but by the time we got once around and completed a full circle of triangles, it was already a self-supporting bowl.

Here's a simple but useful tool to help you construct the proper face angles: make one plywood triangular corner for each face angle in the dome (3 for 3 frequency). Lable them by degrees or code, or better still, color the sides to correspond to the color codes on the adjacent struts. Then when you want to put together struts, strap them loosely to the hub, close them down to meet the angle-template, and tighten in place (see diagram F).

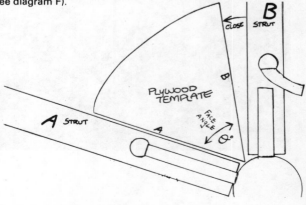

F

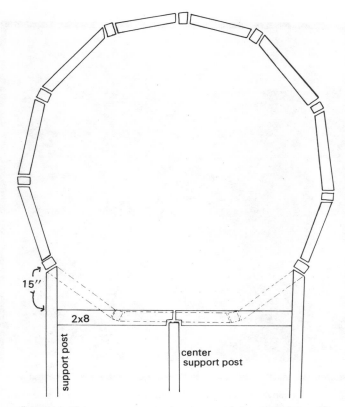

It took four days to complete the shell. Nothing was so satisfying as finding that last top strut fitting in so snugly that it sat in its place even without straps! I had done it! No forcing of the dome into contortions was necessary; not one strut had to be altered! And this by an absolute novice who hadn't previously built anything more ambitious than a tree-house! It was a thrilling experience stepping back and beholding that amazing wooden webbed sphere in the forest. To this day, I think the dome never looked as beautiful as it did then, transparent, like a bubble, with the sky and trees showing through its triangles and pents and hexagons, graceful yet rigid, modern yet cellularly natural. As I sat up on top and watched the sun go down over the trees I thought about how beautiful mathematics could be. I also said a silent thanks to Bucky Fuller.

Being built-in under and after the dome itself, the floor was designed so that its top surface exactly met the plane defined by the lowest horizontal strut members of the 3/4 sphere. I used a pentagonal-radial support system that tied into the same five posts that held up the dome, but the floor beams are supported about 15 inches down the sides of the posts with joist hangers, rather than resting on the tops. This difference compensates for the vertical rise between the floor-plane at the lowest extent of the sphere and the five higher hubs on which the dome is supported. The center post was cut 6 inches lower than the floor plane so that the 2x8's radiating from it out to the perimeter could rest on it with a two inch notch and come out level.

For the longer spans, between the outside posts, 2x10's were used. This created 5 large triangles in the floor plane, which were then sub-divided with 2x6's (at two ft. intervals) into the final pattern (see pictures and diagram). The 2x6 spokes towards the outside of the pattern were double-notched with the 2x10's and extended past them to meet the dome line.

At this point the 2 heavy (6x6) vertical support beams for the second floor were placed in holes in the ground and secured to the floor system. These were salvaged from an old barn and were also creosoted and sealed in plastic bags to prevent rot.

Next, a large sheet of plastic vapor barrier was laid over the whole floor area, and then covered with the first layer of roughcut pine

By the time the third course of triangles was on my dome, it was already strong enough to act as its own scaffolding, allowing us to climb on one level to build the next. After a couple of hours of building and referring to the model one becomes quite familiar with the geometry of the dome, and assembly goes even faster. The one or two mistakes we made were easily spotted and corrected by breaking the straps with tin-snips.

Lonny Brown

Lonny Brown

boards (leaving open the space for the trap door). Over this first sub-floor was then placed a layer of double-faced aluminum reflective foil, to keep in radiant heat. Heat loss by conduction was minimized by creating a complete layer of one-inch deep, 2 ft. square air pockets with a grid pattern of 1x1 wood strips nailed to the subfloor. Over this went the next layer of one-inch pine boards, which at this writing serves as the first floor. Eventually this should be covered with a finished floor for the following reasons: the pine is too soft and rough, catching dirt in its grain as well as between the planks. Also it was installed green and is slowly reacting to differences in moisture and temperature conditions by warping and popping some nails. The advantage of the pine was that it was local and cheap (5¢ / bd. ft.).

Here's an idea I got after it was too late to do it on this dome: With a radial type floor, you can drop one of the triangular sections a foot or so below the others and create a split level floor.

Galvanized plywood nails were used to put up the triangles. I tried to go easy on these, but wound up going over the whole dome again, putting in twice as many nails to get all the waves out of the plywood. Do it throughly the first time. The galvanized nails cost $7.00.

If you have followed me this far, you should have in your mind's eye a picture of a huge plywood ball. Various triangular holes indicate future skylights, windows, and a door. Nothing is in the seams, and the plywood itself, being cheap shop-grade plyscore held together with non-exterior glue, is tending to bubble in places due to exposure to the elements. In short, the application of the waterproofing system is the next step. Here then are the details of how to cover a 24 ft. dome with canvas. Theoretically, this system should eliminate any need for caulking in the seams. This sounded too good to be true to this cautious dome-builder, however, so I spent $10 and an extra two days filling up all the seams with a black gook called Plastic Roof Cement (asphalt base). It looked quite waterproof, promised to remain elastic, and provided a backing where the canvas would have to span the space at the seams. With this precaution under a canvas boat-decking system, I had satisfied myself that I had done everything possible to prevent "the dreaded leak". It is quite possible that the canvas alone would have been sufficient, but it may also be a truism that you can't overseal a dome.

The canvas sealer I used is called Easy-Deck, made by Thorpe Co., in California. One coat goes over the plywood and two or three over the cloth. Since it is fast drying, the instructions recommend working on an area not greater than 3 ft. x 3 ft. at a time.

The canvas sheets I worked with were much bigger in area than that (roughly 5x10), and since I was starting from a near vertical surface, I had to devise a way to hold up the sheets while applying the glue. I did this by stapling them in place along the top edge and letting them hang free while I went under and smeared glue on the plywood. Then the cloth was pulled taut across the glued surface and spread down tight with a yard-stick. Knowing that it might take a few tries to get the flat canvas down on a curved surface without any creases, I started on the back side of the dome. One soon learns to stretch around and away from crease points. A staple gun comes in handy.

Working from the bottom up, a water-shed system was created by making 2 inch overlaps at the seams. Window frames and skylites were leak proofed by putting the cloth sheets over them and then cutting out holes from the centers, bringing the excess around the frames and inside as one continuous skin. It took 6 five gallon pails of Easy-Deck and 2 weeks' work to cover the dome. The canvas and Easy-Deck for 1350 sq. ft. cost $120 and $180 respectively.

Exactly two triangle courses up from the floor of a 3 frequency, 3/4 sphere (vertex zenith, icosa alternate) geodesic are located the bottoms of the five main pentagons around the sides of the dome. It was here that I decided to tie in the 4 horizontal 2x10's from the two large barn beams I had erected in the center of the dome to support the second floor. On the wall side they were simply set into the vertices. At the posts they were double lag-screwed through the side. The rest was a repeat of the first floor procedures: a breakdown of the area with 2x8 headers, and then finally 2x6's at 2 foot intervals. The second floor is shaped like a pie slice with the "point" jutting out into the center of the dome. Still another over-lapping slice will eventually create a third level.

Four high triangular glass windows were installed at the bottom of four sun-facing pents. Another was put in point-down at floor level. It makes a beautiful picture window to watch the seasons grow by. These glass triangles were custom cut against a plywood template which I took into a local window works: 3/16 in. thick, $10 each. The same glass man insisted that I use 1/4 in. plate glass for the five mini-triangle skylights. These are in the down pointing tips of the triangles just below the zenith pent and must take a near vertical snow load. I saved $25 by buying the remains of a broken glass door (supermarket variety) and doing the cutting myself. After a little practice, I got four whole triangles and one busted one, which I repaired with epoxy. The window frames are made from 2x4's. The glass is glued with epoxy into grooves cut in the 2x4 frames. Lips made from 2x6's are framed into the window openings, and the skylight frames fit over the lips like box lids, resting on a rubber strip seat. They can be propped open or removed entirely. Next spring, we will have to screen underneath them for ventilation without mosquitoes. Would like to hear ideas for mechanisms to open them from the inside. Same problem with our small square side windows. These are salvaged small pane types. We simply framed inside the triangles to fit the available windows. They are hinged at the top for ventilation without leaks, and are propped open with sticks. When needed, more ventilation can be had through our trap door, which also allows us to get firewood stored under the dome without having to wade through snow.

A couple of skylights cracked after they were put in. At first I thought it was from expansion-contraction of the dome members, but then I found that they were loose fitting all the time. The reason the glass broke was because it was framed in green wood, which then created too much pressure when it began drying out.

We heat with an Ashly automatic which is more than adequate. We orginally had the heater located in the center of the floor, but the resulting stove pipe was so long that it was distilling turpentine and who-knows-what all over the dome. The original intention was to run the pipe straight up out the top, but a few talks with some veterans and a futile search for cheap water shedding caps led to my punching a hole out the side about 10 feet above floor level. The Ashly is now on one side, but this still gives plenty of inside heat. I have since been told that reversing the pipes to run female to male would solve the leaking problem by dropping all liquids back down to the fire-box for more complete burning and/or evaporation. Next spring!

Here's something neat about domes in snow country: they build walls around themselves! Every once in a while we hear a beautiful swoosh, thump! when some snow slides off. We're waiting for someone to go out, shut the door behind them, and get buried in the resulting avalanche!

Insulating the dome was the draggiest part of the whole project. I would suggest to anyone working with fiberglass to use a cheap breathing mask. Also long sleeves if your skin is sensitive. Foil-faced, 15 in. wide, 4 in. thick roll insulation was used here. Three appropriately cut pieces were stapled together on the floor to make a prefab triangular blanket, which was then carried up into place and gun-tacked in. I used only one aluminum extension ladder, but it would have been a lot safer and faster with some kind of scaffolding.

The snow flew and money ran out before we could do interior walls so right now we are living in what seems like a cross between a space capsule and a silver womb. From the outside, because of the window placement, our home looks like a giant jack-o-lantern, especially at night, with candlelight shining through.

More thoughts: old church pew cushions go well around the inside perimeter . . . have been told that sawdust piled up around the posts will give added protection against frost-heave . . . total costs so far (no second level) $1150. We used some recycled lumber in the floor . . . unlevel doors are dangerous on the backswing if not countersprung . . . We would like to know if anyone around this corner of New Hampshire would like us to build them a dome (We are near Keene, N.H.)

Hope I have been of some help.

Like a brother,

Lonny J. Brown
Yellow House
Hidden Springs Community Land Trust
South Acworth, New Hampshire 03607

Lonny Brown

Our 2V Triacon

Kathe Welles

(Or How We Built a Dome for Love and Money and Found Pieces)
Kathe Welles

I am happy to tell you about our dome, how we decided on it, designed it and built it. It is built in the rainy coastal mountains of Oregon where temperatures are mild and insulation is somewhat optional - or so we thought, but as you'll see, we thought wrong. We were two constructional illiterates when we began but we've learned a lot, which I will try to pass on to you in intelligible form.

Our dome is a 2V triacon 3/4 sphere, about 22' in diameter, 8' on each triangle side. Including the mezzanine we have about 500 square feet of floor. This structure was chosen for personal (aesthetic and practical) reasons and I don't think it's necessarily the best geometry for everyone. For instance, it's wasteful of plywood skin material (but of course we have plans for the scraps) or would require large joins across each face and more framing. It was not the most economical way to build, but even so it has cost only about $1300, exclusive of the very large and therefore very expensive windows.

Our "foundation" is of pilings set in deep (hand dug) holes and surrounded with gravel. Concrete impresses people more, and in many places a continuous concrete footing is required by law, but we're convinced gravel is fine (See Rex Reed's *Your Engineered House* for a good discussion of the good points of gravel. That's what convinced us.)

Our windows are not symmetrical. They consist of a huge hexagonal window on the east (1/6 of the whole skin), a large diamond window on the northwest, a small diamond window on the west and a large fan-shaped window on the north. The doors are on the south. There are also a dormer window and a 4/5 circle "skylight" window.

A. Skylight B. Dormer Window C. The morning window D. The evening window E. The west window F. The fan window G. The door.

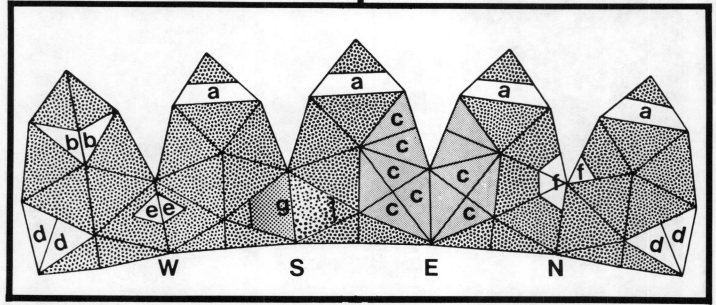

W   S   E   N

As you can see there are additional struts inserted along the altitudes of the triangles in the big windows. We found to our delight that the extra struts in the morning window outline a face of the original icosahedron. The morning window gets us up in the morning and also serves to light the whole place most of the time as it faces the direction in which the sky is most open (fewest trees).

Neither of us was ever in a dome until we began work on ours. We started with a D-Stix model and then built a "final" model of scale model lumber. We worked out the window placement on the model and then began to cut out the real pieces. We precut all struts and skin pieces in town and assembled them in the woods, taking only 8 fairly easy days (2 of us) for the dome proper (the foundation and deck were already in place). We assembled the dome frame loose on the deck and then bolted it down at premeasured locations. For work on the very top, we rented a scaffold.

We used steel pipe hubs and stainless steel strap, as described in *Domebook 2*. We also used their chord factors (after checking them ourselves). *Domebook 2* is good for a) pictures of many nice domes and b) chord factor tables and accompanying diagrams. But a lot of their practical advice is less than practical. For instance: it is *not* necessary to be finicky about how far the strap holes are from the ends of the struts, and they need not, in fact, should not, be drilled parallel to the angled ends, but should be straight across the strut. That way, the pull exerted by the strap is directly along the strut instead of at an angle to it. It matters a whole lot that the steel hubs should be 2 1/2" ID (or 3" OD) for use with 2 x 4 struts, so that six of them will just about exactly fit around the hub. Larger hubs will allow the struts to slither around until the skin is on. I don't recall that *Domebook* mentioned this point at all. It is also not necessary to be too finicky about exact angles on the ends of the struts. On the other hand it *is* necessary to be finicky about the lengths of the struts - outside length especially. I realize these comments wouldn'd make much sense to someone who hasn't read *Domebook*, but I assume anyone seriously interested in building a dome *will* read *Domebook*.

Our dome is a two story structure, in which the upper story is much smaller than the lower story and is entirely surrounded by the dome, which rests independently on the lower story. We arranged the rectangular array of pilings in such a way that every hub and pseudo-hub is located directly over a piling or near a piling and directly over a joist. (A "pseudo-hub" is a flat footing at the point where the half struts around the bottom of the dome meet the deck.) Since the deck and the dome structure are completely separate, there's no reason the mezzanine frame couldn't pass right through the dome frame. The frame is of 2 x 4's and 2 x 3's and the skin is 1/2" exterior grade A-C plywood. The C side is exposed inside (the knot holes make nice patterns - and so do the struts, which are stained dark brown).

Some people apparently think it's esthetically 'wrong' to mix domes with rectangular structure. We don't feel that way (although there *are* some awful examples in brochures of prefab dome makers who propose to squash a suburban rancho into a dome). Besides there are practical reasons for our choice. We tried at every step to make things as easy and foolproof as possible. We'd rather spend a little more money or work a little harder or longer, rather than attempt something tricky or something that would require cabinet-maker's skills.

I can't overemphasize the importance of a scale model. Ours was built to a scale of 1/16" per inch or 3/4" per foot, which is very convenient because inches count in domes, as you know, and this way you can read scale inches right off the ruler. It was the scale model which really sold us on the dome and on the particular geometry we chose. Those big, beautiful, gem-like facets! That lifting-off-into-space look! And it was easy to work out placement of the windows and orientation. Eventually our model came to have furniture, and inhabitants all to scale. Right now, I'm taking the dear old model apart (we really don't *need* it, now we've got a real one) and preparing to reassemble it into a model of our next project.

One of the greatest moments in my life was when I looked at my pile of handmade struts and they looked *exactly* like the ones I had cut for the model. That was when I knew it would work.

As I have said, we tailored our design to our limitations. Everything had to be assembled by two inexperienced people, without power tools, as quickly as possible. It also had to be completely enclosed when the first layer of skin was up although we planned to add insulation and shingles later. And because we liked the look of the

Kathe Welles

big facets we planned to cut the pieces as large as we possibly could using standard sheets of plywood & 2 x 4 struts. We ended up with the very largest pieces we could handle alone.

We settled for a good deal of waste in cutting the plywood in order to avoid large seams across the faces of the panels. The way the cost of plywood has risen, we might very well not use it if we were building now. Our alternative plan was to use lapped siding but we preferred plywood because prefabbing the triangles of siding would be a lot more trouble and so would sealing the dome.

Anyone who has to precut a dome and assemble it without electric power available should assemble trial triangles in advance to check skin size and fit. Strap together the sides and hubs of one triangle, drive nails down the mid line of each strut and cut the panels so they will just drop into place between the nails. No matter how careful you are about this, when you get out in the woods some of the triangles will appear not to fit! This is due to shiftiness of the struts and can be corrected by banging the strut into correct alignment with a hammer.

While putting up the foundation and deck we learned about truss plates, which look like slabs of incomplete nails, and that's just what they are. They're invaluable for joining pieces of wood firmly without much effort - just lay them on the joint and pound the points in - and! they can be bent to go on or into corners. We also learned about galvanized nails - that there are two kinds: smooth classy looking ones (electroplated) and lumpy, funny looking ones (hot dip). The lumpy, funny looking ones look like they were made by hand in someone's basement, where the light was bad, but *they* are the right kind. The galvanized coating slips right off the others under the slightest stress (like being hit with a hammer).

Later, while working on the frame, we learned that there are two ways to make steel hubs. One is by using a pipe vise and pipe cutter and spending hours filing and grinding the sharp edges. The other is by hiring someone to cut them with a power hacksaw, and then filing and grinding the rough edges. This is more expensive. I don't know which is better. We did it the cheap way. We had the five bottom hubs welded to angled iron supports which were drilled for bolting to the deck. Our topmost hub extends about a foot above the skin and is topped by a flat plate welded on.

Incidentally, speaking of hubs, I visited a dome with polyvinyl chloride plastic hubs, and they looked terrible to me. They were attached to the struts with lag screws into the end grain of the wood and appeared to have neither the tensile strength to resist the pull of the struts nor the compressive strength to support the weight of the dome. The ones I saw were failing after only a few months (and think of the work involved in tightening all those bolts inside the hubs!)

We also learned to cut compound angles by hand for the various internal parts of the framing, around windows and doors and between the panes of the big windows, in which each 8' x 8' x 8' triangle was divided into two 4' x 6' x 8' triangles by a 2 x 3 pseudo-strut, or perhaps you could call it a mullion (?!). An aid to cutting and fitting all these fancy little pieces is the use of scraps of rigid insulation board (if you're using it). A piece can be cut out of styrofoam quicker and easier than out of wood, can be set in place, corrected if necessary, and copied finally in wood when it's just right, for a perfect fit.

To make our floor we laid silvered paper over the deck (which is of 2 x 6's with spaces between) and styrofoam boards over that. Between every styrofoam board and the next we nailed a 2 x 4 (used up a lot of scraps this way) and to these boards we attached 1 x 4 fir flooring, which unexpectedly cost *more* than oak (but was less trouble). We used styrofoam insulation because it's cheaper than fiberglass for the same insulating value, and besides fiberglass is dangerous if you get it in your skin or eyes or lungs. I got some fiberglass in my finger once and my hand was disabled for months. I'd *hate* to breathe any. While making the floor we learned that not all 1x4's are the same size. We wished we had bought all of the flooring at the same time and place. For ventilation we placed heater grids in our floor around the edges. To clear the deck they had to be an inch thinner than the ordinary ones. We found the skinny ones at a trailer manufacturer's place. This is a good place to look for all sorts of odd hardware and so are boating supply places.

Back to the frame again: we used stainless steel strapping because *Domebook* recommended it, and because it is lots stronger. Here's a hint about stainless strap, given us by our sympathetic stainless strap dealer: it's fairly stretchy-thus you may have more spring in the structure than you anticipated until the skin is on. This doesn't mean it's weak - on the contrary. It's stronger because it will give and spring back. But it can be unnerving. When it starts to stretch it visibly changes texture, so we tightened each strap until it began to stretch, then let off slightly and fastened it. Tell Lonny Brown that the reason for using stainless steel strap isn't to prevent rust, but because it's stronger. Rustoleum probably won't help. The skin should protect the strap anyway.

Also as recommended in *Domebook* and because it sounded right we used half round pegs in the strap holes to provide a flat bearing surface. We used soft wood because we had already bought the strap and drilled the holes when we discovered we couldn't get half round hardwood 5/8'' wide. But because they were soft they squashed up something awful and with other factors contributed to a general looseness of the structure that we would rather have done without (another factor, we think, was the shrinkage of the struts, which were mostly new lumber). I have since visited a dome in which half round was not used but the holes were drilled oversize.

We suspected that contrary to *Domebook* the strapholes need not be uniformly distant from the ends of the struts, and time seems to have proved us right. We really like the irregular sunburst effect of the varied lengths of strapping around each hub.

The buckles on the straps should be on the inside as much as possible to avoid fitting problems with the skin, but some places just can't be reached from inside.

When we got to the skin we learned that careful fit in town is a little different from exact fit in the woods. Luckily this method of assembly is tolerant of small mistakes. And we found out a very interesting thing about leaks. People who have mysterious leaks that look like they are in the seams may have another problem altogether. People seem to think plywood is solid. Actually, there are all kinds of large and small voids in the inner layers. We found several leaks where water entered through a tack or staple hole, ran between layers to an edge and appeared alongside a strut looking for all the world like a leak in the seam. We might have believed it if we didn't know how tight the seams were. Even so we looked for pinholes in the seam sealing. These leaks were cured by rubbing Tuff Kote into the tack holes when we found them. We knew it was them because we could *see* the water running into some of them.

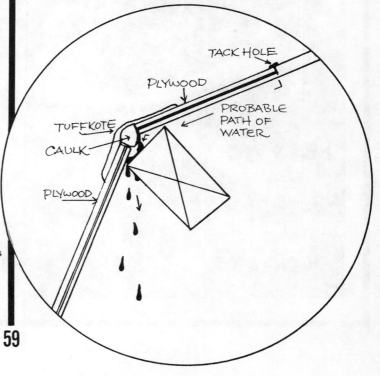

TACK HOLE
PLYWOOD
PROBABLE PATH OF WATER
TUFFKOTE
CAULK
PLYWOOD

Other than that, putting on the skin was uneventful until we got to the windows. Time and money considerations prevented us from putting in rigid windows right away, but our original plan to use roll vinyl windows the first year or two until we could afford plexiglass didn't quite work out. We had assumed that it would be a simple matter to staple vinyl across the openings and seal the edges with tape, but it was not. The stapling went well (we used pieces of folded IBM card under each staple for padding) but the taping was another story. It seems there are very few tapes that will stick well to either vinyl or wood and only one that will stick to both. It took us quite a while to find it (it is Mystik Tape #5803, made by Borden, comes in 8 or ten colors).

Unfortunately for the vinyl windows it was by that time nearly summer and we found ourselves able (barely) to afford plexiglass. We also found that we really didn't like the ripply look of roll vinyl.

So we proceeded to the buying of plexiglass. I called a local place, described our situation in detail, and received assurances that they could handle it. But when I went to actually but the stuff they suddenly realized we were talking about *triangles*. We had been all along. Seems they can't make diagonal cuts.

So we quickly called some other places. And what do you think we found? Well, we found that acrylic sheet is made in the U.S. by big names (Plexiglass, Lucite, Acrylite) and elsewhere by not-so-big-names. Not so big in the U.S. that is. We ended up buying "Shinkolite" made by Mitsubishi (a pretty big name actually) for a price including labor, about 15% below the price for plexiglass material only. A bonus which we can't make use of now is that Shinkolite comes in over 30 colors, most of which are described as fluorescent in the brochure - as opposed to 6 or so for plexiglass.

We set it into aluminum channels using silicon caulk as per plexiglass installation manual (we weren't able to get Shinkolite's manual). Buying aluminum extrusions is a whole 'nother trip which I won't go into yet, except to say that it appears that Colo-Trym makes more shapes than anyone else. (*Thousands,* my mouth waters and my gears spin when I look through their catalog.)

Now a word about fitting. We did it wrong because we couldn't afford to do it right. Right would have been to do it all at one time, plywood and plastic panels together. Our windows with one exception were meant to be simply transparent panels or parts of panels and since the dome had been up a while and settled some, the spaces for the panels that were meant to be transparent had also changed shape some. We had to measure for each window separately. We think if we had to do it again we'd buy a roll of cheap thin linoleum type stuff and make patterns for the windows by nailing it up as if it were plywood and marking directly on it, then taking it down and copying it onto acrylic sheet.

Acrylic was our choice because it costs about half of what polycarbonate costs, and much, *much* less than glass. Glass would be expensive because it would have to be safety glass for such large overhead windows, and because due to its weight it would require professional installation. People always ask why I didn't "just use glass" but it's a good thing I didn't. Picture raising a 4 x 6 triangle of glass over your head to set it on an ethereal looking framework of struts. Picture carrying it 20 feet up an extension ladder and sliding it off the roof into the waiting hands of a helper hanging by a rope. No no no! Plexiglass is dangerous enough!

Acrylic looks safe compared to glass, but sand the edges anyway before handling it at all. I didn't until after I cut my hands all to shreds carrying it from the car to the dome. It has to be smoothed on the edges anyway to increase its resistance to breakage. Ideally it should be *polished* but we let the jeweler's-rouge step go by. Acrylic is pretty easy to crack which makes it hard to cut. Having everything cut in the shop by professionals would be better but we found we had to make some cuts ourselves. I tried a scriber but I could *not* make it work. So I had to reluctantly go back to sawing. The thing about sawing acrylic is, if it vibrates it will crack, so it has to be clamped firmly, right along the cutting line. I used giant C-clamps and 2 x 4 or 2 x 3 scraps, clamped it to the deck and sawed in the spaces between the deck boards.

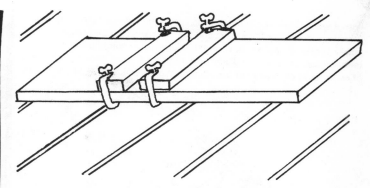

Acrylic comes covered on both sides with masking paper. The instructions say to take it off before installation but you'll prevent a lot of finger prints and scratches if you just turn it back from the edge only, and that just before you put it up. Then when it's finally in place you can peel it and admire it.

This masking paper has a tendency to peel back during transporting and handling and then it won't stick back down. The line along which it still adheres will be visible after the paper's removed and is *hard* to take off. So, next time I will cover all the edges with masking tape to hold the paper in place.

Our method of installation is pretty unwieldy although it looks nice when done. I like it as well as any others I've seen.

As we progressed with the windows we learned about 1. climbing on the dome with ropes; 2. aluminum moldings; and 3. silicone caulk.

In order to climb up and down the dome on ropes I purchased rope and webbing as recommended on page 117 of *Domebook 2*. Luckily I bought extra. Following *Domebook's* instructions exactly, using 2 yards of webbing for the big harness, I constructed a harness too small for me to wear (I'm skinny). I made another, trying it on first - it turned out to take 8 feet of webbing, forming a loop, when tied, about 7 feet long. I'd advise people who try it *not* to position the strap around their waist. After a few minutes of hanging by it I got pretty nauseated. Pressure on the kidneys or something I guess, because when I slid the strap down to bear across my hipbones I felt fine immediately. Otherwise, like it says in *Domebook 2*, it's easy to get the hang of it. There's no need for me to duplicate their getting-around instructions. It is best to wear many-pocket overalls or a tool apron, because you'll find there's nowhere up there to lay your hammer down.

There never seems to be ideal weather for working on top (this probably applies to all roofs). If the sun shines it's hot and the glare is terrible. If it's cool, it's *cold*.

We used a lot of aluminum extrusions, of 2 types - H-bar, also called mullion strip, and bar edging. We're very pleased with our decision to treat the windows as part of the skin. There are no windows that don't touch an edge. Otherwise we'd be faced with some tricky framing. At the point where the skin changes from plywood to plexiglass we use 1/2" H-bar - we laid a bead of silicone caulk down the bottom of the trough on one side and forced it onto the edge of the plywood. Then we laid a bead on the inside lip of the remaining trough and let it harden. Then we inserted the window and laid a bead between the window and the outside lip to serve as sealant, tooling it to form a concave surface.

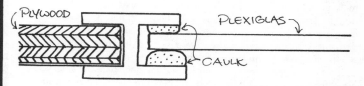

PLYWOOD   PLEXIGLAS

CAULK

Where window panes meet edges (struts) we did it a little differently, but not much. We laid a bead along the strut where the window would touch, let it harden, placed the window, held it in place with a few nails driven in next to the edge. Then we caulked between the exposed edge of the acrylic and the strut and clamped the bar edge over the acrylic window and the edge of the neighboring panel (either wood or acrylic) and screwed it tight. Later we added a tiny line of caulk beside the edge of the aluminum extrusion, on the window.

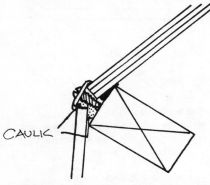

CAULIC

The numbers of these extrusions are: mullion strip #SW-2152 and edging #1993BMC, both from Trymtex which is a dealer for Colo-Trym, a division of Futura Industries Corp., Seattle, Washington 98134.

The extrusions situation is funny. Apparently there are many local fabricators - often outlets for some manufacturer of aluminum. They make some shapes that they keep in stock and some they make to order (they have the dies on hand but you have to order some minimum weight of aluminum) and some are exclusive for certain customers. You may locate a lot of interesting shapes but if you have something specific in mind you probably won't find it. Trym-Tex, on the other hand, has a catalog the size of Monkey Ward's, and can order anything therein in under a week. Unfortunately they don't sell retail. The trick is to find out exactly what you want and order it through a cabinet shop, or hardware, or building supply store. A cheaper but not entirely honest trick is to temporarily become XYZ contractors, buy everything at one time and then drop out of sight before they're on to you.

Cutting and smoothing aluminum is easy, but making the corners of the strips meet nicely is impossible for such as us. We did our best, filled the gaps with caulk and covered most of them anyway (sigh of relief) with Tuff Kote, like the seams.

Silicone caulk is recommended in the Plexiglass installation manual - specifically GE Construction Sealant or Dow Corning 790. I looked all over for DC 790 and couldn't find anyone who'd ever heard of it. But I kept running into DC 780, so maybe it's a misprint. I also kept running into people who wanted to sell us stuff plainly labeled "for interior use only". Couldn't get any explanation anywhere of the difference, but I felt better not buying it. So I got GE clear construction sealant and was happy ever after. Until I ran out. This kind of thing (triangular joints and poor fitting) takes 3 - 4 times as much as anyone imagines you'll need. When we ran out of GE, we couldn't find it locally so we bought DC 781 (just like DC 780 only for non-porous surfaces - or something - no one seems to know exactly *anything* about what they're selling). Compared to GE, it's so milky it's actually white, takes much longer to harden and is harder to wipe up. The slow hardening might be useful in some applications but mostly it was a drag.

A couple of practical hints from one "thumb" to others. 1) It's vital to "tool" it immediately and then leave it strictly alone till it's hard (tough). The easiest "tool" to use is the finger. 2) It's vital to use masking tape on joints that are to be tooled. A couple of times we didn't (it was down there and we were up here) and boy, are we sorry! It gets very, very tough and is very hard to remove from wrong places. 3) It's a good idea to wear a pair of jeans you can spare because you are always wiping your hands and no kind of rag or towel is as good and as handy as a pair of jeans - but it never comes out. This silicone caulk by the way is excruciatingly expensive. But obviously, nothing else will do what it does. I guess there's a Japanese source, but I couldn't locate any (probably Mitsubishi again and it would probably

be worth one's while to look for it.)

After we had been working on the windows for some time I finally got some MEK (methyl ethyl ketone). It is mentioned in all the silicone caulk brochures and on the tubes as the correct solvent for cleaning up, but no place that carried the caulk had the faintest notion of where to get it. I finally asked at a paint store and there it was along with untold numbers of other weird solvents. MEK is powerful stuff, very volatile and very toxic. But it really cleans up silicone caulk - it doesn't dissolve it, but after patient rubbing it sort of separates the caulk from whatever it was stuck to and it can be just slipped off. It also turns out to be very good for removing a lot of different kinds of ick from acrylic, which because of its soft surface has to be handled gently. I used some to remove the peel marks from the masking paper. A little MEK on cheese cloth cleans the acrylic without much effort or scratching, but I don't know whether in the long run it will weaken it, so I'm going very light with it.

The effect of the big windows from inside is indescribably delicious. Especially at night. First while the lantern is lit, each of the huge radiating panes of the large window reflects a slightly different view of the interior - it's like being inside a kaleidoscope. Then, turn off the lantern and watch the moon rise - ! -

A lot of factors I won't bore you with brought work on the dome to a halt last fall when it was habitable but not really comfortable. The last thing we did was paint it with gray porch and deck paint which in no way interferes with its fairy bubble-spaceship appearance but makes it less conspicuous and more water repellent.

During the winter an unprecedented cold spell (temperature dropped to 11 degrees below zero!) drove the sole inhabitant into town and while it was empty, one of the skylight windows cracked and leaks appeared at the corners of some of the windows. The acute corners were a real sealing problem - we never were sure we'd gotten caulk everywhere it was needed. We didn't have time to do anything but wrap it all in black plastic (we nearly froze doing it). We used black because we've found that transparent polyethylene degrades in mere weeks. It becomes very, very thin and brittle and just flakes away. I believe it is the ultraviolet that causes this - anyway, black lasts longer.

Our future plans include fitting a regular door (regular as to function, not shape) and other similar details. Later we may shingle it, if we can work out a method that satisfies us. As always, work stops while we think about it. We also plan an improved water supply system, more domes, etc., etc.

Here's another possibility for ventilating that I wanted to try but couldn't talk my friend into (actually I like our roof with skylight fine). Raise the top ring of triangles "above" the rest by using five extra long hubs drilled for straps at top and bottom and set louvers, screens, or windows in between. It was suggested by someone who, after seeing an item about fireman's poles (seems they aren't too expensive) proposed that the central hub of a dome could be a fireman's pole extending to the ground. I like that idea too, but I can't quite fit it into any of my projects/plans/dreams.

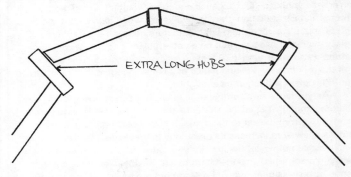

EXTRA LONG HUBS

Here's a brief summary of costs. Remember that most of these things cost more now than they did when we bought them.

foundation (railroad ties, gravel)	$ 68.20
deck lumber (2 x 8 joists, 2 x 6 stringers, 2 x 6 decking)	308.25
deck hardware (bolts, nails, trussplates)	62.39
dome frame (hubs, welding, strapping 2 x 4's 2 x 3's, stain)	159.95
dome skin (1/2'' exterior plywood, butyl caulk, Tuff Kote, resin sealer, nails, paint)	335.42
interior (upper story framing, floor framing, insulation, ventilators, 1 x 4 flooring, nails, stain, sealer)	234.06
windows (acrylic sheet, aluminum extrusions, door screws & washers, silicone caulk	694.17
TOTAL	$ 1,969.78

Actually we spent somewhat over $2,000.00, including little extras that just don't fall into any of these categories, and I have not included the cost of tools which can be used again, ropes and plastic tarpaulins, and gross mistakes.

Among the tools we used are hammers, saws (coarse and fine), hacksaws, brace and bit, wood rasps (Surform) and files, Weldwood resin glue, nailsets, screwdrivers, strapping tool, single edge razor blades, straight edge, bevel gauge, C-clamps, wirebrushes, paint brushes & rollers, masking tape, tape measures, lots of sandpaper, sanding block, extension ladder, stepladder, scaffolding, and last but never least, vise grips. In town we used a circular saw and electric drill, but we did *not* use a radial arm saw and we didn't do anything that couldn't have been done, more slowly, in the woods. We had several of most tools, or ended up buying extras so we could all nail at the same time, or saw, if that's what was happening.

A really striking thing about this project is how much stuff we have left over. Actually I don't believe we have any more left over bits and pieces than the builder of a conventional structure (in fact some of our dome parts came from the discard bins of conventional builders), but it looks a lot different when you know *you* bought it (or scrounged it) than it does when you're scooping someone else's scraps into the van to use for firewood.

This dome is really only a small cabin in which we propose to crouch while planning our ultimate home. Unfortunately it impressed the local tax collector as being a veritable palace - and we can't protest because our *land* is underassessed and it will be jacked up to par if we open our mouths - Boohoo and all. I guess everyone has local government problems of some sort.

I've been visiting other local domes. So far I haven't seen any as beautiful and airy-light as ours and I haven't seen anything really good in the way of window solutions. Ours I'm not satisfied with, but I haven't seen anything better.

Kathe Welles
Central Oregon Coast Range

Kathe Welles

How to raise a dome singlehanded

Fred Barger

Care must be taken to avoid excessive proselytizing of dome construction. The day will soon come when the landscape will be polluted with little plastic domes, stamped out of machines and poured into endless rows of geodesic ticky tacky. Domes are even more inflexible in design than the eyesores of slurban tract homes. Yet, life in a dome has an excitement that is unattainable in a rectilinear structure. But the enduring reward of a dome is the *self-built* dome, (although possibly any self-built home might be comparably exciting, especially with the use of scrounged and/or native materials).

I built a 30 foot, 3 frequency dome, which is more than adequate for two but would be a cauldron with young 'uns around. Through ingenious scrounging, I have been able to hold the cost to $1300, and it is nearing completion after a year and a half of spare time work. This cost includes complete wiring, indoor plumbing, carpet, cabinets, and a generally decent, modern interior with basic amenities for comfortable living.

However, there is a myth that has been perpetuated about the time and expense of dome construction. As in most any construction, the interior consumes much more time and money than the structure. The shell of my dome cost me $54 . . . the rest going to the interior. As promised, the framework went up quickly . . . two weeks in my case. After it was covered, painted and sealed, we moved in only two months after starting.

It is exhilarating to raise a framework or one with minimal cover in 45 minutes at Whiz Bang Quick City or in two weeks by oneself. But when you set out to provide a hassle-free, liveable environment, only then does the work and expense begin . . . and the unusual shape of domes only complicates matters further.

Cabinet work is a nightmarish frustration. Fitting cabinets to a curved floor is hard enough. But trying to make them conform to triangular panels which alternately slope inward and outward provokes screeching curses. And with cabinet locations unpredictable with respect to a wall whose 5/8 level locations likewise cannot be predicted, the plumbing rough-in riser dimensions are generally unknown when the floor is built—not exactly the most desirable situation. Our semicircular bathroom with sleeping loft on top would have driven a carpenter mad. In general since workers react rather than think, labor costs would have been prohibitive, which is exactly why a self-built dome is virtually essential.

The shell consisted of 2 x 4's, covered by 3/8'' exterior grade plywood—not the most desirable covering—but the plywood was scrounged and was at least of natural origin. The half sheet plywood was cut as shown in Fig. 1.

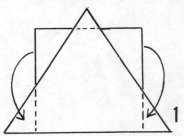

The excess pieces were flipped over and spliced to the main body of the triangular panel by nailing to 1 x 3 backing (Fig. 2).

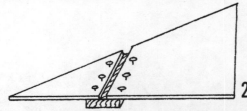

Surely there are better ways, but there was virtually no waste, and considering the inevitability of splicing whenever any standard size pieces are fit to triangles, these were probably the optimum sized sheets. Overall, it was a time consuming process, but it was the cheapest possible method I could conceive under the frenzied conditions at the time.

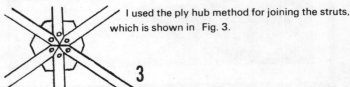

I used the ply hub method for joining the struts, which is shown in Fig. 3.

The hubs were cut from pieces of 1/2'' plywood into hexes and pents which were 3 inches from the center to a point at the tip of the hub. Care must be taken to allow enough clearance on the slot in the strut (Fig. 4) to avoid splitting the end of the strut while fitting the hub into the slot. The strut will also tend to split if there is any inward or outward *movement* of the hub.

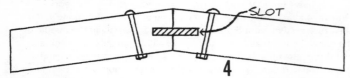

The cuts on the beveled ends of the struts require skill, especially with a skill saw. Due to the complexities of the compound angles (Fig. 5), four cuts were necessary on each end, even with a weird jig, because the blade wouldn't cut through the depth of the 2 x 4. A radial arm saw would have greatly simplified this procedure.

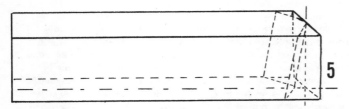

In retrospect, Fig. 6 shows a method by which the number of cuts on the strut ends might have been reduced to two without the necessity of a radial saw.

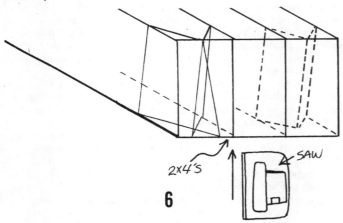

By stacking the struts together as shown with pipe clamps or whatever might be devised, a skill saw, cutting perpendicular to the strut ends, would have the adjacent struts as a surface to stabilize the saw table. The compound angles are therefore cut simultaneously by tilting the saw blade to one half the axial angle to allow for the axial angle on the strut and cutting along the two planes shown to allow for the dihedral angle.

I attempted to predrill the hubs and struts in prefabbed hexes and pents before erecting the framework, but the beveled points didn't pull together satisfactorily during the actual fabrication. Instead, I drilled them in place after using a 1/2'' wood bit as a counter sink for the nut and washer. I used $32 worth of 3/8'' x 3 1/2'' carriage bolts. It is almost mandatory to have a socket wrench to tighten the nuts since they are recessed. Since the 2 x 4's are not always 3 1/2'' deep, some bolts will inevitably protrude beyond the outside surface of the strut. Fear not. It does not interfere with the plywood panel. Just bang on the panel with a hammer at the protrusion and the plywood will lie flat on the strut.

To my knowledge there have been no comparative studies made on ply or metal hubs vs. pipe-strap hubs, although the overwhelming majority of self-built domes have utilized the pipe-strap hubs. Personally, I chose the ply hubs because they were made very cheaply

in only 30 minutes by stacking six pieces of plywood and cutting little pents and hexes from patterns drawn on the top. I had an inescapable feeling that a ply hub in conjunction with strut ends was stronger and sturdier than a pipe hub. I would rather have bolts supporting my dome than skinny little bands of steel.

Of course, bolts are expensive since 360 carriage bolts are hard to scrounge. But then again, pipe hubs require pipe cutting and an expensive banding tool. Metal hubs would have been the strongest of all, but the cutting and drilling would require expensive tools and/or labor, even if made by laminating several pieces of sheet metal, which I tried and abandoned. Perhaps one alternative method to the time consuming cutting of beveled struts is shown in Fig. 7 and Fig. 8, whereby the ends of the struts are cut only once. The savings in time, however, would be at the expense of sturdiness. Perhaps it would even be possible to have a hub with no cuts at all on the end.

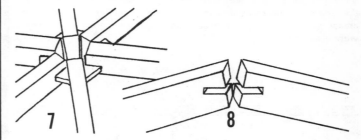

My framework fabrication was rather curious. I chose to build from the top down and raise each successive layer as I went, which would have been fine had a centerpole been used to suspend the framework. But in my usual revulsion at spending money when a cheaper method might be available, I elected to avoid the cost of the pole, cables, block-and-tackle and do it the hard way.

I started by prefabricating the top pent on the floor and then supporting it on five piers. The support at the pier is shown in Fig. 9.

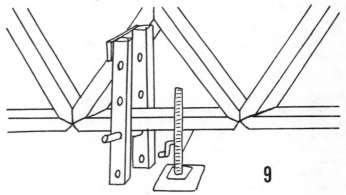

The piers were slightly taller than the altitude of the largest triangle (about 6 feet in my case) with holes drilled at approximately one foot intervals. I started at one pier and raised the framework at that point above the 1st hole and stuck the 3/4'' pipe through the two holes in the pier. The same procedure was followed at each pier all the way around, raising the framework one foot at that point each time until the entire dome was high enough to install a new layer of triangles at the bottom.

This method is clumsy at best. But it did, nevertheless, allow me to go as far as the 3/8 level entirely by myself, and only two friends were necessary for the final two levels. Perhaps the use of a car jack might have eliminated the need for any supplementary labor. The distinct advantages of top-down erection are that it eliminated the custom cuts normally needed at the top in bottom-up erection due to accumulated errors; and more importantly, all the fittings at the hubs were performed at ground level. Since my goal was to leave the beautiful framework exposed to the interior, obviously, for aesthetic reasons, it was imperative that the beveled ends of the struts at each hub come as closely to a point as possible. Therefore, I often used a fourteen foot 2 x 12 at various pressure points for the required leverage to push or pull the six 2 x 4's to a point at each hub, and this would have been virtually impossible on a scaffold 15 feet off the ground.

A word of caution: Don't skimp on the supporting piers. Use at least 10 or more piers and brace them well with at least two 2 x 4's at each pier. My dome fell twice with great drama each time. It fell once while the entire dome was 6 feet off the ground before the final layer of triangles was in place. I thought it was going to roll off into the woods. Perhaps as an extreme testimony to the dome's strength, the only damage was to four hubs whose bottom halves broke off, having absorbed the entire impact of the fall. How many FHA homes could match that?

After the usual frustration with leaky seams, by trial and much error I finally settled with a combination of aluminum duct tape (mainly because it was free), caulk and paint. Evidently, the secret with the tape is to crease it as shown in Fig. 10, and therefore allow the crease to absorb the thermal expansion and contraction of the panels without splitting the tape.

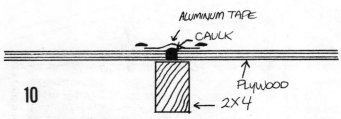

10

I caulked the joint, applied the tape, caulked the edge of the tape, and painted the entire surface with a white vinyl roofing compound. I used a caulk called Acryl R by Schnee Morehead (advertised in *The Whole Earth Catalogue*). The roofing compound was called Permaseal. Perhaps there are better materials, but they worked. The type of caulk is probably not too important. I also used a duct sealer (rubber glue), silicone, and three types of Schnee Morehead's caulks with apparently no appreciable difference in performance. The Permaseal may be a local trade name, but I'm sure similar materials could be found locally almost anywhere by looking under "Roofing Contractors" in the Yellow Pages. Two coats cost $70. Most of the caulk was available free as samples from a friend. The long-term effects of my method may make a fool of me, but at least I'm dry now. There's always shingles.

For insulation I taped up triangles from scrounged pieces of fiberglass duct board used in air conditioning. I used two layers with the foil on the inside layer facing in and the outside layer facing out. This eliminates thermal transfer by radiation as well as conduction; however, I have since learned that three layers of aluminum builder's foil is about the best for the money. Evidently my method is quite effective because a small 15,000 BTU gas floor heater keeps us warm in 20° weather. It would have definitely been more effective had I known to insert spacers between the foil and the surfaces they faced because the dead air space would have provided more resistance to heat flow.

I also botched the interior wall. I chose to recess the 1/4" sheetrock panels 1/2" inside the 2 x 4 cavities to accentuate the framework and eliminate the visual monotony of a monolithic inner surface. It took me all summer to cut the panels, which were then fitted into place, resting on small nails tacked 1/2" back from the inner surface of the 2 x 4.

My naive hopes were to have a suspended ceiling with easy removal and avoid the expense of backing or trim. Unfortunately, the sheetrock settled around the nails and bowed terribly at the middle of the panel. Thus, I was forced to remove all the panels (amidst curses and thrown hammers) and install a 1 x 2 backing at the edges and a 2 x 3 strip in the middle to provide stiffening support. After painting, I hope the effect will justify my anguish. In retrospect the best method would have been to lap the sheetrock over the framework as the plywood was done and simply nail a suitable trim down the seam, such as a rough cedar strip.

Perhaps my worst mistake was using vinyl to cover my window openings—which is what I get for relying on a plastic. Vinyl should at best be thought of as temporary. I used $10 of vinyl to cover 15 triangles, mainly to give me time to complete the dome and contemplate a permanent window covering. I read that vinyl gets brown and brittle after approximately one year of exposure. After a year it was milky but not brown, and like a fool, I tried to get as much mileage as possible out of it. Lying in bed one night, I knew the time had come when I casually stuck my finger through the window while flipping at a raindrop. My fears were confirmed one week later when a moderate hailstorm blew out five windows and thoroughly drenched everything inside. Avoid this trauma.

Plastic does have its limited place, however, but heavy reliance on it is a no-no. The plexiglass I now use for windows is doing fine, but it still bears the plastic stigma and has to prove itself to me. Plexiglass is difficult to control at best, mainly due to the tremendous thermal expansion and contraction. I attempted to use my tape-caulk method, but it pulled apart and leaked. I have no remedy as of yet, but eventually it will be resolved. Plexiglass scratches easily, collects dust and is expensive.

Either due to my incompetence or the extreme Texas heat, Bucky's upflow method of natural air conditioning was a dismal failure despite a 1/2 HP forced draft. Perhaps my four 16 x 5 supply ducts in the floor and five 16 x 5 exhaust grilles at the top failed to meet Bucky's description of large openings at the top and bottom. It did cool to 105° inside one day, but somehow I can't imagine that bringing 109° air inside will ever cool the dome to a liveable temperature inside, regardless of the method. Regretfully, I'll have to scrounge up a small window air conditioner.

The most persistent and perhaps unresolvable problem with a dome manufactured by my method (without resorting to gross foam sprays) has been winter condensation. With only one layer of window material, it literally sprinkles inside if a window is overhead. It is a nuisance trying to find a dry place to sit while dodging large droplets of water.

Obviously, a second layer of glass or plexiglass will remedy this problem, but the dilemma of condensation removal *inside* the walls is

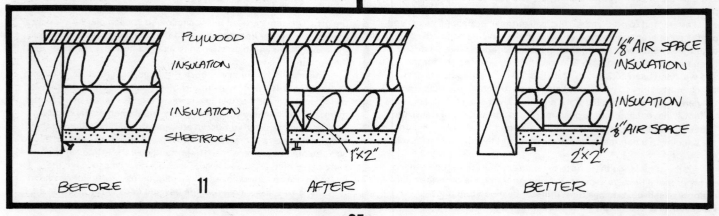

perplexing. Standard houses trap condensation on a vapor barrier just inside the outer wall, which is then free to fall unimpeded by the vertical studs to the bottom of the cavity and to the outside. However, the horizontal struts in domes become a barrier for any such motion. As a consequence, moisture condenses on the duct board foil (and rots the inner layer of plywood since I failed to provide an airspace), travels down the foil, and accumulates on the horizontal struts (Fig. 12). From there it either passes by the strut at the seam to do further damage

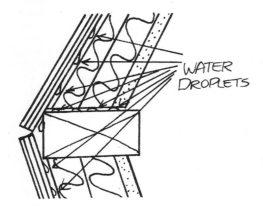

WATER DROPLETS

down stream or rots the strut or soaks through the sheetrock joint at the strut and stains the wall paint as it drys below. Does anyone have a cheap solution?

Despite all these difficulties, if one is flirting with the idea of building a dome, he should. The methods I have described allowed me to do about 97% of the work with no need of help, but a larger crew would have been fun and much more efficient. Although I could probably build a conventional house, I doubt that I would have attempted it. Boredom and lethargy would have frozen me. The skills for building a dome are rather basic. Almost any question regarding plumbing, wiring, nailing, etc. on a dome can with a little intelligence be extrapolated from books about standard houses.

The dome dweller must prepare himself for attracting all types of people especially if he is located near a large city. Unfortunately, being located on a well-traveled road near Dallas, we draw the foolish as well as the fascinating. Our visitors have ranged from touristers in ranch wagaons, wanting to show the kids the weird jack-o-lantern; to hucksters, trying to sell ice machines; to hippies in Cadillacs, who sour our ears with "Far Out! Outasite! This is really groovy!" Put your dome in the trees, folks.

Fred Barger
Rt. 1, Box 60A
Coppell, Texas 75019

Photo: Geodesic Structures, Inc.; Hightstown, New Jersey

Better Domes & Gardens

Andrew Ralph

(A few thoughts, suggestions; a little pointing)

Dome interiors are a problem for most people who are used to dealing with four-walled rooms, all variants on the cube. Yet the spherical shape is the essence of what a dome gives; low cost, completely unobstructed volume.

Since a number of people who want to build domes seem genuinely puzzled about how to arrange and furnish a dome's interior, I decided to put down some basics. They are not hard and fast rules, just possibilities and directions. The basic difference in furnishing a dome is not the need for new or different furnishings, but the need for your own attitudes to change to consider integrating familiar objects with a spherical shape.

A house is an expensive structure, both financially and in terms of the time and effort (or yourself) invested in it. As well, you have to live with your creation. Don't rush it. Plan carefully in terms of money, space usage, your own tastes and interests. Collect all the information you can. Buy books and magazines, clip articles and pictures, note ideas, leaf through catalogs, take brochures. Use the library for back issues of magazines—and please don't rip'em off—libraries aren't rich—and someone else may want to use them after you do.

The first and fundamental fact you'll have to work with is all that unobstructed volume. The second, and often more confusing aspect of dome interiors is the circle. If you are used to living in a cube, thinking "square" (I'm sorry) is a mental bind—things don't seem to work: a cube doesn't fit a sphere—leading to visions of all sorts of wierd inaccessible nooks and crannies, buying new furniture, acquiring a permanent crook in your back from huddling under sloping walls—needlessly.

Since you are not seriously restricted by arbitrary heights in a dome, try split-level living in all the floor plans you can develop. I'll give a quick, incomplete rundown of some ideas for a dome, each of which represents an entire spectrum of ideas and treatments of floor plans. This is just to start you thinking—then go ahead, fantasize—your fantasy may work—and well. Your imagination, your ingenuity, your *brain* is your best and cheapest tool—get all you can out of it.

A two story living room is a natural. It could occupy from 1/4 to 2/3 of the ground floor space. I say living room—living area is better,

encompassing the dining area, the traditional living room, and a private or semi-private library, along with a sizable amount of open space if you just crave room (I do).

Depending on the size of the area and your own needs and finances, this could be all one level, undivided, or go the route: a dining area at one end of a semicircle, a free form sunken pit or entire lower floor for your living room, a raised library. Or would movable bookcase/partitions suit you better?

Fireplaces can be in the middle of the floor, accessible from all sides—a dome has enough height so a fireplace will draw well.

The upstairs would be bedrooms and a bath, perhaps a studio. A balcony can go inside and/or outside. An observatory? A solarium? Don't forget: stairways can be pretty original if you desire.

The second aspect of a dome is its circularity. Learn to work with windows, because your circle is upward as well as around, especially in the living room. See *Domebook 2* for some fine window treatments. Great fantasy seeds.

Built-ins are a part of any modern, efficient house, and non-rectangular furniture arrangements also will be a basic feature of a dome (more on furniture later).

The circular shapes of rooms such as kitchen and bedrooms (actually pie slice shapes, but the word fits) can produce both unusual effects and aid efficiency if you think with the shape. In the kitchen for example, the work area traffic pattern will be smaller yet keep all available surfaces and cabinets much closer than in a rectangle. Place tall appliances on inside walls, to avoid any conflict with the wall slope.

Bedrooms can be lightly personal in shape and will take modern or traditional furniture with ease. Remember—contrast in furniture and interiors is as valid a concept as matching. The dome's angularity could be softened by color, and met with deeply toned wood to add warmth. Any antique of good design will go well. Skip Victorian, baroque or rococo type stuff in most cases (this is my opinion). Brief thoughts: murals, not pictures. Texture or pattern walls, using triangle motif. Skylights are easy in bedroom window treatments.

Sound in a dome: domes reflect sound with incredible efficiency. So contemplate the use of textured or soft materials, enriching your visual experience and at the same time helping the acoustics. Try: cork panels (unpainted are best); carpet—do an abstract design with scraps; commercial egg box liners (waffled cardboard—spray paint 'em); burlap; you name it. Both stereo and quad sound systems should sound sensational and require less power: try hanging speakers on the wall, above eye level.

Lights in a dome should be modern. Fixed lights can be sunken spots in the ceiling or wall mounted swivel spots. Lightolier, among others, makes a light bar mounting several movable units for store use that would go well in a dome. More on lights under furnishing.

Built-ins are a natural part of any efficient house. By providing great amounts of storage space without the attendant expense and clutter of chests and shelves, they allow carefree low maintenance living and better aesthetics.

The most important built-ins are the kitchen cabinets. I find the kitchen cabinets, especially the upper ones, an enduring if not obvious movement to male chauvinism. They are designed by six-foot tall men for six-foot tall men. The uppers are too high and too deep to be readily accessible and lower ones are too deep also. Large accessible work areas do not exist, and at the same time the kitchen's layout precludes any added table to solve the problem. Good conventional designs shown in the home and workshop magazines solve some of these problems. For a dome, I would recommend shallow (18″ or so) lower cabinets and counter, with a curved top and a free form bulge to create a deep working area. The curved bulge does not project into floor area while giving a lot of space. A lazy-susan arrangement may be used to keep most of the space accessible under the bulge:

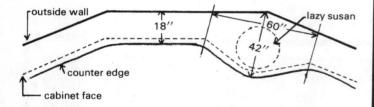

If, in a larger dome, a table is desired, no bulge need be used or a pair of smaller bulges may be placed to suit (see tables below).

Upper cabinets are generally too high and too deep, rendering much of their space useless, as it is out of reach. Try 6-8″ depth instead of 12″. Lower the bottom to within a foot of the counter. Use an open spice shelf to avoid opening cabinets at all. You shouldn't, and shouldn't have to store large items above. You still may need a foot-stool, but less often, and it should be easier to use.

Built-ins can be used elsewhere to deepen walls for soundproofing, while giving storage, and are conventional in all respects on interior walls. Again, think shallow. How often do you put something away deeper than 8″? Hang things from pegboard. Should you have two sided shelves, accessible from a utility room and a hall? Hit the house design books and magazines for ideas here. They've got lots of good ones and so many variations they may actually have just what you want.

Bookcases can be built in or add on. Movable ones used as dividers can define room space in accordance with your desires. They could also be suspended from the dome frame. Abstracta makes a nice non-movable display frame in stainless tubing. It's modern, spare and delicate looking. A real minimal structure and maintenance free. Presses together, from the look of it (address below).

Furniture in a dome can be anything you desire. If you are buying modern, look into the better grades of office furniture. Doesn't look office at all, is rugged and generally simple in design, well upholstered, and though expensive, cheap compared to a "name" designer's stuff that may or may not practical. Steelcase, Hon, Cole, Oxford, Lyon, and more or less in just chairs, All-Steel and Cosco are big names. Others abound. Go into an office supply and browse. Cities are the place to go here. Use the Yellow Pages. Small towns can't give you a deal. If it's too expensive, take ideas. You may find the same thing someplace else cheaper or you can make your own. Sears' selection is limited, but 30-50% cheaper than usual list.

In desks and tables borrow ideas. For example, Oxford makes a cluster 120 series of desks meant to be modules in a three part office work station. Each module is a fine 120° desk with all that area and because of being wrapped around you, 95% efficient, they claim. Not cheap. Build your own.

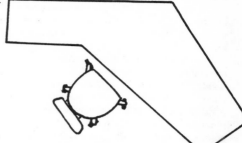

an approximation - desk can be asymmetrical left or right

Tables: again the circle-square conflict. Table corners jut out making you move the table into the room center before it can be gotten around. To boot, the table center is too small for serving dishes. Answer: an oval, or—

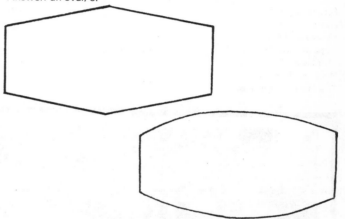

make your own. These are commonly $500-$700. Sears $300-$400.

Chairs, sofas, etc. Except at unreasonably high new prices there seem to be only three ways to get well made furniture of any design: used, kits, and made from scratch.

Used furniture includes second hand stores, dumps (unlikely), auctions, and newspaper ads. Luck enters here—read up on auctions and learn a bit about furniture construction before you buy. Try not to buy damaged stuff unless you are a middling successful handyman, or are sure you can learn fast. Be fussy about materials and construction—if you buy cardboard and staple furniture, and it's damaged, it won't even make good firewood.

Kits: a number of firms will sell you knockdown furniture. Kits of a specific good item are considerably rarer. In all cases, you just assemble and finish. Actual work varies with the quality of cutting and the wood used. Ask questions, order brochures. Perhaps friends have done this, and can inform you—and give leads on where to buy them. Magazines of the mechanic, handyman, and home sort carry ads for kits. Yankee, too. The only reproduction outfit I know of is Cohasset Colonials; good materials and fit, finishing supplies included. Copies of authentic pieces. Savings 50%-60% over store bought. There may be other reproduction firms around. Tell me—I'd like to know.

From scratch: The Whole Earth Catalog Craft Section, and books for sale in museums. A favorite of mine: *The American Shakers and Their Furniture*. Beautiful, functional. Bucky would probably love the stuff—very efficient.

Lamps—I'm death on most table lamps and the old fashioned floor lamps. Inefficient, clumsy, expensive and lots of clutter. Multiple pole lamp fixtures, tensors and well-chosen spots are cleaner and cheaper. While you're at it, your fixed lighting should include dimming. It's cheaper to design in when you're building from scratch.

An excellent discussion of lighting appears in *Tomorrow's House* (see below) and I am sure in other layman's books on design. It was said then and is probably true now as well, that the single most neglected area of house design is lighting. Another area where so little expense can mean so much to your living conditions.

Shop on price: often the identical item is sold in gift shops at a real rip off, furniture stores for too much, and discounted in chains or available through electrical firms or builder's supply stores at a fair price.

I'm at a loss on interior finish and color, carpets, and nifty decorating ideas. Play the sponge. House and garden magazines are good for this. *Better Homes and Gardens* has an annual feature, 100 ideas under $100—A how-to approach, using a lot of ingenuity. A good source. *House Beautiful* is $, good taste. *House and Garden* is gimmicky to me, that is, more than the others. Suit yourself. Paint companies sell, and often give away free brochures. Keep looking. A list of things referred to in this article appears below.

Magazines:

House Beautiful
Better Homes and Gardens
House and Garden
Popular Mechanics
Mechanix Illustrated
Popular Science
The Home Handyman

Books:

The American Shakers and Their Furniture
   John G. Shea
   Van Nostrand-Reinhold, NY, NY, 1971

Tomorrow's House   1945   Simon & Schuster
   George Mellon
   Henry Wright
   of Architectural Forum
   (Old, but it seems to be a basic book. Look for newer on same idea.)

Office supply firms

Abstracta Structures, Inc.
101 Park Avenue
New York, New York 10017

A few last words: take your time. "Act in haste, repent at leisure." Time invested in understanding and exploring will not only make life better at home, but could save you a bundle. Taste doesn't mean money. Good Luck!

Andrew Ralph
86 Maple St.
White River Jct.
Vermont 05001

Carey Smoot

Thoughts, Ideas, and Dreams of Domes

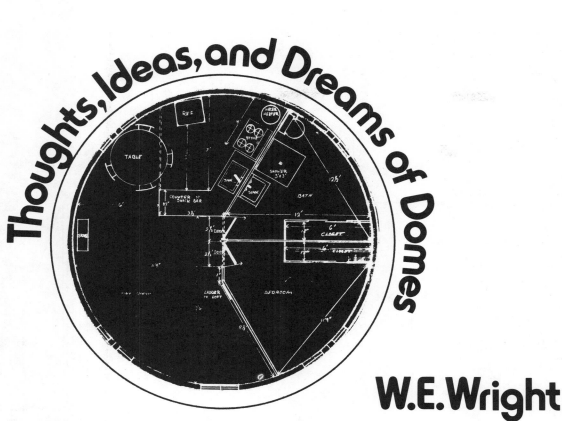

W.E. Wright

All figures and thoughts in this material are mine and no rule says anyone has to go along. Most figures are based on the building of a 24' 3/8 dome used for a garage and the present construction of a 24' 5/8 dome to be used for my mother as her home. All other figures are from drawings of mine for two dome and three dome dreams right now, but I'm hoping to start construction someday. I feel like anyone else that's into domes—that they are the strongest, cheapest and fastest homes to build. I won't go into chord factors or too much into foundations to use, as anyone into domes just about knows what sort of foundation he wants, plus where to find the chord factors for the size dome wanted. All I can throw at you now are some floor plans and costs and ideas of mine.

We'll start with the 24' 3/8 dome my brother and I and a few friends built in Missouri, on his 20 acres where he moved last June. We used 1 x 2's for struts and plywood hubs all bolted with carriage bolts. We built it mainly as a model to gain information for bigger and better ones. We did use it as a garage and tool shed after finishing. We threw a 30' x 50' circus tent over it for a skin. Took us about 7 hours (3 hours work—4 hours goofing off). Total costs were $30 for the old tent, $40 for lumber and bolts. The height is 9 ft, but it seems three times larger when you first walk inside, a really far out feeling of space and room.

The dome I'm going into now is the 24' 5/8 3 freq. now being constructed in Missouri for my mother. It will have a concrete foundation only around the circumference. A wood flooring will be laid on this, and the dome built on top. This will give her dome about a 2 or 3 foot crawl space if she ever wants to add anything under the floor. The struts are 2 x 4's with 1'' thick hubs. They will be covered with 1/4'' to 1/2'' plywood, then with roofing paper and then with shingles. We feel that to stop leaks from happening shingles is the cheapest and easiest way. It will take approximately 44 sheets for the outside plywood covering and approximately 1200 sq. ft. of shingles to cover the outside. Inside walls will be insulated and then covered with plywood or pasteboard or maybe even cardboard which can be painted. All interior work can be done at a later date if money is low and time is too valuable. The dome will have a bath, kitchen and living room, and master bedroom on the lower level. This gives a total of about 450 sq. ft. The upper level or loft is above the bedroom and kitchen and bath, and gives extra room for more sleeping space or storage. There will be a skylight in the top pentagon for lots of light, so the loft could be used for a reading or sewing room also. A simple ladder is used to reach the loft. All doors and window glass are to be bought second hand and as cheaply as we can. The approximate total cost for the dome is $750. The interior costs would run about $125,

W. E. Wright

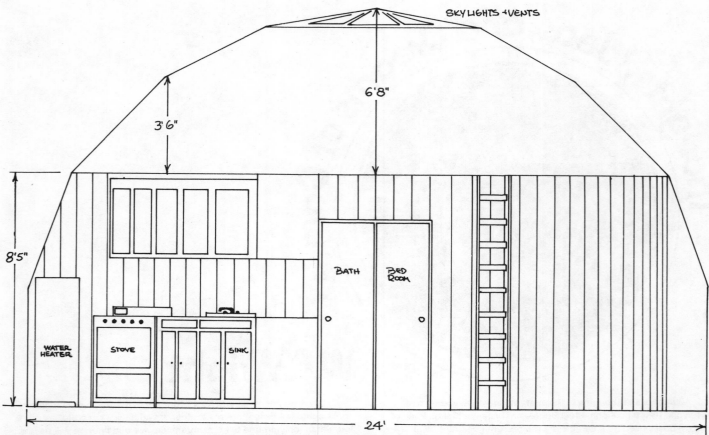

SKYLIGHTS + VENTS

6'8"

3'6"

8'5"

WATER HEATER

STOVE

SINK

BATH

BED ROOM

24'

depending on how much of the counter space we build and how cheap the bath fixtures are. To be on the safe side, we're figuring on $1000 for all. Of course my mother already has a lot of furniture and inside additions, so the costs for that will be about nil. This price of $1000 is for a well constructed dome and we expect it to last "forever". Now on to other domes.

The domes Judi and I are planning to build for our future home will be two domes at least and maybe three, all connected by hallways. They will include solar heating to save costs of fuel, and to cut pollution. A back up heating system of oil or gas stoves will provide heat for really cold days when the sun is clouded over.

The solar collector will be built to provide approx. 200,000 BTU's with a storage capacity of about three or four days. A rough estimate for building the solar heater is $2 per square foot, doing all the labor ourselves. We'll use all the cheapest materials we can dig up, wood for the framing, and plastic for the collector windows. The collector will be located between two domes and the hallway will serve as the heat duct. The wall between the collector and the hallway will have vents for adjusting the rate of heat entering the domes. A system of shutters will close at night to prevent loss of heat and in the summer to cut down heat not needed. A door will lead from the hallway into the collector so that it can also be used as a greenhouse in the winter. Building the collector into the domes will cut down on heat loss and costs of materials will be less. I'm figuring on 600 sq. ft. for two domes, and will have to figure for a bigger collector for three domes or two larger ones. Enough of that, and I won't go into using windmills for electric power, another plan of mine. After the domes are built, the interior layout is going to be a big argument between Judi and I, but I'll show some of the plans I have made up. The darkroom in the main room plus water heater will probably turn out to be a storage room if I don't watch out. With a three dome system the darkroom could be located in another dome. What I am thinking of now is keeping the waterpipes as short as possible. The bathroom could be located in the main dome to further cut costs and shorten pipes. I haven't really made up my mind yet on this point, but all pipes and wiring should be as short as possible.

The main dome will house the living room and kitchen plus darkroom and will have a loft over the darkroom and kitchen area. All the counters will be built by me (as much as I can, anyway). I plan to have eight foot ceilings to make buying lumber, etc. simple. To save costs, a ladder will be used instead of stairs to all lofts. The lofts have about seven feet of ceiling height at the center and three feet at the roof, or outside diameter of the loft. A sky light at the center of the dome will provide extra light for the lofts and main floors. The lofts can be used for extra bedrooms for guests, or for storage, or reading-sewing room. A four-channel system would sound wild in the loft too. Right?

Room dividers would be studs covered with fiberboard, plywood, or whatever, with doors or folding doors. Everything would be as conveniently placed as possible, including outlets, doors, windows, speaker switches, stoves, shelves and closets. In the kitchen the stove pipe can be run out the wall at the 7'-8' level and one of the windows can be changed to a vent. For two domes, the total floor area just on the main floors would be 900 ft. for 24' domes. The loft areas would give another 400 ft., plus the storage areas which would give lots of hiding space. Everything would be out of the way. The bathroom will have two doors, one from the hallway and the other connected to the master bedroom. The closet space in the main bedroom is 12 feet long and 18 inches wide; plenty of room for the wife and her gear. There will be a small furnace in the living room and in the second dome as back up heating. The second dome will house the master bedroom, bathroom, and den or recreation room. If a three dome system is used the third dome will be a work shop and possibly a darkroom and extra guest bedrooms. What we plan on doing is building the two domes first and adding the third as we save the money and as room is needed. The third dome can be joined to any hexagon on either of the first two domes when needed. All the domes now planned are 24' 5/8 3 frequency covered with plywood and then with shingles. The foundation is to be cement around the circumference with wood floors on that. I will try to have a three or four foot crawl space under all floors. If ever in the future we want a big furnace instead of the wall

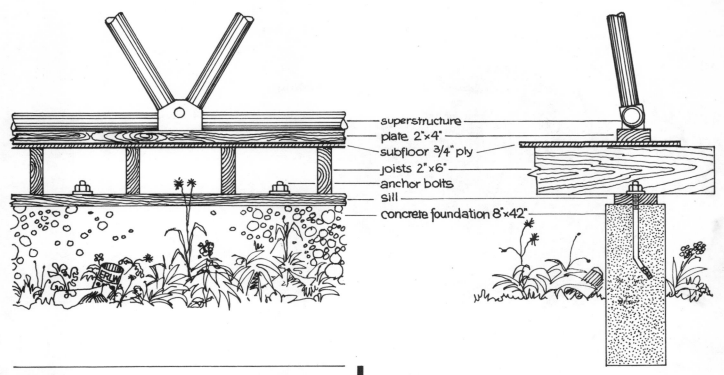

superstructure
plate 2"x4"
subfloor 3/4" ply
joists 2"x6"
anchor bolts
sill
concrete foundation 8"x42"

furnaces, it can be put in the crawl space. Could also be used for hiding little things you don't ever want found by anyone, ya know?

Right now the plans for our domes are waiting while we're saving the money for them. As of now, we're not sure where we want to build, but it will be either Missouri or Illinois. If we get lucky, we'll move to the western states and build there. Anyway everything is ready to start building except money and location. All we need are those two things and it'll start. The costs are figured at about $1000 to $1500 for each dome plus the cost of the land. It seems like everyone I talk to about domes first comes to the idea that I'm half nuts for wanting such a far out weird house. Then they can't believe that it can be built for such a cheap price. I guess everyone is used to square rooms and houses, but if they want to spend $20,000 to ?00,000 for a house that they could build for $15,000, then let them—I'm through talking and trying to make them see that the dome is the best

type of house for *ANYONE*. These are the same people that leave the lights on all day and night and turn the heat up till it's 90 or 100° inside and think nothing of throwing trash out the car window or taking 30 minute baths to use all the water they can. They can't seem to understand that a dome uses the least amount of the cheapest materials. But some people act as if they have all the money in the world to throw away, even if they only make $80 to $100 a week. People not giving a damn and thinking that the other guy is going to do it, not them, is what's tearing this planet to hell. If they could imagine themselves the only ones on earth and see how they are polluting the earth, maybe people would watch things a little more. OK, enough of that—I got carried away. At least to give the people some ideas will accomplish what I started out to do.

W.E. Wright
5106 Main St.
Downers Grove, Ill. 60515

Zomes

Dave Mielke

"Zome" is a word popularized by Steve Baer, meaning a structure based on a zonohedron. Zonohedra are solids that have one or more bands of parallel edges circling them. You've seen some in this book already—the cube, the rhombic dodecahedron, and the rhombic triacontahedron are all zonohedra.

Because the edges in a zone are parallel, a zonohedron can be stretched or compressed by stretching or shrinking a whole zone, without changing any angles.

This feature makes zomes more flexible than domes. On the other hand, zomes are not triangulated, so stresses must be resisted by a rigid skin, rigid joints, or extra bracing.

The zome Dave Mielke describes is based on the rhombic dodecahedron. It's called an *exploded* rhombic dodecahedron because the original faces are expanded radially outward, producing new faces between the old vertices and edges.

The new solid is also a zonohedron. This treatment can be applied to many other solids with interesting results.

Several of the Archimedean solids are zonohedra. Among these are the truncated octahedron and the small rhombicuboctahedron, which Doug Lais uses in his structures.

Rhombic dodecahedron

Exploded
rhombic dodecahedron

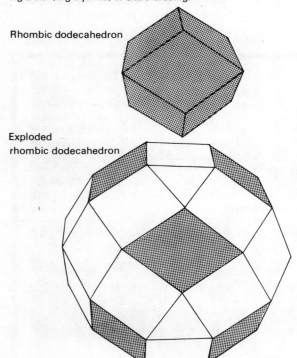

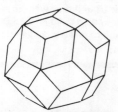

A rhombic triacontahedron

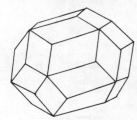

One zone stretched

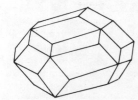

A second zone compressed

Great Lakes Zome

Dave Mielke

We started building domes as part of a school project, but split off to form Great Lakes Domes and experiment with domes and zomes on our own.

I'd say our zome is our most successful project. The shape is an exploded rhombic dodecahedron 19 feet long, 14 feet wide and 11 feet high. It was designed with a slide rule and ideas picked up from seeing Steve Baer's work in New Mexico. For more on zome design, get a copy of the *Dome Cookbook* and the *Zome Primer,* both by Baer.

All the panels were pre-fabbed using beveled 2 x 4's and 1/2" plywood. The panels were fastened together with metal plates and nails. This method seems to work pretty well, since the completed shell was dragged by a jeep about 150 feet to the site without any joints separating. Since we never did develop a cheap and efficient method of sealing, caulking the joints was a constant job.

Cost—About $300 for the shell material including about 20% scrounged lumber—mostly wood packing crates used for the flooring.

Erection Time—Prefabrication took three weeks and the actual erection time was about ten hours with five people helping. People were needed to keep the panels propped up while they were nailed together.

Foundation—Since this was supposed to be a "temporary, experimental" building, the zome did not have a real foundation. The floor was placed on a layer of gravel topped with a vapor barrier. Frost heave was a problem. We ended up caulking each spring.

The interior was insulated with plastic-backed aluminum foil. The foil covered interior was pretty wild, especially with candlelight, but we eventually panelled the lower course with 2 x 4 ft. acoustic tiles. This finished off the interior nicely, but it was mostly done because the materials were free and we wanted to make the structure more appealing to the straight folks who were constantly dropping in for a closer look. All in all, I'd definitely use sprayed foam next time. It was really a big hassle piecing 90° materials into our wierd geometry.

We put small triangular windows into the two triangular panels, at the low end of the zome and the triangular panel above eye level at the high end. We used 1 ft. triangular pieces of thin acrylic with caulk and batten strips to hold them on. We had no leakage problem. Even this small amount of glazing made the zome less cave-like and let us see out without sacrificing inner privacy.

Ventilation is accomplished by opening panels on both sides of the base course and a hole covered by a 1 ft. triangle on top. We had a triangular chimney on top, but the wind would cause the joints to open and leak profusely. There were some condensation problems, but given the experimental nature of the structure, we didn't try to do too much to prevent this. The ventilation system kept the interior pretty fresh. The top vent was always open and one bottom vent was open even in winter. The ventilation and insulation is adequate, since the zome isn't intended as a permanent living structure.

One thing worth mentioning about the zome and other domes we've been in is the illusion of great interior volume enclosed by a shell that doesn't seem big enough to hold it. Almost everyone mentions this no matter whether the interior is bare or loaded. The place looks much bigger inside than outside.

As far as building codes go, we have our zome classified as an "experimental structure." We don't even have the damn thing on a foundation, which causes no end of hassles in the spring, when the stove end sinks faster than the other end, but it hasn't caused any trouble with the Man. The inspector did pay a visit when it was being constructed; we had five stout American males jumping up and down on the top to show him that it would stand (a crude but effective structural test, but he bought it). Our only restriction is that it can't be used as a permanent living quarters or office. The lack of plumbing and permanent electricity had a lot to do with that, however. It's been used mostly for discussion groups and weekend parties. The biggest objection that can be used around here is the "appearance" clause in the codes. A dome just doesn't blend in harmoniously with the ranch houses and split-levels in our suburban area.

We've put Great Lakes Domes on the shelf for the time being. Personal hassles scattered our energy. The land the zome was on has been sold, so right now all our building is done in our heads.

Dave Mielke
520 Lakeview
Box 3
So. Milwaukee, Wisc. 53172

Domes and Zomes

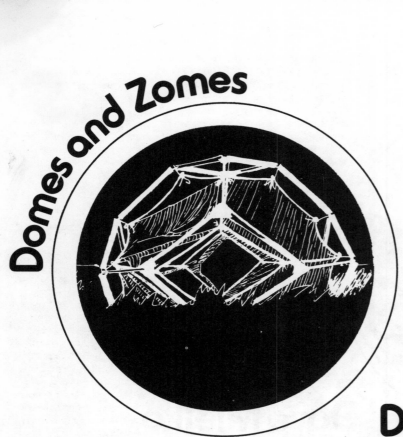

Doug Lais

The following is a concise summary of my dome building experience.

1) My first dome was a 2V 6 foot diameter cardboard dome model, with stapled seams.

2) My next dome was a 2V 11 foot diameter cardboard dome with the seams taped with masking tape and the whole dome covered with tar. It stood up to 3 days of rain before it collapsed. Then the neighborhood kids used it as a crawling snail shell, a tank tread, and an enormous bowl, and the soggy thing stood up to it all without ripping apart. It was just stapled with regular small staples too. Fantastic.

3) So next I built a 2V 11 foot diameter carboard egg dome, with the panels bolted together. I had no purpose other than experimentation, so its final resting place was the county dump - minus the bolts.

4) I decided to try something more ambitious, so I built an 11 foot diameter icosa greenhouse dome, made of 8 foot long 1 x 3's, and sheet metal hubs, bolted together. The plastic was stapled onto the outsides of the struts and left temporarily until slats could be stapled over the easily torn plastic. The dome was not staked to the ground and so became airborne late one night. My wife ran outside in a bathrobe and western boots, armed with a pitchfork, and slew the ailing beastie before it could fly into the road, exposing to public view the "thing" we had harbored in our back yard.

5) After the disaster, I built a truncated octahedron tent zome 10' diameter, with 1 x 3 struts, plywood hubs, and an interlocking notch system of assembly (John Prenis' idea). Being a mathematical idiot, I computed all the angles wrong, but it fit together anyway. The tent was made from extra bedsheets sewn on a home machine. I just tied rocks into the apexes and strung it up. The day I cut it down I went out with a knife and started whacking away at the strings. I had two left right at the top. I cut one of them and all the weight of the tent was hanging from one apex. Amid crackings, creakings, snappings and groanings I wildly slashed at that stubborn rope. When I had finally felled the hanging destroyer my frame was cocked at a jaunty angle on the lay of the land. I stood in the sunset trying to swallow that, with my trembling knife gleaming in the sun, but finally relaxed, bundled everything up and carried it home. Praise the Lord that it was just a prototype.

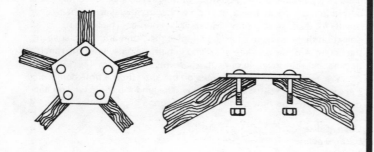

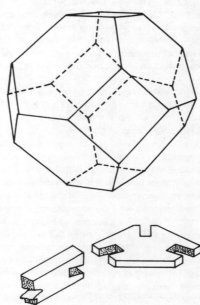

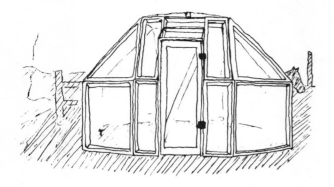

6) The next project was a small Rhombi-cubo-octahedron greenhouse zome 13 feet in diameter. The 2 x 4's were all free for the removal of the fence they constituted. The construction techinque was sun-dome type with the plastic stapled on before construction. There were actually 3 shapes instead of two in my dome. I used 5 squares 6' x 6', four triangles, and eight rectangles around the base, 4' x 6'. The unit was bolted together. The top square had a 2 x 4 set across it to

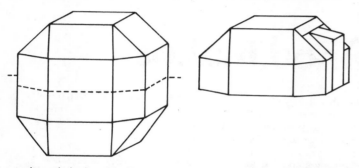

make a pitched roof for the plastic. The door was quite nice and easy to build. I built the door frame into a base rectangle and stretched a canopy of plastic from the door frame to the upper square. I goofed up the dihedral angles and axial angles, so I won't bother writing them down. I almost hate to tell you the same disaster story again, but . . . as heavy as that dome was, sixty-four two by fours, mostly all six feet long, and soaked with condensation, you wouldn't expect it to blow away. Well, it didn't . . . at first. First it exploded (eyewitness account) and *then* it blew away. We were having gusts up to 45 m.p.h. that day, and Bernouli's Principle was proven again in an unusual way. About twenty feet from the original site I was shown a pile of splintered wood and plastic by my wife. I investigated. It *was* a small pile for a dome of that size. Yes, some of it *was* missing. Half of it, to be exact. Where? I looked in front of the house, behind the garage, behind our neighbor's house, in all the nearby fields and pastures from a high hill - I even looked on top of my house! Nowhere - gone with the wind. I can see it now; some poor farmers wife running out into the night with a pitchfork to valiantly slay the evil flapping beastie chicken-eater. I salvaged enough parts to build . . .

7) An A-frame, 6' square greenhouse, now in use. It's set up on two 40 lb. logs with plastic side walls - the whole A-frame unit is therefore elevated about one foot. That's all the space we ever needed in the first place. So far, the total spent on these domes is about $75 at the utter maximum; we never kept close track though. The next one I finish (I'm in the process of building it now) should cost me about $25-$35, the most expensive yet, but neither is it another prototype.

8) It's going to be a weather proof, functional playhouse for my daughter. I have a 1/2" conduit frame, an icosa 5'9" diameter, which I plan to cover either with plywood or sealed triple-layered cardboard painted with aluminum-abestos trailer roof coating. I'll use fiberglass cloth strips sealed with some special gook they've got for the purpose to seal the edges. I'll attach the skin to the conduit with either U-bolts or rope (maybe wire, smaller holes to seal). With a door, a floor, and some windows it should be fantastic. A slightly larger version could be nice for adults. With a little wood burning stove it would be really cozy and light to transport. I'll fill you in when I've finished.

Know anybody who has experimented with resin (or whatever) impregnated paper mache? The reason I'm spending (some people call it wasting) time on such non-permanent materials is because I have never made enough money to lavishly buy the best pro-model unit. My conduit came from a dump; so did most of my cardboard. I'm just an amateur scrounger, though. I have heard it said that the way to success is to risk everything, to go in over your head and keep a 'goin. If you have a good product, you'll probably survive. But, anyway, paper mache should be a good permanent material if handled properly.
Doug Lais
Rt. #2, Box 3222
Sacramento, Cal. 95826

Ferro-Cement "Domes"

Thad Matras

Ferro-cement is made by plastering a mortar consisting of a mixture of ordinary portland cement, clean masonry sand, and water into a thick wire mesh. The components are much the same as in ordinary reinforced concrete. The main difference is that a wire mesh is used almost exclusively instead of just steel reinforcing bars and there is no gravel, crushed rock or other aggregate in the mixture. There are no exotic ingredients in ferro-cement. Ferro means iron; in this case referring to the thick wire mesh.

The resulting shells are both light, strong and thin, rarely exceeding 3/4 of an inch. To use this medium properly to gain its maximum potential strength, it is necessary to make the shells curved. The principle that applies here is that curved surfaces are stronger than flat surfaces.

The ferro cement shells must be constructed over a framework of some kind. We have used a variety of flexible materials to form the curved frameworks of our domes. We have used 1/2'' x 3'' select white pine, saplings, and 1/2'' steel reinforcing rods, as well as scraps of wood and even old t.v. antennas scavenged from dumps for additional bracing. The framework can be considered a temporary armature which will have little if any structural value after the ferro-cement shell has cured. Its chief function is to serve as a fairly strong and rigid frame to walk and work on, and of course to support the wire

mesh and the wet concrete during the cureing and hardening process. The framework could theoretically be removed after the concrete has hardened. However, a framework could be useful in the interior as a convenient support for electrical wiring, for attaching insulation, or for plastering. To make our frames more rigid we strengthened them with as many supporting posts in the interior as we thought necessary.

Our experience in building with ferro-cement demonstrated the practical advantages of certain materials over others. We tried always to be conscious of costs but considered first the practicability of the materials to be used. Selecting a film of some kind to cover the framework as a retainer for the wet mortar presented some problems which we eventually solved by trial and error. While the applied wet cement is supported to a great extent by the wire mesh covering the film, it does press down with the force of its own weight plus the pressure exerted in the plastering process. With these pressures many of the films we tried would belly down and sag or even rip and tear away

The plastering started from the top of the structure and fanned outward and downward with more people joining in as the space widened. Cement was conveyed to the plasterers in a bucket brigade on ladders leaning against the structure. The plasterers all wore heavy vinyl gloves (available at most hardware stores) as cement is quite caustic and sharp wire in the mesh can cause severe cuts. The mortar was rubbed into the wire mesh by hand. This is a very important part of the process and is hard work. The mortar must be very thoroughly rubbed into the mesh leaving no voids or air spaces. Covering the wire and leaving no strands exposed is very important.

The curing process is another vital part of ferro-cement construction. A minimum of seven days damp curing is advisable. Up to a month is ideal. The dome should be covered with a plastic film to retain the moisture or covered with burlap, rags, etc. and kept wet.

The first ferro-cement dome we built was on a lumber frame, generally using select 1/2'' x 3'' lumber, making sure there were no knots or splits that would give under the stress of bending while

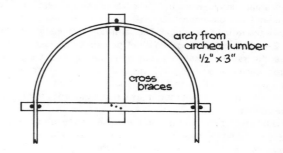

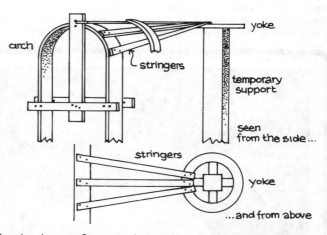

between the frame members. Without the retaining film, the mortar would fall through the wire mesh. We tried 4 mil polyethylene plastic, burlap (from old feed bags) and metal screen. Metal screen was the best in itself but too expensive unless scavenged from discarded screen doors and windows. Burlap and plastic needed support. We found that one layer of 1 inch chicken wire stapled to the frame would give adequate support to any film. Here we also discovered that the plastic was the best in combination with the chicken wire underneath because it was transparent, making voids and air spaces visible from the inside while the plastering was being done.

After the mortar-retaining film is stapled to the framework, the wire mesh which is to serve as a body of the ferro-cement can be applied. One inch galvanized chicken wire seems to be adequate. This wire can be readily purchased in almost any lumber yard, hardware store or agricultural supply store. It comes in rolls of from 25 to 150 feet and in widths of 4, 5, and 6 feet. We found that the best width was 4 ft. Our experience suggests that not fewer than four layers of this wire applied in such a way as to make a fine tight mesh was adequate for most small domes not exceeding 30 feet in diameter. It will be assumed that because of some overlapping in applying the wire there will be strips and sections that will have five layers. The wire should be compressed and stapled with considerable force to make it as flat as possible and of uniform thickness. An ordinary Bostitch stapler or other brand can be used. They can be bought or rented from lumber yards or hardware stores as they are used quite generally in stapling ceiling tiles.

Since ferro-cement dome designs have almost infinite possible dimensions and shapes, each builder will have to use some ingenuity in discovering the best way to apply the chicken wire. In general we found the wire must be applied one layer at a time starting from the top and working downward and outward. Where there are ends or edges terminating with no frame member underneath to which to staple, the wire can be tied to wire underneath or to succeeding layers over it. Care should also be taken to tie down any loose strands of wire. These will stick up through the cement and rust, causing discoloration of the surface and also leaks at a later time. In making the mortar, the ratio that we used successfully was about 2-1/2 parts sand to one part cement. The mixture should be kept as dry as possible. A general rule is that the drier the mix the stronger the cured concrete. A good test is to form a ball in the hands; if the mortar holds together without collapsing or splitting apart the mixture is about right and should be plastic enough to be nicely workable. We mixed all of our mortar in an ordinary cement mixer. We mixed 2-1/2 shovels of sand to one of cement, then 2-1/2 more to one more, continuing in this manner until the full capacity of the mixer was reached. This assured a thorough mixture.

forming the arcs. Cross members and braces were made of scrap lumber, old t.v. antennas, and miscellaneous articles scavenged from the local dump. The window and door arcs were built first, by bending the good 1/2'' x 3'' lumber and securing them with straight cross pieces of 1 x 3 lumber tacked from the outer edges of these arcs to a center support. This center ring or "yoke" served as an axis for the "stringers" or "arched ribs". The old t.v. antennas and scrap lumber were used to stiffen the shaky frame by tacking them transversely across the ribs. The completed frame was supported by many interior posts using one and two inch diameter saplings and available 2 x 4's. We used mostly screen wire, but also some plastic, cloth, and burlap from old sacks to retain the wet mortar. These were stapled as tightly as possible to the wooden frame. Then, one layer at a time, we stapled 4 layers of 1 in. mesh chicken wire over that. At seams we had 5 and 6 layers, but we tried to stay within a 1/2 in. thickness by using many staples and by wire-tying the chicken wire where there was no stapling surface.

Unlike the next two domes we were to build, we had a scaffolding to work from on this one. Using one mixer and a crew of about six, we finished most of the cementing in one day. Plastering is one of the most important steps in ferro-cement dome building. Much care should be taken to work the cement into the wire and to keep any wire from surfacing. The quality of the work done in this step directly affects the outcome of the finished shell.

To seal the shell, we first washed it with a muriatic acid solution, then painted on a clear silicone sealer, and finally a masonry paint. About a year after the cementing we had it sprayed inside with urethane foam, for insulation and a finished interior. Windows and doors were scavenged from the local dump, and with a little ingenuity fitted very nicely into the arcs.

The dome has weathered two winters, having been completed in October 1971. It has no defects such as cracking or flaking, and it has not leaked. Recently a section of cowling was struck accidentally by the bucket of a 7 ton front-end loader. The damage was minimal with only a localized wedge shaped break, approximately 2 feet on each edge, developing. This experience checks with that of ferro-cement boats.

Our second ferro-cement structure was built over a frame of 1/2 inch steel reinforcement bars. The frame was tacked to a conventional cement block basement, 30' x 50', and spot welded in various areas to make the re-bars more rigid. The semi-rigid frame was supported by 1 to 2 in. diameter saplings. Four mil. polyethylene plastic was stretched over the frame to retain the cement mixture while setting. A layer of large mesh hog wire (2-4 in.) was used on the inside to assist shaping, give the plastic a base to which it could be stapled, and support it while retaining the wet mortar, as it had a tendency to belly down from the weight.

Our first step in constructing the frame was to form the arcs, which were to define the basic exterior shape and serve as window openings and cowlings over the windows and doors. These were first set in place, then attached by long arched re-bars to a very crude "yoke" or center ring atop a 14 ft. pole in the center of the floor. Basically, the frame construction was a matter of supporting the preformed window arcs by running the long re-bars to the center ring, which gave form to the arched roof. A great deal of improvising and logical placement, together with a general idea of the desired shape led us to the finished product.

The large mesh hog wire was attached by "wire tying" it to the interior of the frame. The plastic was laid over the top of the frame and stapled from underneath to thin slats of masonite and plywood. These slats were also used to tighten the chicken wire and keep it within 1/2 in. thickness. Many spots had to be hand tied to re-bars with 5-6 in. long wire loops (utility wire) to bring down the bumps.

The cementing was done in one day, with the exception of ridges and areas under the cowlings. Two cement mixers were used and a crew of about twenty. We have a very unique free form ferro-cement "dome", although we can't recommend this particular frame of steel reinforcing bars, as it required too much labor. The cost of this house was 1/3 less than a conventional house of the same size, even though all other aspects of building (electricity, plumbing, heat, etc.) were done in a conventional manner.

Our third ferro-cement dome was built in the same manner as the first two except for the frame. A desire for economy and a readily available supply of saplings suggested their use as a framework. We selected long and slender saplings and bent them within their breaking limits to form a unique free-form shape. The saplings formed an extremely rigid framework that was suggestive of a primitive native hut. All other construction techniques were the same as in the first two domes.

The advantages of ferro-cement over conventional structures are numerous: they are less expensive, more durable, and fire proof. They have no gutters as the roof and wall sections are molded as one. They are technologically simple, putting them within the building skills of the average craftsman. Last, but not least, they are more pleasing to the eye than the average house being built today.

Thad Matras
Box 307, RD. #1
Highland, N. Y.

Thad Matras

Big Foot Foam~Imagination and Reality

John Prenis

Bob Schuler

Today because of our dwindling resources anyone working with materials and/or energy justifies their use by throwing in with one or the other of the extreme views of man's future. We have our choice between the optimism of the Bucky Fuller who sees the world in a state of surplus or the pessimistic Club of Rome report which reveals a world soon to break down through over population, over production, and exhausted resources, not to mention possible social disintegration. One tends either to embrace technology, expecting it will in time solve all problems, or, seeing the handwriting on the wall, drop out to found a new culture based on natural power and materials. In fact most of us must operate somewhere in between such blind technolgical faith and nostalgic yearning for utopian clan cultures.

A. The Theory

Man is now technological: We do not believe that returning to natural life styles based on pre-technological cultures can begin to solve the living problems of the four or more billions of people expected on this planet by the year 2000. Nor do we expect that massive doses of power applied to discarded and renewable resources will appreciably reduce the problem. The natural energy sources are still pouring into our planet at a rate that we have not as yet begun to tap. As we begin to understand in more detail how plants and trees efficiently trap energy new technologies will develop which will convincingly mimic nature. The history of technology traces our cleverness in improvising on nature's themes. Technology is with us and in us. It dies with us and we with it. It is not reversible. We scream because technology let us down or led us astray. Yet nature is constantly erring. Species prove impractical, too heavy, too small, too this, too that. We tend to think in terms of technology versus nature as if nature were the perfect model. We have overstepped the bounds of nature, we say. But is that possible? Are we and our products not part of nature? If man succeeds in blowing up this speck of dust in the sky will it even be noticed more than a few light years away in space? Compared to a super novae the exploding earth would be no more than an insignificant spark. Can we, knowing the infinite extent and complexity of the universe, truly believe that we can overstep the bounds of nature? We pride ourselves on our consciousness and believe we are perfectable. Many would say that nature is not

consciously motivated, it being in a sense super-conscious. Nature errs without consciousness; we with self-consciousness. Why the constant separation of man from nature or man's products for that matter? Technology is natural. After all, one could in high spirits say that nature has made more disastrous mistakes without technology than man has with the help of all his artificial hardware. Is our technology part of another universe? The unnatural universe? A world that can never be reconciled with nature's? That is what many would have us believe, or is it that we outrageously exaggerate our accomplishments? We must continue to examine nature closely and hope to make fewer mistakes.

B. Theoretical Solution

Technological mega-cultures must be decentralized.

All the inputs to mega-technologies must be broken down into packets to fit minimum group size.

That is, mega-capital into micro-capital

mega-power sources into micro-power

mega-resources into micro-resources

mega-organizational structures into micro-organizational structures

mega-structure personnel and technologists drop out to form technological micro-structures

This can be accomplished in the following possible ways (from least probable to the most probable)

1 mega-structures decentralizing of their own volition

2 slow metamorphosis from a few stagnating mega-cultures to a proliferation of small micro-cultures loosely interconnected (several centuries)

3 after total violent, disintegration of present mega-systems.

This can be accomplished only in conjunction with some massive cathartic political change.

Big Foot Foam is presently interested in energy/shelter technologies. Our interest in building is not with object architecture, but with process architecture. To us hard architecture, stone, wood, and concrete buildings are too inflexible, too unwieldy, too expensive as solutions to world building problems. Lightweight semi-permeable membrane structures enveloping areas the size of Los Angeles may replace our present monument oriented structures. In the past the skin of a building has had only two major functions, strength and impermeablility. A closer look at natural membranes like plant leaves reveals the necessary strength as well as an ability to absorb energy from the sun, air, and earth to suppy its life functions. We are at the threshold of discoveries which will make it possible for us to literally soak up the earth's energy through the skins of our houses and convert them to heat, chemical and electrical outputs, much as plants photosynthesize life functions from CO_2, sunlight, and water.

C. **The Practice**

At present we are working with lightweight membrane structures using urethane, paper, stretch cloth, teflon coated fibreglass, and flexible coatings. Urethane has been our major material to date because it's readily available, it's reasonably inexpensive, and the urethane molecule

$$[R\text{-}NH\text{-}C\text{-}O\text{-}R']$$
$$\overset{..}{O}$$

is extremely flexible. It is formulated as flexible, semi-rigid, and rigid. It can be as soft as cotton candy or as hard as slate. It adhers to most materials, stone, glass, metal, cloth, wood, paper, and many plastics. And of course it is an excellent thermal insulator. It can be tailor-made to almost any specifications, structural, thermal, acoustical and flexible. It can be sprayed on the spot even in areas with no power. Big Foot Foam now designs and produces chairs, lamps, beds, play houses, camper tops, boats, floating houses, and large domes.

My partner will explain some of the common questions asked about foam.

Formwork for foundation of 35 ft. diameter dome. Flexible plastic pipe is in place for use as conduits after slab is poured. The entire form was made in less than two hours of masonite and cable, covered with foam. Underneath the concrete slab is 1-1/2″ of foam plus a polyethylene vapor barrier.

After the slab was completed, this vinyl bag was inflated. With all electrical conduits in position, 6″ of 2 lb. foam was applied. A layer of 30 lb. foam was sprayed on the outside. Finally the vinyl bag was pulled down and the inside was painted.

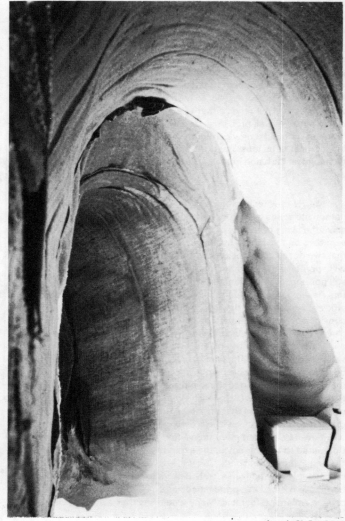

photos by Big Foot Foam

Polyurethane Foams and Dome Structures

Gary Allen

Polyurethane foams are relatively new; in many ways they are a totally new experience. Their properties rarely fail to arouse curiosity, if not awe, when seen for the first time. Consequently, as a foamer, I have met many people, each with a whole list of questions about the material. Needless to say, the questions have often been asked before, and no doubt will be asked again. In an attempt to simplify the whole process, and perhaps clarify it a little, there follows a list of the most asked questions (and, hopefully, their answers) geared to the needs of dome designers and builders.

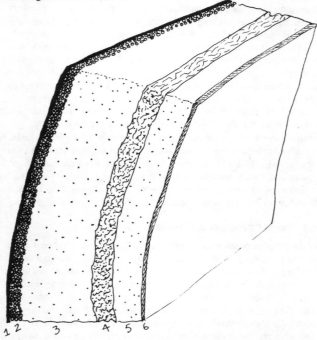

Possible laminar structure for foam dome (section through wall)
1. Elastomeric coating   2. High density foam   3. 2 lb. density foam
4. Open-celled flexible foam   5. 2 lb. foam   6. Plaster or flame retardant paint.

Q1   WHAT IS IT?

Basically, polyurethane foam is a two-component plastic material which, when mixed under the proper conditions, froths up into a liquid foam (much like fine textured soap suds) that cures before the bubbles can burst. Polyurethane foams have been around for many years, for instance in cushions where it is mistakenly referred to as "foam rubber". In the early sixties, sprayable urethenes were developed. This meant that for the first time, it was not necessary to have a plastics factory at your disposal in order to experiment with polyurethane foams. The equipment needed is portable, and the actual spraying techniques can be quickly and easily learned.

Q2   ARE ALL POLYURETHANE FOAMS SOFT AND FLEXIBLE?

Not at all. A given foam's properties are determined primarily by its chemical make-up, which is formulated by the chemical company that sells the raw material. You can get rigid closed-cell foams in almost any density, from 2 lbs./ft.^{3} (standard, insulation-type foam) up to 60 lbs./ft.^{3} (very hard and tough; essentially solid, resinous material . . . not like a foam at all). There are rigid foams of this type (closed-cell) made specifically for use in cold weather. Or you can get open-celled rigid and flexible foam. (There are no sprayable closed-cell flexible urethane foams yet. EN-SOLITE is a trade name for closed-cell polyethylene foam which is strictly factory production). The characteristics of a given foam cannot be altered by the foamer, but all foams can be sprayed through the same equipment.

Q3   IS IT EXPENSIVE?

The main savings are in time and labor costs. Material costs are usually about $.50/lb. ($1/ft.^{3} for 2 lb. density foam), depending on which type, which company you buy from, how much you buy, etc. The liquid foam is usually purchased in two 55 gallon drums, a "system." One drum contains the resin, liquified fluorocarbon (Freon gas kept just below its boiling point), and a minute quantity of catalyst. The other drum contains the bulk of the catalyst (isocyanate) needed to complete the reaction.

Q4   WHY USE IT AS A BUILDING MATERIAL?

Lots of reasons. It's light in weight, strong, waterproof, and it has five times the insulation efficiency of fiberglass batts of the same thickness. It doesn't rot, and it is not affected by mildew or termites. Most appealing is the fact that it allows total freedom of form. When you're working with a liquid, the restrictions of rigid, rectilinear materials such as plywood are meaningless. Due to foam's light weight, you don't need the elaborate (and heavy) form-work necessary with concrete. Aside from the technical reasons, there are of course esthetic and ethical reasons. Esthetics do not stand up well in the presence of justifications, but in a book on domes I can expect to find readers who appreciate curvilinear spaces. If we must use wood in building, let's not waste it. Use it where it can be seen; trees are too valuable to hide inside walls. At least equally important, personally as well as generally, is the fact that foam is the most efficient insulator available. This means, that in a time when most people are using ever-increasing amounts of energy, it is possible to use less and be just as comfortable as everyone else. America grew up on the idea that there was an infinite supply of wealth (ENERGY) available to everyone. The habits developed while under that misconception are hard to break, and we still use too much to do too little. A house insulated with six inches of foam would have one eighteenth the energy requirements of a conventional house of the same size and standard of living.

Q5   HOW LONG DOES IT TAKE TO HARDEN?

Within seconds the foam rises to its full volume. With most foams, it is dry and firm in less than two minutes. Final curing is complete in about a day. One of the reasons it can cure so quickly is the small amount of isocyanate in the resin component. This allows the resin molecules (monomers) to start forming long chains immediately (cross-linking or polymerizing). It is similar to adding a "seed" crystal to a super-saturated solution of sugar to grow rock candy crystals. Also the two components are heated to 140°F. to accelerate the process.

Q6   ISN'T THERE ANY WAY TO GET AROUND THE HIGH
         EQUIPMENT COSTS?

I only know of three ways. Unfortunately, they aren't ideally suited to the building of domes. There are: 1) Slab stock. This is factory-made boards or sheets of foam, with or without paper skins. Either way, you're back to rectilinear materials. It is, however, an inexpensive and efficient way to insulate a geodesic dome. 2) Pour foams. These are essentially the old style foams, in which excess isocyanate reacts with water to liberate CO_2 (instead of freon). This forms a foam that has an uneven texture. It has large gas bubbles scattered through it, spoiling the foam's structural properties. Also, CO_2 filled cells are not as efficient as freon filled cells in terms of thermal insulation, although pour foams are still better than fiberglass in this respect. The pour foams are used at room temperature, thus they cure rather slowly. They flow in the form of a frothy liquid, which is good if you are filling in between 2x4's or under floors. Using pour foams on curved or overhead surfaces can be very tricky. They are best suited for insulation and casting. 3) Froth-packs. These are essentially pour foams in a more convenient package. The components come in two pressurized cans and are extruded through plastic hoses, then mixed in a somewhat clumsy nozzle. This allows you to spray onto vertical surfaces. As insulation, or for touch-ups and repairs, they have some value.

Q7   IS IT DANGEROUS TO WORK WITH?

Like any other building material, certain precautions must be observed. The most important of these is the avoidance of vapors. All you have to do is wear a mask bearing the label "FOR USE WITH ORGANIC VAPORS". If you don't you'll soon develop a dry sore throat and sometimes a headache. The fumes linger for about a day (depending on temperature and ventilation), so plan on sleeping somewhere else for the first night. If you work with foam repeatedly without a mask, in a couple of years you'll have an irreversible respiratory condition. Wear the mask. Some people complain that the foam gives off fumes for

long periods, causing headaches. This is an exception, but a coat of any kind of paint will seal the surface (unlike styrofoam, paint solvents have no effect on polyurethane foam). I would also recommend a hat and overalls; foam can be quite unpleasant in hair and on skin.

Q8   DOESN'T ANYTHING ATTACK POLYURETHANE FOAM?

Just two things: 1) foam stripper—this is a liquid available from UNITED PAINTS MFG., Spokane, Wash. It will soften and remove foam from anything, but be careful . . . it will also remove all paints and attack almost every plastic. It costs about $10/gallon and is reusable. 2) Ultraviolet light—when foam is exposed to the UV in sunlight, the surface is broken down to a fine brownish orange dust. This will eventually be washed or blown away, thus exposing the fresh foam underneath to the UV, etc. In sixty years or so, a five inch thick dome will have crumbled to dust. However, any opaque material will screen the foam from UV, making it very durable indeed. As a screen you can use any house paint, roofing compound, asphalt, ferro-concrete (if you want the extra strength and weight), even sod! There are a number of elastomeric coatings on the market that remain flexible and waterproof down to very low temperatures, for up to twenty years. To last outdoors, foam has to be protected, and it seems worthwhile to spend the extra money at the beginning and eliminate the job of painting the house every three years.

Q9   WHAT ABOUT DOORS AND WINDOWS?

This can be as simple or sophisticated as you wish to make it. You can merely cut a hole in the wall, hold a piece of glass or plexiglass in place and foam it on. We've considered foaming old car doors in place, to have roll-down windows. For doors, a conventional doorway can be framed out, foamed in place. Esthetically speaking, doors have always been a problem with domes in general. It's an area that needs some serious attention, as standard doors (and windows) have been designed for flat walls.

Q10   IS IT STRONG ENOUGH TO SUPPORT
         SNOW LOADS, ETC.?

Architect Stan Nord Connolly of Boulder, Colo. has designed and built several large foam domes, mostly multiple dome structures. They were all designed with large snow loads and winds of 125 mph. in mind. They are six inches thick (2 lb. density, with the outer surfaces covered with higher density foam; inner surfaces are covered with plaster). There is no other supporting structure, just foam. Charles Haertling (also of Boulder) on the other hand, originally worked in reinforced concrete, but switched over to foam on steel (re-bars) and wire mesh. Foam can be sprayed on inflated plastic forms (don't use polyethylene, it deforms from the heat generated by the foam's curing) or gov't. surplus parachutes. Forty feet seems to be the limit for an unsupported clear span, with parabolic cross-sections being stronger than hemispheres. If all the radii of curvature are kept small (ie. by building clusters of small domes, as opposed to single large spans) the strength is increased, while wall thickness doesn't have to be as thick as in large spans. This is basically what Felix Drury of Yale did when he built his first experimental building on the Yale golf course. Drury was one of the first architects to realize foam's potential as a building material.

Q11   WHAT CAN GO WRONG?

The two things most often at fault when something goes wrong are dirt and moisture, usually moisture. The isocyanate will react with moisture and clog spray equipment, resulting in improper mixture and foam that won't cure. Foam is sensitive to water at all stages of the process. One drop of sweat or rain will eat right through uncured foam. Foam that has been sprayed on damp surfaces will rise and cure beautifully, then pop off. Among the reasons the foam rig is so expensive are the elaborate defenses built in to keep water away from the chemicals. Primers are sometimes necessary when spraying on smooth metal, such as sheet steel, aluminum, or zinc, as in galvanized steel.

Q12 CAN YOU USE FOAM FOR SOUND-PROOFING?

For some reason, many people think that foam must be a barrier to sound. Unfortunately, rigid foams transmit sound well. To stop sound transmission, you need heavy, massive walls (such as stone or concrete), so that the wall itself is not vibrated by the sound wave, thereby becoming a sound source. Alternatively, you can use walls made of some "dead" (inelastic) material such as lead, which damps vibrations internally . . . by absorbing them. To cut down reflected sound, you can use a material with a maze-like structure, so that sound-waves are bounced around in these baffles, gradually losing energy (this is the principle behind "acoustic tile"). Rigid foams (closed-cell, especially) can never meet these requirements. Open-cell flexible foams in the higher densities seem to be exactly what is needed, but there has not been enough testing in this area. Also, flexible foams are not yet available with the flame retardent qualities needed for habitable foam structures. Perhaps a layer of flexible foam can be sandwiched between layers of rigid foam. Smooth, curved surfaces are typical of all dome structures. This fact, more than any other, is responsible for the terrible acoustics in domes. The larger the diameter, the longer it takes for sound to reach the wall and bounce back to the listener, exaggerating the effect ("reverb"). The smaller the diameter, the shorter the reverberation time. So, by keeping domes small you can minimize perceived echoes. The main problem is that the inside of the dome acts as an acoustic lens focusing sound in the center, reinforcing or amplifying it. This can be prevented by breaking the strict symmetry of the single dome structure, or by including some large "obstacles" to the sound (many small echoes tend to even out, soften the sound).

Suppliers of foam

Stephan Chemica Co.
Nopco Division
175 Shuyler Ave.
North Arlington, N.J. 07032

Reichold Chemicals, Inc.
RCI Building
White Plains, NY 10602

Witco Chemical Co.
Isocyanate Products Division
P.O. Box 1681
Wilmington, Del. 19899

Coatings

United Paint Mfg., Inc.
1130 E. Sprague Ave.
Spokane, Wash. 99202

Equipment

Gusmer Corp.
P.O. Box 164
414 Rt. 18 & Spring Valley Rd.
Old Bridge, N.J. 08857

Designers & Contractors

Big Foot Foam, Ltd.
Box 198 RD#2
Highland, N.Y. 12528

Stan Connolly Architects
P.O. Box 1255
Boulder, Colo. 80302

Felix Drury
Dept. of Architecture
Yale University
New Haven, Conn. 06520

George Beggs
School of Architecture
Oklahoma State Univ.
Stillwater, Oklahoma 74074

Upper Ptarmigan Creek Design Co.
P.O. Box 3202
Aspen, Colorado 81611

Deeds Design Association
1706 W. Arbor
San Diego, California 92103

WARNING: Even "fire resistant" foams are flammable. Exposed foam on interior surfaces should be covered with plaster or intumescent paint.

Big Foot Foam

Dome 7072

Don Butler

Don Butler

Don Butler

In 1970 a group of students at the School of Architecture in Copenhagen started working under the theme "Practical Building Experiments". This group was got together at the instigation of a teacher who had become rather disillusioned with the "normal" type of education at the school which was very theoretical and seemed to give people a very strange view of what building actually involves, both technically and socially. This is, of course, a widespread malady at schools of architecture.

We're trying in this group to work out alternatives to the ever expanding, indestructable, reinforced concrete flip and all that it entails in social and economical problems. Through this work we're hoping to find out how to build cheap "environment shields"—basic building shells or parts of such, which people would be able to buy (or scavenge) for a reasonable cash price without having to get involved in the banking and loan jungle.

We hope we can perhaps make a little positive inroad in the growing centralization of building and all things material. We hope to evolve then, cheap, practical materials and methods which can be put together according to individual motivation and with a maximum of individual participation.

We believe that you can learn a great deal about the technical and

social complexities of building by doing it with your own hands as much as possible—everyone should have the opportunity to build their own home or "base" or influence their immediate environment in a meaningful way. Why don't children learn about building like they learn other subjects at school?

We learned a lot from this dome we built—about building and about us. We made a lot of mistakes too. Here's what we did supported by the drawings we used and some photographs. We've unfortunately not got many black and white photographs although we took lots of color slides and color films of the whole process. This left us in a bad situation when we needed to reproduce the material for this book. So take *lots* of black and white photos of all your work. You may want to communicate without A-V media sometime.

I happen to be writing the story of this dome, but if we are naming names, then I think it's important that everybody involved is mentioned. The regular group when we built the dome consisted of: John Risgård Johansen, Flemming and Sten-Ove Østergård Nielsen, Carsten Hoff, Per Boelskifte, Barry Rimm-Smith, and myself, helped by numerous other people whose help was immeasurable at crucial moments.

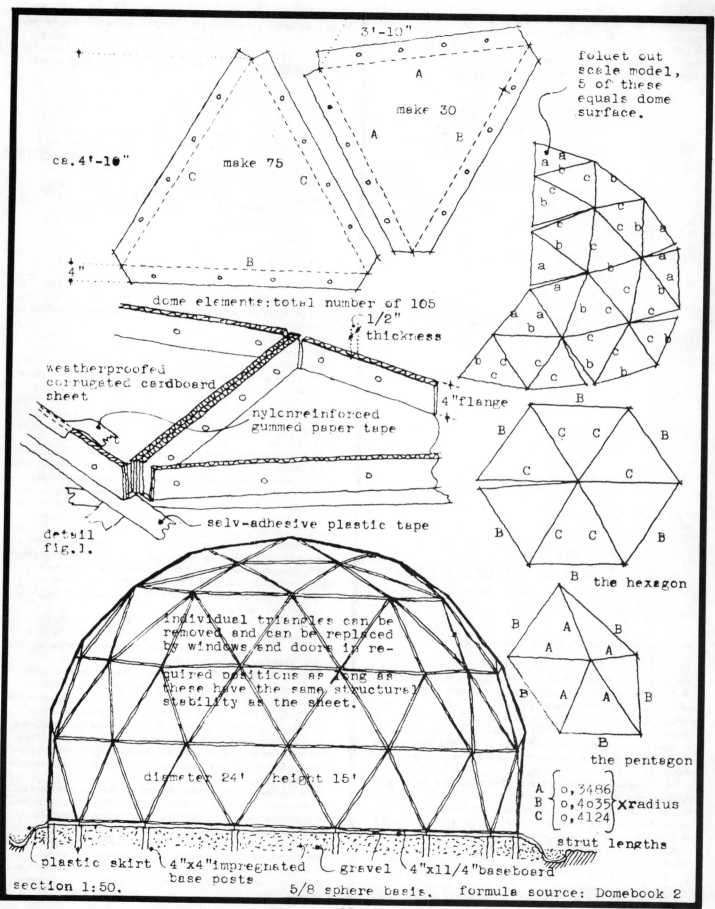

3'-10"

make 30

A

A   B

foldet out
scale model,
5 of these
equals dome
surface.

ca.4'-10"

make 75

C   C

A

B

4"

dome elements:total number of 105

1/2"
thickness

4"flange

weatherproofed
corrugated cardboard
sheet

nylonreinforced
gummed paper tape

B

B   C   C   B

C   C

detail
fig.1.

self-adhesive plastic tape

B   C   C   B

B   the hexagon

Individual triangles can be
removed and can be replaced
by windows and doors in required positions as long as
these have the same structural
stability as the sheet.

B   A   B

A   A   A

diameter 24'   height 15'

B   A   A   B

B

the pentagon

A ⎰ o,3486
B ⎱ o,4o35 Xradius
C ⎰ o,4124

strut lengths

plastic skirt   4"x4"impregnated   gravel   4"x11/4"baseboard
                base posts

section 1:50.   5/8 sphere basis.   formula source: Domebook 2

86

This dome's geometrical and structural principle is such that forces from wind, snow and its own weight theoretically run down to the base via lines on the dome surface which accumulate to 15 points of contact at the base. There are the centers of the half hexagons and pentagons forming the bottom row of elements.

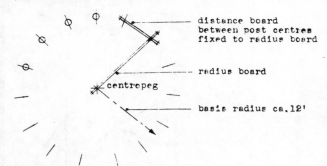

fig.2. marking out of post holes
plan 1:100

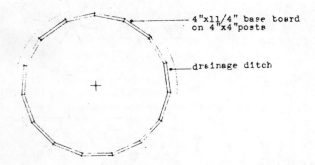

fig.3. finished base construction

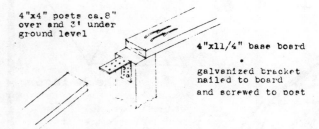

fig.4. assembly detail of base board and post
1:10

We constructed a base consisting of 15 posts joined together by boards to form a continuous ring on which the dome could be built. (See Fig. 2,3,4) We tried to place the posts very accurately according to these 15 points of contact. The holes were marked out with boards as shown in Fig. 2. These were then "dug out" with a motorized drill (the type used for collecting earth samples for analysis), but this leapt about on stones and such so much that we ended up by digging them out again by hand.

It was impossible to place the holes with the accuracy we thought necessary—the posts had to be plumb too. We eventually got them down with a tolerance of +/-1" from the center and each other. We then cut them off at the required height according to the domes base-line, which in this case is irregular (see 5/8 sphere, 3v)

It quickly became evident that this base principle was wrong. Instead of this we should have built a strengthened *platform* of posts and boards—a kind of circular "bench" about 1' wide. On this we could then have marked out the form of the dome's bottom line easily and with more accuracy. We wouldn't have needed to be so accurate

in placing and plumbing the posts either. We could also have better used this platform for adjusting the domes irregular base line, as the posts we had cut off were wrongly cut anyway—it was almost impossible to work out the correct height for this line relative to the horizontal. This platform would have also given us a shelf inside on which

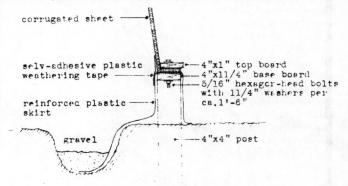

fig.5. section in base construction

we could have built up a first floor. Maybe we could have built something into the cardboard shelf for a floor support—it was very strong in its original form before it was damaged—but we didn't get that far.

Calculations on the possible loading of the base construction due to wind, snow and the dome's own weight showed that the most dangerous loading would come from wind suction on the leeward side. We therefore secured the base boards to the posts with a "tie down" as shown in fig. 4. The ground we built on was calculated to give enough resistance around the posts that they wouldn't be wrenched out by this wind force on the dome. Around the base we made a drainage ditch with a gravel drain to take the run-off from the dome sphere. (fig. 5)

The triangles were cut out of cardboard, rolled along the edges to give a "bend" for the flanges and drilled for bolts at the saw mill which provided the material. On site we taped all the open edges with a nylon-reinforced gummed paper tape. We were skeptical about the claims made by the manufacturer as to the material's water resistance, so we brushed them all with one coat of a 2-component thermo-plastic laquer. (After the dome was erected we brushed it once more on the outside with this laquer). This laquer is quite nasty to work with and a carbon filter mask is to be strongly recommended, although it makes hot work. When the elements were finished we bent the flanges on the edges by putting them down between two strong planks—a kind of big vise—and bending them over to 90 degrees along the lines we had rolled earlier.

The work with the second coat of laquer showed that the shell could easily stand the weight of a man working on it as long as he kept himself spread out. We made ladders of plank with short blocks nailed on, just leaned up against the dome.

We're not too happy about the use of this thermo-plastic laquer now, as we consider it to have been an exaggeration both from a technical and an economic point of view. We could perhaps have used a fluid that's normally used in Denmark as a water protection for concrete, and also used as a fire-retarding agent on theatre scenery. This might have suited us better as we also had the problem of fire-proofing our dome. The fluid is called "Vandglas" in Danish—I don't know the English. It's very cheap and can be bought at any hardware store here.

Over the base construction we draped and nailed a reinforced plastic skirt which hung down in the drainage ditch and also inside the base. The first row of elements was then bolted down with a ring of boards on top of the flanges so that these were sandwiched between the two layers of boards. The plastic skirt should have been trimmed off inside the dome but we failed to do this, with the result that a dense plant growth rapidly grew up in this "greenhouse" and subsequently carried dampness up to the lowest elements. Several of these were severely damaged in this way.

The elements were bolted together using 5/16" x 2" hex head bolts and 1-1/4" washers—4 bolts per flange. The whole shell was assembled using small adjustable spanners and some C-clamps for holding while bolting. We used two light scaffold towers with planks across inside the dome for fixing the two topmost rows of elements. These were rented for the occasion and are included in the price shown for the whole dome.

The seams between the elements on the outside of the dome we covered with various types of self-adhesive plastic and nylon tape. These were of several widths and colors, the latter being quite important when using dark colored tapes as these absorb a lot of heat from the sun, causing them to "slide" as the adhesive melts. We had intended this outside taping to have two functions. Apart from being a weatherproofing of the seams it also acted as a "net" of restraining bands to tie the structure together. There was no way of calculating the strength of this "net" but loading tests previous to the actual erection showed that the taping increased the strength of the structure considerably.

None of the tapes we used, however, could stand the changing temperature and humidity during the summer. On the most exposed area of the surface (facing south-west) and on the top, the tape lost its grip and allowed water to seep into the corrugations via the bolt holes. Some of the elements in these areas were subsequently pressed inwards by wind pressure. In those areas where the tape held and no water had seeped into the material, the elements retained their original strength and position.

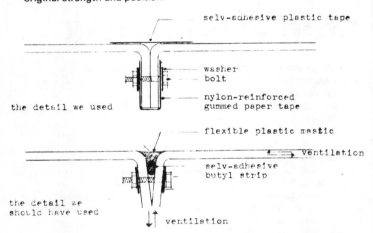

selv-adhesive plastic tape

washer
bolt

nylon-reinforced gummed paper tape

the detail we used

flexible plastic mastic

ventilation

selv-adhesive butyl strip

the detail we should have used

ventilation

ventilation

Later experience showed that we should have used a more refined jointing method—for example elastic butyl strip pushed down into the seams as shown on fig. 6. The butyl strip we experimented with afterwards had an elasticity of 50% and when we "stuck" two element flanges together with it they could not be separated without ripping the surface off the cardboard sheeting. The strip would have had the same function as our "tape net" but with less sticking area on the sheeting—it wouldn't have come unstuck either.

The strength of this jointing lies of course in the surface strength of the dome elements. The cardboard was therefore primed first with a silicone primer, where the strip was to be stuck. This made, all in all, a very tight seam, but for maximum security against water this joint could be supplemented with a silicone mastic (elasticity of 300%). This would therefore be able to take any movements whatsoever in the seam and still stay "tight". The one disadvantage with this type of jointing is the price—it would have cost about a 1/4 of the total price of the dome! But as one of the biggest problems with domes is the seams—maybe it's well spent.

During construction we made a temporary door opening by removing one of the elements in the bottom line. Later we removed a whole hexagon at this point and built up a hexagonal timber frame which was intended to function both as a (temporary!) door and window module with the door taking up the center "rectangle" and the remaining triangles t the sides forming windows when covered with plastic. We intended later to experiment with various window

positions, materials, sizes, shapes, etc., but never got around to this

We knew that we should have ventilated the shell better than we did—the only ventilation was the door-triangle! But there was difficulty getting people together at that time and it just didn't get done. This lack of ventilation undoubtedly contributed to the great damage the dome later suffered.

Most interesting structurally speaking and concerning the optimum use of the material, is the fact that there were no actual "struts"— these were replaced by two flanges bolted together. There were no hubs either! In fact there was just a hole where the hub should have been and this state of affairs was much criticized by engineers who saw the construction. But this dome was perfectly stable in *that* respect—the engineers are working on structural theories which certainly are applicable, but we've shown that the dome was working satisfactorily even though the forces had to run *around* the non-hubs—said in theory to be our biggest mistake. Domes are evidently still difficult to erect and understand with theory alone.

The corrugated cardboard sheeting was quite expensive in itself, but when we considered we needed no strutting, it became very cheap. The price of the completed dome-shell including taped seams totalled 5000 Danish Kroner. The man-hours used are difficult to calculate as the construction time was very spread out over about a year with intensive days and non-productive weeks. But the actual erection of the dome-shell was relatively short, whereas the preparation of the elements themselves prior to erection was quite lengthy.

We had planned to live in this dome for short periods to "test" its various qualities and to work on it according to the feeling it gave. But everybody in the group had something else going when the school year was over. So no one actually had time for this experience.

The dome had suffered a lot of damage during the summer but was still surprisingly strong when autumn came around. We decided therefore to try and repair it and continue the intended work with its development.

The dome is based on a 5/8 sphere and the diameter of the sphere is around the height of the first horizontal element seam. By removing a triangle as we did for the temporary door, we weakened the shell in the worst possible place because of its theoretical tendency to "spread" at the diameter. The sides of the triangular opening were thus overloaded. We checked some of this spreading by fastening a thick wire to the diameter line inside the shell. This went all round and could be tightened with a tourniquet which pulled in any spreading. This (too!) was regarded as a temporary measure until the door could be arranged in a better way. During this period and after more inspection of the damage and fruitless attempts to repair failures in the joints, we could see that about 30 elements would have to be replaced (of a total of 105). We decided therefore to leave it and see just what it could stand and how long it could remain standing in its "natural" state—it was still quite strong despite the damage. During the inspection period we had made the mentioned hexagonal door-opening but had not covered it sufficiently against the weather: subsequently during a violent early winter storm the wind got in under the weakened shell through this opening and tore the dome to pieces.

This report doesn't do full justice to the feeling we got out of working with this type of building and the social complexities we ran into as we worked together. But even though the description I've given seems to indicate that this dome was a failure it was always regarded *by those involved* as a howling success—we have realized so much about social processes and domes in general.

This group is now continuing with other practical experiments concerning, for instance, small scale latrine/methane gas plants, ferrocement, light weight building systems and general recycling of materials, the latter overlapping all these experiments where it's relevant and possible.

We hope to publish something about these in 1974-75.

Don Butler
Willemoesgade 31, 5.TV.
2100 Copenhagen Ø
Denmark

My Building Career

Stan Vandenbark

The motivation for building my first 40′ diameter dome was the need for inexpensive shelter for a workshop. Also the novelty of the idea impressed me. I had been spending a lot of time with metal sculpture, and had been working in a nearly converted stable with a slanting concrete floor. There didn't seem to be anything to lose—but a lot to gain. As I evaluate my efforts at this point, however, I seriously wonder whether the results are worth the effort. The consequences of following a dream to the bitter end are sometimes hard to accept. First of all, experimentation often is costly in a financial way, which in turn in my case has jeopardized my happy home. But back to the dome idea. The concept of the vaulting ceiling intrigues a person—especially, I suppose, because we are so unused to large volumes of space except in public buildings.

Buckminster Fuller has influenced my thinking for the last ten years. I have carefully studied all the literature available about him and his work, and I'll have to admit that I have been very impressed by him. I thought about building a dome for several years before actually undertaking the project. After beginning, the technical hurdles were handled one at a time; basic dome design, size, material, structure, skin, sealing, sky lights, door, floor, wiring and heating. When all was

finished, I discovered that what I had discovered was what I had suspected all the time. The cost was only $.67 per square foot for materials in the shell, another approximately $.33 in the concrete floor, for a total of about $1200, plus 90 man hours in its construction, including painting.

After the dome was completed and all seemed fine because of the low cost, the happy sightseers, the attention and discussion, it was distressing to find that it was almost impossible to seal weather tight. Apparently others have had the same problem, but I didn't know that or how to profit from their experience, so it took at least three attempts to get favorable results. Metal strips and caulking worked for about a month, until the differences in expansion rates allowed the seams to pop open again. Resealing with heavier roofing compounds had the same dismal effect. Aluminum sheets from the Twin Falls newspaper printing department applied with staples worked much better. The most positive way to roof a dome that I have found is shingling. Asphalt shingles are easier to apply than cedar shingles, also the former cost less. On my second dome, a 26′ diameter vacation cabin near Sun Valley, I spent three weeks shingling with cedar shingles, but the finished building looked good and fit the environment, I thought.

Stan Vandenbark

Stan Vandenbark

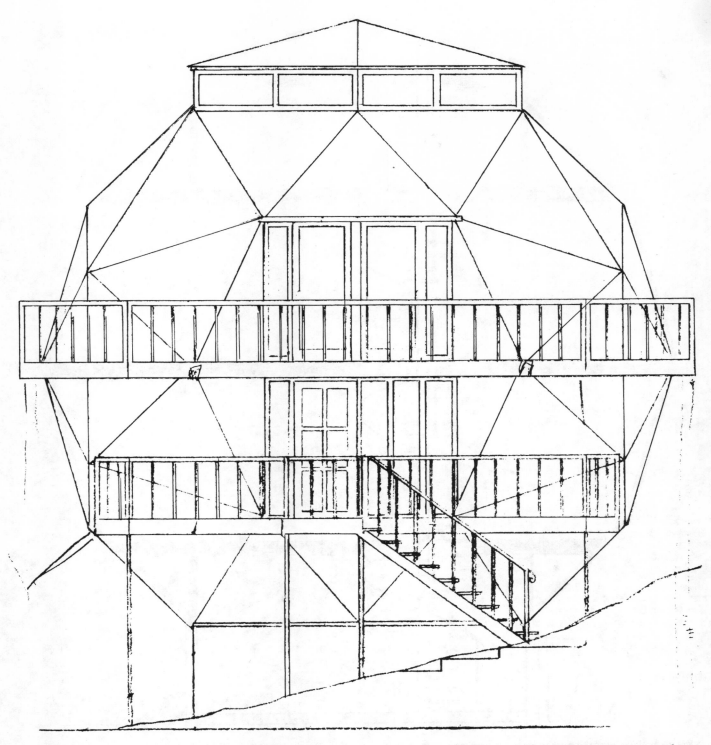

The third dome, for the Boy Scouts of America at Camp Roach on the Snake River near Hagerman, Idaho, was first coated with asphalt composition material, applied with roofing brooms. When that failed in about six months because of a too-thin coating, we re-roofed with asphalt shingles, which are still serviceable after five years. The fourth building, a 1400 square foot home for the Ted Loveday family, Kimberly, Idaho, was fabricated with a shallow-domed geometric roof coated with urethane foam and two coats of sealer.

My experience in getting a building permit for this structure may be instructive. The building was a compromise from the very beginning, so there were very few problems with the building inspector, because most of the house is quite conventional. Only the roof structure is controversial. There were two original objections:

First, the inspector and zoning commission had no way of knowing the strength of the building, especially the roof. Second, the urethane foam on the roof required some scrutiny.

No compromise was required on the external appearance of the building. The engineer determined that a steel tension ring would be required to meet the loading requirements—in this area 20 pounds per square foot live load and 15 pounds per square foot additional dead load. The steel is completely hidden.

Originally I had planned to have eighteen brick columns support the roof, but the engineer pointed out that without structural steel inside they couldn't support the lateral thrust that would be imposed by the roof, so we then incorporated the tension ring.

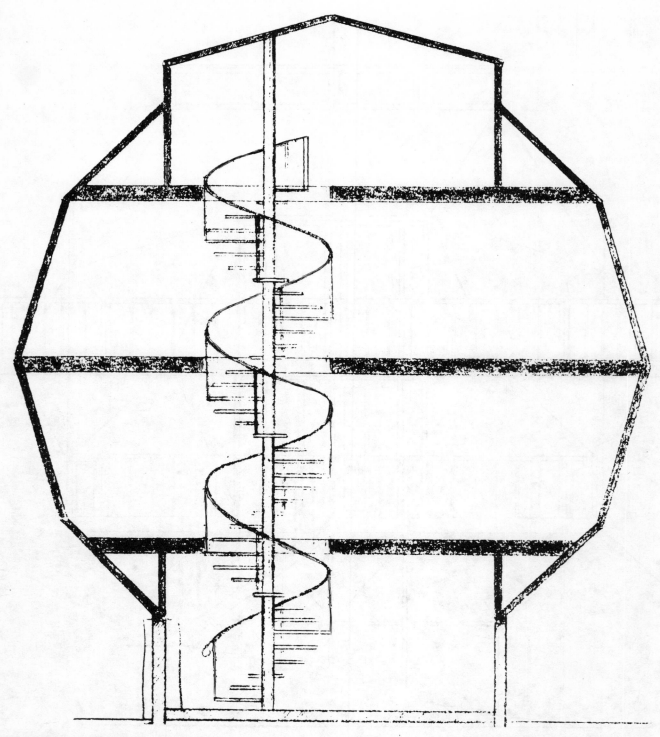

We went ahead with the brick work as planned, and I'm sure that the columns do serve some structural purpose—maybe only a larger safety factor, if nothing else. Incidentally it took five weeks for myself and another fellow to lay the bricks.

As it turned out, it is much more difficult to find a sympathetic engineer to do the work than it was in this case to satisfy the inspector. Not any engineer will do—he has to be a qualified *structural* engineer and one licensed in your state. Very likely this could be true in most states—that the engineer must be licensed for the state in which the construction is planned. Also, if a second structure is planned it would have to be identical to the first or additional engineering would be required, even if only slight changes are made.

Number five has asphalt shingles covering its two 600 sq. ft. modules and a layered shingle-over-hot built up roof on the 300 sq. ft. center section. Buildings six and seven are homes. They have sprayed-on foam for roofing and insulation combined, and consist of 10-sided vertically walled units with shallow domed roofs, and connecting halls with built up composition coverings. Building eight is my 500 sq. ft. shop, also 10-sided, topped with a shallow dome covered with fiber-glas cloth and asphalt coating. Number nine is an addition to an older farm home near Jerome, Idaho; a basement and two stories above ground totaling 1600 sq. ft. The tenth is the apparently ill-fated sphere in Ketchum, Idaho (Sun Valley area). It is 29′ in diameter, and was planned as a four-level ski cabin with 1300 sq. ft., but remains framed only, a skeletal form. Problems with financing and the Ketchum village

91

building inspector have produced an impasse. Buildings eleven through sixteen were short-lived, half-sized models (12' to 20' dia.) and fair booths, but deserve mention because of the additional experimentation made possible through their construction.

When a project is of extended duration, I think it a natural tendency for a philosophy to develop in conjunction. For example I think that one must be especially wary of aesthetic indigestion, commonly caused by compromise. In the name of economy, ruinous shortcuts may be allowed, or in an attempt to incorporate conventional ideas, the impact of the geometric structure may be greatly diluted, causing it to lose its effect.

The compromise that I specifically have in mind is that of attempting to partition off too many rooms inside a geodesic or geometric structure, with the result of very difficult carpentry in addition to confining spaces. Another bit of philosophy pertains to the customer-contractor relationship. I have noticed that often appetites for finer and finer quality furnishings grow as the project nears completion, which of course can be a real thorn in the side of the contractor. Also, what about the possibility of creating a monster? A very real chance indeed, it turns out. Poor engineering encourages built-in booby traps in the experimental structure. Just think how thrilling it is to become aware that your balcony just collapsed with 29 of your guests. Your legal department must now be prepared for overtime. Or ponder this: The fantastic geometric house you sold last May is occupied by perfectionists who insist that the plumbing must perform. In spite of objections, you decide that in order to avoid a nasty law suit, repairs must be made at your expense since this is only March and the year warranty period will not expire for two months yet. Goodby vacation money. And what about those windows that leak every time the wind-driven rain zeros in from the east? Creaky floors, sticking doors, gurgling johns, frozen pipes, family gripes.

Even though there are problems inherent in new concepts and methods, the overwhelming fact that assaults you is the minimum amount of material required for domes and related goemetric structures. A pickup truck load of pieces will produce 500 square feet of living space, or should I say hexagonal or octagonal feet of space?

In spite of the complications in my life stemming from this affair with geometric volumes, I am still intrigued by the romance of the exotic in architecture, and would probably go the same route again if given the choice. It has occurred to me that a new system of measurement could very well be instituted to deal with geometric building; hexagonal feet, triangular and tetragonal inches . . . .
Write for a list of building plans from:
Vandenbark Geometric Construction, Inc.
P. O. Box 907
Kimberly, Idaho 83341

Jim Wilson

Chord Factors

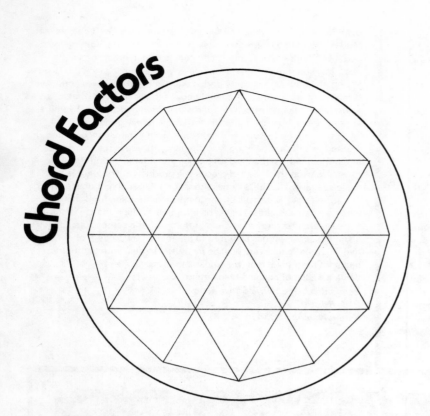

Dome math is not difficult. All you need to know is how to add, subtract, multiply and divide. That, plus the ability to think things through and use your common sense, is all you need. All the hard work has been done for you and summarized in the following pages.

For each type of dome there is a diagram and a table. The diagram shows how the struts are assembled and gives face and dihedral angles. The table beneath gives central angles, axial angles, and chord factors.

The *central angles* are the basis for all the other figures. Think of the dome struts as curved arcs drawn on the surface of a sphere. The central angle of a strut is the angle between the ends of the arc and

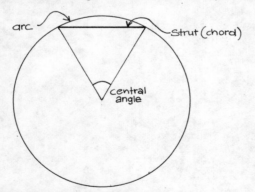

the center of the sphere. (In spherical trig, the central angle is used to define the length of its associated arc—an arc of X degrees has a central angle of X degrees.) The central angles are not of direct use to most dome builders, but they are included here in case you want to check or make further calculations from our figures.

The *chord factors* are the figures of interest to most dome builders. They are calculated from the central angles by means of this formula:

$$\text{Chord factor} = 2 \sin \left(\frac{central\ angle}{2} \right)$$

Once you have a table of chord factors for a particular dome, you can calculate strut lengths for any size dome you like.

Strut length = radius x chord factor

The result will be in feet if your radius was in feet, meters if your

radius was in meters, and so forth. If you want to know the size of the largest dome you can build with a certain length of material, the chord factors can tell you that too:

$$\text{Radius} = \frac{\text{strut length}}{\text{chord factor}}$$

Axial angles are useful in hub design. They are the angles the strut ends make with the center of the sphere.

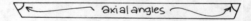

They are found by the formula

$$\text{Axial angle} = \frac{180° - \text{central angle}}{2}$$

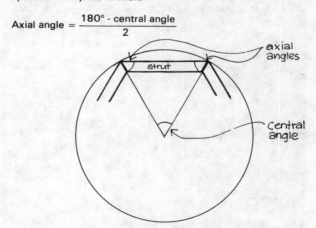

Face angles are the angles you should find at the tips of your skin panels. Rather than clutter the diagrams by labeling every angle, each

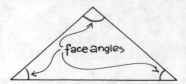

angle is given only once. Since the triangle is symmetrical you can easily find the other places it belongs by turning and flipping the triangle.

Dihedral angles are the angles between triangles. They are useful if you plan to bevel your skin panels or use beveled struts.

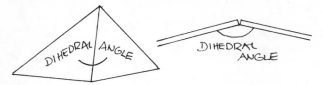

Calculating face and dihedral angles requires fairly elaborate trigonometry, and where we did not have the time for this, we made the measurements from models and indicated them as approximate.

The icosahedron is not the only solid from which domes may be derived. We give here analogous breakdowns derived from the octahedron. The tetrahedron can also be used. In fact, any irregular network of lines that can be drawn on a sphere can be used to design a dome, although no one has yet been willing to go *that* far.

Octa based breakdowns have the advantage of easy separation into hemispheres without the need to cut any members. This is true in all frequencies and both alternate and triacon breakdowns. Octa alternate breakdowns have the additional advantage of being easy to attach to ordinary structures.

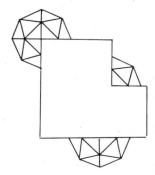

To make a complete sphere from an icosa breakdown, you have to repeat the basic triangle 20 times. For a octa-based breakdown, you repeat the basic triangle only 8 times. You will find that in order to get an equally smooth appearance with an octa breakdown, you will have to use a higher frequency.

For still other variations, like elliptical domes and higher frequency breakdowns, see *Domebook 2*.

ICOSAHEDRON

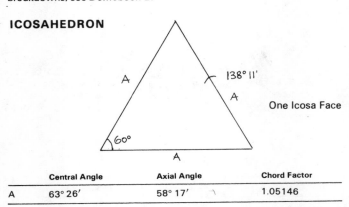

	Central Angle	Axial Angle	Chord Factor
A	63° 26'	58° 17'	1.05146

2V ICOSA ALTERNATE

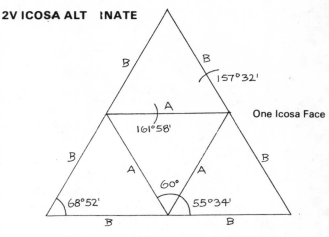

One Icosa Face

	Central Angle	Axial Angle	Chord Factor
A	36° 00'	72° 00'	0.61803
B	31° 43'	74° 08'	0.54653

3V ICOSA ALTERNATE

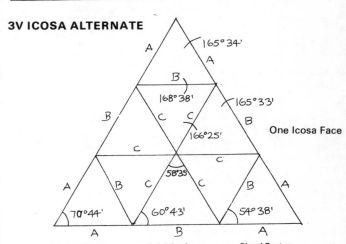

One Icosa Face

	Central Angle	Axial Angle	Chord Factor
A	20° 05'	79° 58'	0.34862
B	23° 17'	78° 22'	0.40355
C	23° 48'	78° 06'	0.41241

4V ICOSA ALTERNATE

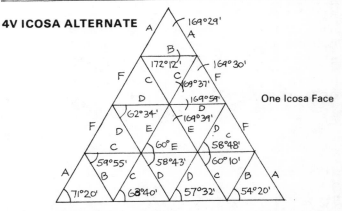

One Icosa Face

	Central Angle	Axial Angle	Chord Factor
A	14° 33'	82° 44'	0.25318
B	16° 59'	81° 31'	0.29524
C	16° 56'	81° 32'	0.29453
D	18° 00'	81° 00'	0.31287
E	18° 42'	80° 39'	0.32492
F	17° 10'	81° 25'	0.29859

2V ICOSA TRIACON

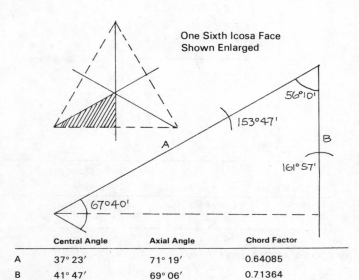

One Sixth Icosa Face
Shown Enlarged

	Central Angle	Axial Angle	Chord Factor
A	37° 23′	71° 19′	0.64085
B	41° 47′	69° 06′	0.71364

4V ICOSA TRIACON

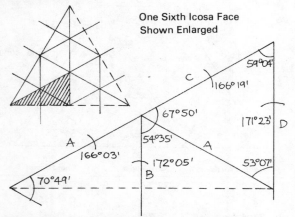

One Sixth Icosa Face
Shown Enlarged

	Central Angle	Axial Angle	Chord Factor
A	19° 22′	80° 19′	0.33609
B	22° 27′	78° 46′	0.38948
C	18° 02′	80° 59′	0.31337
D	20° 54′	79° 33′	0.36284

OCTAHEDRON

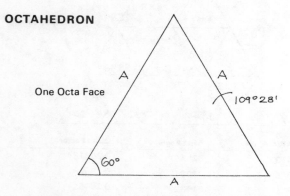

One Octa Face

	Central Angle	Axial Angle	Chord Factor
A	90° 00′	45° 00′	1.41421

2V OCTA ALTERNATE

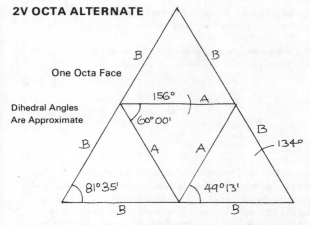

One Octa Face

Dihedral Angles
Are Approximate

	Central Angle	Axial Angle	Chord Factor
A	60° 00′	60° 00′	1.00000
B	45° 00′	67° 30′	0.76536

3V OCTA ALTERNATE

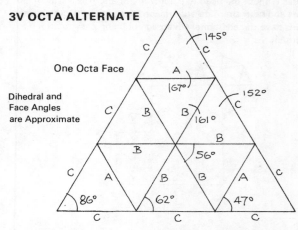

One Octa Face

Dihedral and
Face Angles
are Approximate

	Central Angle	Axial Angle	Chord Factor
A	36° 55′	71° 33′	0.63244
B	39° 15′	70° 23′	0.67152
C	26° 34′	76° 43′	0.45958

4V OCTA ALTERNATE

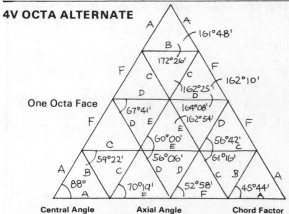

One Octa Face

	Central Angle	Axial Angle	Chord Factor
A	18° 26′	80° 47′	0.32036
B	25° 50′	77° 05′	0.44721
C	25° 21′	77° 19′	0.43887
D	30° 00′	75° 00′	0.51764
E	33° 35′	73° 13′	0.57735
F	26° 34′	76° 43′	0.45951

2V OCTA TRIACON

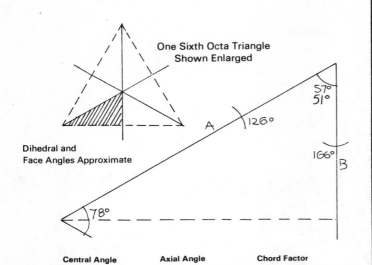

One Sixth Octa Triangle
Shown Enlarged

Dihedral and
Face Angles Approximate

57°
51°
126°
A
166°
B
78°

	Central Angle	Axial Angle	Chord Factor
A	54° 44′	62° 38′	0.91936
B	70° 32′	54° 44′	1.15470

4V OCTA TRIACON

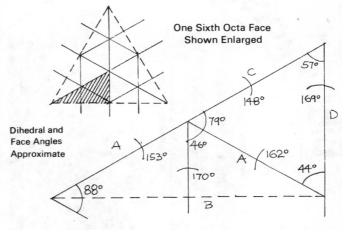

One Sixth Octa Face
Shown Enlarged

Dihedral and
Face Angles
Approximate

57°
C
148°
169°
D
79°
153°
A
46°
162°
A
170°
44°
88°
B

	Central Angle	Axial Angle	Chord Factor
A	30° 17′	74° 51′	0.52242
B	41° 54′	69° 03′	0.71510
C	24° 27′	77° 47′	0.42350
D	35° 16′	72° 22′	0.60584

Manufacturers and their products

The following manufacturers all offer information and literature on their products.

Cadco of N.Y. State, Inc. P. O. Box 874 Plattsburgh, N.Y. 12901	Plywood dome kits
Expodome International Ltd. 3737 Metropolitain E. Suite 1005 Montreal, Quebec, Canada H1Z 2K4	*Suspended skin domes* *Custom dome skins*
Dome East 325 Duffy Ave. Hicksville, N.Y. 11801	Dome model kits Large tent domes Computer calculations
Domebuilders Co. Box 4811 Santa Barbara, Cal. 93103	Dome Kits, hubs Recycled materials optional
Dyna-Domes 22226 N. 23rd Ave. Phoenix, Ariz. 85027	Dome Kits, hubs (Octahedral geometry)
Intergalactic Tool Co. 1601 Haight St. San Francisco, Cal. 94117	Portable tent domes
Geodesic Structures Dept. 15, P. O. Box 176 Hightstown, N.J. 08520	Plywood dome kits
Redwood Domes Aptos, Cal. 95003	Dome Kits

Synapse Box 554 Lander, Wyo. 82520	Custom-made prefab domes
Timberline 2015½ Blake St. Berkeley, Cal. 94704	Steel dome hubs Dome kits
Domaine Box 55 Mount Desert Maine 04660	*dome design, kits* *contracting*

Bibliography

Anyone who is sincerely interested in building a dome ought not to begrudge a few dollars for some of the books listed below. The expense will be only one or two percent of the cost of the dome and the information gained will pay for itself many times over in mistakes avoided and greater livability.

GENERAL DESIGN AND BUILDING TECHNIQUES
THE OWNER-BUILT HOME
Ken Kern

Ken Kern Drafting
Sierra Rt.
Oakhurst, Ca. 93644
300 pp $5

This book is full of useful details on all phases of house building. It is particularly good as a source of information on innovative and low cost building techniques, information often difficult to find anywhere else. Extensive lists of references are provided.

The urge for a dramatic architectural effect usually impels the modern designer to place the structure on the most prominent position of the site. Or, for ease of construction and access, the house is located on the most level portion of the site, irrespective of associated outdoor functions. Actually, it is the outdoor functions which require level ground; the house itself can be located on precipitous topography often to great advantage. It is usually a mistake to build upon the most beautiful, most level section of the site. Once this area is covered with massive structure, its original charm is destroyed.

About one percent of the cost of a wood house is for nails. If threaded nails (which have twice the withdrawal resistance) were used throughout, the cost of a $5000 house would be increased by $20.

If nothing else is learned from the series of chapters in this volume, it is hoped that the amateur home builder will at least be in position to ridicule the main slogan of the organized trades: "Relax—let an expert do it." We should not think of an expert builder as a special kind of man. We should rather think of every man as *a special kind of builder,* planning and working, perhaps with his wife, to meet the unique needs of his growing family.

At a recent American Institute of Architects convention, psychiatrist Humphrey Osmond said that the most carefully designed buildings today are *zoos.* An animal will die if not properly provided for. A human, however, learns to adjust. The emotional cost of this adjustment can hardly be assessed, but it must be considerable.

YOUR ENGINEERED HOUSE
Rex Roberts

J. P. Lippincott Co.
East Washington Sq.
Phila., Pa. 19105
237 pp $8.95

The engineered house is built to make sense, and it can give twice as much value for the money as an ordinary one. This book tells not only how to do things, but why, in a clear and graphic manner.

There isn't any name or type for your engineered house, no pigeonhole to put it in. For one thing, it most emphatically is not "modern". The first modern architect was a man who looked at his family, his needs, his location, his available materials, his tools, his strength, his resources, then built accordingly. He lived a long time ago.

The sun comes up in the east and goes down in the west. Your engineering must begin with this obvious but all-governing fact. If bacon is to be fried by daylight, the kitchen will look southeast. If shaving is to be by daylight, the bathroom will be close by.

Two vital work areas have been located on your previously blank piece of paper. You spend crucial morning minutes at lavatory and stove, and you have given the southeast sun a chance to make those desperate minutes as warm and cheerful as your nature will permit. The house, at least, will begin its day pleasantly.

A cry, "The eggs are boiling", can be heard through the bathroom wall. Your house, while pleasant is also efficient.

Since both kitchen and bathroom run on running water, the closer together they are, the shorter the pipes. Your house, already pleasant and efficient, is on its way to being inexpensive.

SHELTER
Lloyd Kahn and Others

Shelter Publications
P. O. Box 279
Bolinas, Cal. 94924
$5

Lloyd Kahn has been moving away from domes toward structures that use old building techniques, hand labor, and natural materials, with a minimum of flashy technology. *Shelter* will be a gigantic collection of hand-built shelter ideas from cultures primitive and modern all over the world. Recent refinements in dome design will also be included. *Shelter* is expected to appear in the fall of '73.

Here is a quick summary of some things I've learned about shelter:

1—Use of human hands is essential, at least in single-house structures. Human energy is produced in a clean manner compared to oil-burning machines. We are writing for people who want to use hands to build.

2—It took me a long time to realize the formula: Economy/ beauty/durability: time. You've got to take time to make a good shelter. Manual human energy. For example, used lumber looks better than new lumber, but you've got to pull the nails, clean it, work with its irregularities. A rock wall takes far more time to build than a sprayed foam wall.

3—The best materials are those that come from close by, with the least processing possible. Wood is good in damp climates, which is where trees grow. In the desert where it is hot and you need good insulation, there is no wood, but plenty of dirt, adobe. Thatch can be obtained in many places, and the only processing required is cutting it.

4—Plastics and computers are way overrated in their possible applications to housing.

5—There is a fantastic amount of information on building that has almost been lost. We'll publish what we can, not out of nostalgia, but because many of the 100 year old ways of building are more sensible *right now*. There are 80 year olds who remember how to build, and there are little-known books which we'll be consulting in transmission of hand-owner-self-build shelter information.

Lloyd Kahn, from his booklet "Smart But Not Wise".

BOOKS ABOUT DOMES
DOMEBOOK 2
Lloyd Kahn and others

Shelter Publications
Box 279
Bolinas, Cal. 94924
128 pp. $4

This is an indispensable book. It contains information on geodesic geometry, chord factors, models and the experience gained from the building of a dozen different kinds of domes, plus feedback and information from dome builders all over the country. If you get only one book from this list, it should be this one.

The 38 ft. plywood "Pease" dome that was being used as a temple burned down in less than an hour in July 1970. It burned so quickly that there was little chance to save it. The only thing interesting to note is that domes cave in not out and thus contain themselves. Please take fire into account when designing domes.

Because I was in too much of a hurry in sealing our dome, it rained inside during the first rain storm. It was a traumatic experience to have our floor and belongings covered with water in the middle of the night. The three of us ended up huddled in a dry spot on the floor in the least wet sleeping bag.

Domes get built out of whatever is available, whatever you can afford, or whatever you have the tools to work with.

DOME COOKBOOK
Steve Baer

Cookbook Fund—Lama Foundation
Box 422
Corrales, N.M. 87048
40 pp. $1

This should be called "Zome Cookbook". It discusses zonahedral geometry in a loose, informal way and includes experience with actual zome structures built with a variety of materials, including old car tops. The side ideas are as much fun as the main work. Nowhere else will you find the practical aspects of zomes discussed so well. Unfortunately, Lama Foundation has allowed it to go out of print. Bug them about it.

These are instructions on how to almost break out of prison. The prison is the paucity of shapes to which we have in the past confined ourselves because of our technology—industry— education—economy. There are no dramatic disclosures here; those have already been made to us when as children we first drew polygons, patterns, and messes of straight and squiggly lines. At anyone's finger tips lie many more solutions to the architectural geometric problems of enclosing areas and volumes than a life time of study of geometric regularities and systems offer. But we have sensible reasons for not breaking out into the huge freedom of irregular shapes—once done we would no longer have the aid of our machines, tools, and simple formulas. Our first move can be to explore the territory we have confined ourselves to; it is far bigger than we think. Eventually we must, aided by different kinds of tools and methods drawn from as yet unrelated branches of our sciences, go forward so that we find ourselves back with the man who works with branches, reeds and mud and who needn't worry about the angle a saw blade was set at years ago in a mill in another town.

GEODESICS
Edward Popko

University of Detroit Press
4001 West McNichols Road
Detroit, Mich. 48221
124 pp. $4

This was the first book to be devoted exclusively to geodesic domes. It contains very clear drawings of dome geometry, showing different breakdowns, orientations, truncations. Most of the book is taken up by 87 pages of photos of big industrial and exposition type domes, useful chiefly as a source of ideas and fantasies.

Although somewhat basic, it is necessary in our development from polyhedra to spherical structures to point out that spherical bodies may orient themselves in an infinite number of positions in space. In dealing with domes, however, only three basic conditions are considered: edge, face, and vertex zenith.

To this point our concern has primarily been with the basic icosahedral forms and their related duals. We have chosen to limit ourselves to this category of geometry for this family offers the greatest degree of regularity when translated into the spherical structures of which member length and joinery conditions become factors.

In dealing with the great range of conditions that the dome must geometrically satisfy (span and height most commonly) it becomes readily apparent that the basic icosahedron cannot remain in a pure state. This brings us to the matter of a geometrical breakdown. This can best be described as an attempt to expand the icosahedral form to satisfy the space requirements and allow the components from which it is made to remain within structural fabrication and erection limits.

FULLER PATENTS

from U.S. Dept. of Commerce
Patent Office
Washington, D.C. 20231
50¢ each

If you can untangle the patent language, you'll find a wealth of interesting ideas in Fuller's original patents. Especially recommended are the laminar dome and the tensile—integrity patents.

Building Construction   2,682,235
Fuller's first patent, which defines the geodesic dome concept. Illustrates a 16V dome with hub and truss details.

Laminar Geodesic Dome   3,203,144
Shows how to make domes out of folded diamonds. Chord factors for 3V and 4V domes are given. Also shows how a dome may be stretched.

Geodesic Structures   3,197,927
Ideas on how to construct domes from hexagons and pentagons.

Geodesic Tent   2,914,074
Illustrates a 6V dome with a suspended inner skin. Details on skin construction.

Self-Strutted Geodesic Plydome   2,905,113
Shows a 6V triacon dome made of overlapping plywood sheets.

Tensile-Integrity Structures   3,063,521
Contains many ideas for tensile-integrity domes and masts, with instructions for making a 270 boom tensile-integrity sphere.

Octahedral Building Truss   3,354,591
Defines the concept of the octet truss and suggests its use in masts and domes.

Synergetic Building Construction   2,986,241
Shows how the octet truss may be used in buildings.

Building Construction   2,881,717
Suggests ways of making domes and other structures from folded cardboard.

Other Interesting Patents

Plywood Domes—A. E. Miller   3,114,176
Construction details of the Pease plywood dome.

Method for Erecting Structures—Dante Bini   3,462,521
How to construct a ferro-cement dome by plastering an expandable mesh stretched over an air-tight membrane and then inflating it.

THE BIOGRAPHY OF A DOME
Robert Harding Wright

P. O. Box 1500
Salt Lake City, Utah 84110
84 pp.   *$4*

This book is especially interesting because it describes the construction of a large (63 ft. diameter) high frequency (10V) dome with vertical walls. Not many dome projects are this ambitious.

Like all things, building and living in a dome has some problems. Assuming you will have to borrow some money for construction as we did, the first problem is the bank. Banks are in the business of making money, which means protecting their investment. Therefore, the banks loan money on safe risks, which means on homes that could easily be sold if necessary. Therefore, conventional mass-type housing is what appeals to the banker. So it is really the banker who controls to a large extent the architecture of our homes. They base their thinking on the here and now, and if there is a revolution in the architectural styles of housing, it will be in spite of them, not because of them.

Sometimes problems crop up from completely unexpected sources. Ours was with subdivision approval. This had nothing to do with building a dome. The area, where we bought our lot had not been subdivided before, and no building permit could be issued without a subdivision approval. So we had to apply for a one lot subdivision, which involved getting approval from the flood control department. Well, it seems the county flood control department was engaged in a lawsuit with an irrigation company, which happened to have an irrigation canal going along the low edge of our property. This canal had been there since pioneer days. The flood control department, however, said they could not approve of our vast subdivision because the water from our house would run off into the canal and cause the canal to flood. After pointing out that this water had been doing exactly that for many years and after many other arguments, we finally got approval from the flood control department. Patience and persistence are great virtues when you get involved with this type of problem.

POPULAR SCIENCE DOME PLANS
Popular Science Plans Division

355 Lexington Ave.
New York, New York 10017

Sun Dome Plans #5519 $5

This was one of the first easily available sources of dome information. It gives chord factors and dimensions for a 3V 3/8 wood and plastic dome to be used as a greenhouse or swimming pool cover. See P.S. May '66. The same information can also be found in Domebook 2.

Hexa-Pent Dome #5544 $15

This is Fuller's plan for a 3V plywood dome that will withstand a load of 60 lbs. per sq. ft. For the price, you get complete plans, plus a structural analysis with which to impress building inspectors. See P.S. May & June '72.

Frame-Hung Dome #5556 $5

This plan is for a 3V 5/8 tube frame dome with a plywood inner shell. The hub design puts the frame in tension, and the shell in compression, thus increasing the strength of the dome. See **P.S.** November '72.

THE MOTHER EARTH NEWS

P. O. Box 38
Madison, Ohio 44057

issue no. 9 $1.35
subscriptions $6.00 (one year)

For those who would like to go a little deeper into dome math, *Mother* no. 9 contains an article on the subject by this editor (beware of mistakes in the worked example). The pages of the *Mother Earth News* frequently contain articles about novel shelter ideas that will be of interest to the amateur builder.

DOME COOKBOOK OF GEODESIC GEOMETRY
David Kruschke

2135 West Juneau Av.
Milwaukee, Wisconsin 53233
46 pp   *$1.50*

Here is a digest of basic dome math which demonstrates how to find chord factors (etc.), yourself if you're the sort who doesn't like having to depend on a computer.

The purpose of this book is to show the *actual derivation* of the chord factors and planar angles without the use of jargon, co-ordinates, and strange names. Also, there has been an attempt to use as few formulas and trig functions as possible.

Unlike *Domebook One* and *Domebook Two*, the chord factor results here are in close agreement with those of Buckminster Fuller. Oddly enough, this confusion and *this book* would have been unnecessary if Fuller would have published his derivations.

During the winter of 1970, this writer met some people who were writing *Domebook One*. These people *refused* to believe that there could exist chord factors that would determine a three frequency dome where *all* of the vertices at ground level would be in exactly the same plane (in spite of the fact that Buckminster Fuller has accomplished this years ago). As a result, both *Domebook One & Two* have incorrect statements about three frequency domes.

BOOKS THAT GO BEYOND DOMES
NATURAL STRUCTURES: TOWARD A FORM LANGUAGE
Robert Williams

Eudaemon Press
Box 236
Moorpark, Cal. 93021
263 pp.   *$6.50*

This book is an excellent compilation of information on regular polyhedra, Archimedean polyhedra, and their duals. Also covered are polygons and planar tesselations, space filling and sphere packing, and general techniques for generating forms. There is an abundance of excellent drawings. This book is invaluable as a general reference, bringing between two covers material previously scattered among half a dozen other books. Williams' premise is that we are cramping ourselves by using only a small fraction of the forms available to us.

An important manifestation of the lack of a *Form Language* can be seen in the complete awe of certain forms that are intuitively generated.

Consider, for example, the form called the *geodesic dome*. Originally designed as a solution to problems of space utilization, economic considerations, and mass production techniques, it is being replicated in various sizes for various human environments by both amateur and professional builders under the assumption that it is somehow the best solution to any problem. This fad thinking is, unfortunately, particularly characteristic of many people who have "dropped out" and consider that they are creatively seeking enriched environments. Since they have little understanding of the great variety of forms that may be appropriate for desired patterns, they rely on a few existing forms appearing to represent revolutionary concepts and ideals, but which really represent only an impoverished design vocabulary.

SHAPES, SPACE AND SYMMETRY
Alan Holden

Columbia University Press
440 W. 110th St.
New York, N.Y. 10025
200 pp. $11

This is a fine source book of 3-D design, dealing with all the primary forms and their evolution into more and more complex shapes. There are 202 handsome photographs showing the inter-relation of various solids. Just looking at the pictures is a stimulating experience. It's a model maker's delight.

Space provides no three-dimensional blackboard. We learn about space only by living in it. A child climbing in his jungle-gym may learn more about it than he will ever learn again, for his books will be made of two-dimensional sheets of paper.

The ideas of *duality* and *symmetry* are powerful intellectual instruments, often providing quick routes to conclusions that may otherwise seem hard to reach. Think again of the observation that each of the Platonic solids can be inscribed in a sphere. Then recall that each of them can also be inscribed in its dual, in such a way that its corners fall at the centers of its dual's faces. Then the sphere that inscribes it will touch the center of each of those dual faces. But the dual solid is also a Platonic solid. In other words, a spherical soap bubble, expanding inside a Platonic solid, can touch the centers of all its faces at the same time. Thus any of these solids cannot only be *inscribed in* a sphere but can also be *circumscribed around* a smaller sphere, just as a square can define both a circumscribed and an inscribed circle.

POLYHEDRON MODELS
Magnus J. Wenninger

Cambridge University Press
32 East 57th St.
New York, N.Y. 10022
208 pp. $14.50

Here are instructions for making models of 119 different polyhedra. Some of them are of fearsome complexity, but all of them can be built, and have been built, as the author's photographs testify. This should keep even the most die-hard model builder busy for quite a while.

In any convex solid, a theorem of Euclid tells us that the angles at a corner must add up to less than 360 degrees. After making a few models for himself, the reader will soon discover that the amount by which the angle-sum falls short of 360 degrees is quite considerable when there are few corners (e.g. 90 degrees for the cube, which has eight corners) but much smaller when there are many (e.g. 12 degrees for the snub dodecahedron, which has sixty corners). This observation was fashioned into a theorem by Rene' Descartes (1596-1650), who proved that the angular defect, added up for all the corners, always makes a total of 720 degrees.

To make a model of this polyhedron, you will have to prepare 76 parts for each faceted decagram alone, not to mention the other parts which serve as connectors. It may interest you to know that the total number of individual small segments of surface area generated by all the intersections of the three regular polygons belonging to the facial planes of this polyhedron reaches the imposing figure of 1232.

MISCELLANEOUS USEFUL BOOKS
IDEAS AND INTEGRITIES
Buckminster Fuller

Collier Books
The Macmillan Co.
Order Dept.
Front & Brown St.
Riverside, N.J. 08075
318 pp. $1.95

This is probably the best overview of Fuller's thoughts and ideas now available. Fuller is not easy reading. His use of the English language is not always conventional, and he has a way of packing several ideas into a single sentence. However, it is well worth the effort. Fuller has some very interesting ideas on the origin and development of domes, not to mention his ideas for the world of the future.

Class One of all history's domes is comprised of the hundreds of milleniums—old upside-down baskets which include the later evolution of baskets into boats and the re-upside-downing, once more, of boats to form the roofs of community meeting places and its later derivative *cathedral*. The nave (navy; Naga, the sea serpent god of the sea) is the upside-down boat. In Japan, the word for "ceiling" or "roof" means also "the bottom of the boat". In this oldest category of upside-down basket domes, there exists a word identification linking the earth's extreme territories which seems to tell us that men in their wooden basketry boats, rafts, catamarans, and canoes had once indeed conquered the whole dominion of earth. The once only oral words of South Africa and the Eskimo, designating their domical enclosures are now spelled respectively INDLU and IGLOO. Only man's later invention of phonetic spelling and its interpretive application by geographically remote, different men, in the documentation of these extreme Northern and Southern Hemisphere sound-words, must alone have occasioned the difference in spelling.

THE SENSUOUS GADGETEER
Bill Abler

Running Press
38 South 19th Street
Phila., Pa. 19103
144 pp. $3.95

The progression from nail-bender to craftsman need not be a long and difficult one. It's partly a process of acquiring a feel for the relations between tools and materials, partly of getting into the proper frame of mind. This book tells how to go about building something that feels right when it's done.

When you hit a nail with a hammer, keep your eye on the nail and hit hard. Press the nail into the wood with your fingers to set the point so that it will not skip aside when the hammer hits. Press the nail into the wood as you hit. First tap the nail to start it, and after that, hit the nail HARD. Hitting a nail hard reduces the chances that it will bend and fold up. Hitting the nail hard reduces the chances of injuring the work because the nail will accelerate too quickly to drag the work along with it. If a nail is hit softly, the friction bond between the wood and the nail will not be broken, so that the nail will pull the wood with it and break the wood. A slowly moving hammer will easily be deflected (onto your fingers) when it hits the nail.

Avoid driving nails parallel to the grain of the wood, especially small sticks of wood, and avoid driving nails parallel to the surfaces of plywood. Not only will this split the wood, but it will yield the weakest nailed joint. Nails hold in the wood because the wood fibers grip the nail, and if the nail travels parallel to the fibers they have no leverage to grip it. If you have to drive a nail parallel to the grain, you may want to use glue to strengthen the joint.

CLOUDBURST
A Handbook of Rural Skills & Technology
Edited by Vic Marks

Cloudburst Press
Box 79
Brackendale, B.C.
Canada
126 pp. $3.95

The people at Cloudburst have very kindly allowed us to reprint the first chapter of their new book (The 16 ft. Personal Dome) but if you are at all interested in home-built solutions to the problems of country living, you'll want to see the rest of it.

The design of a waterwheel is done according to the following steps. First the height of fall, and the volume of flow of the stream are determined. The amount of power available can then be computed. Next, the type of wheel should be selected: overshot wheels are easier to build, breast wheels can use lower falls; the selection of wheel will determine its diameter. The form of bucket is next determined. The computed edge speed of the wheel, and the volume flow of the stream will determine the volume capacity of the bucket necessary (Note: the buckets should never be more than 1/3 to 1/2 filled). The volume capacity of the buckets will fix the necessary breadth (width) of the wheel.

THE UNIVERSAL TRAVELER
Don Koberg and Jim Bagnall

William Kaufman, Inc.
One First Street
Los Altos, Cal. 94022
119 pp. $2.95

This is not a book about hitch-hiking. It is a book about creative problem-solving that uses the concept of the journey as a metaphor. It contains tips, techniques, habit breakers, games and suggestions for finding new pathways through the process of design. It should be useful to anyone who finds himself with a new problem to solve.

The desire for fame (social acceptance) and fortune (financial security) is a great human dream which sets up pride and fear barriers to the solution of problems. Acceptance of problem situations is often deterred by such fears; i.e., we are afraid to accept a problem because we think it will hold back our chances for social acceptance—someone will not like us if we get involved in this thing—or that it will cost us too much money.

One way to attempt to break this habit is to imagine that you have all the money you need and that your friends are liberal enough to be tolerant of your decisions.

Example: Imagine you have just won the Nobel Prize for Architecture. This brings a large cash award and great respect from professionals around the world. After you play this inflated role for a while, see how easy it would be for such a secure person to tackle the problem which faces you. Then realize that fears of losing something you do not have should not stand in your way any longer.

LAST WORD

We hope that you have enjoyed this book. Now that it's done, we have to admit that it has its faults. It's sort of lumpy, rather vaguely organized, and not at all complete. Maybe a better name for it would have been *The Dome Builder's Scrapbook*.

We want there to be a bigger and better second edition, and for that we need your help. We'd appreciate your comments and suggestions. And we'll need contributions from a lot more people. If everyone who built a dome stopped to write about it, there would be so much information in print that all of us could build perfectly functioning domes the very first time. We hope that this book has inspired you to make your own discoveries, and that you will add your experience to the next book.

John Prenis
161 W. Penn St.
Phila., Pa. 19144

Stuart Teacher
Running Press
38 South 19th St.
Phila., Pa. 19103

Vision

At first the eye is confused, dazzled. Unfamiliar figures fill space with an arbitrary jumble of lines. Slowly, a pattern takes shape. Lines and angles meet with perfect certainty, forming designs of rich symmetry. A basic element is discovered, then repeated; thus complexity arises from simplicity. From the repeated meeting of lines and angles the pattern grows, swiftly enfolding space in its own logic of unity until it stands complete in its own crystalline purity of form.

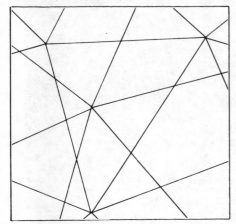 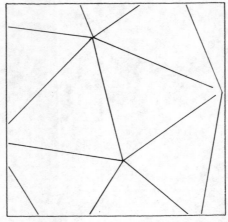 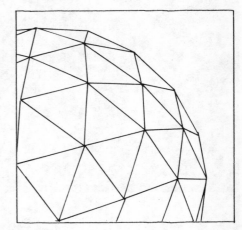

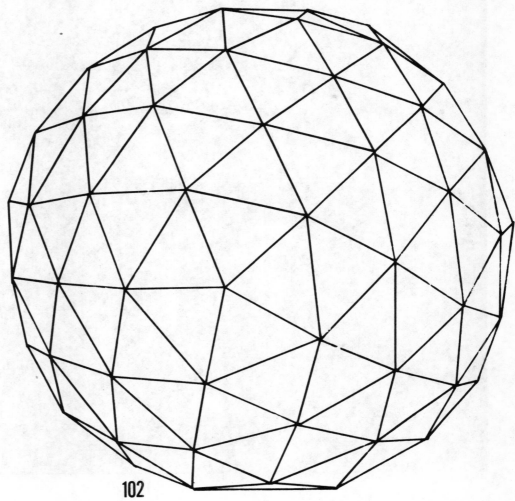

102

Dome Builder's
Handbook
STEREO VIEWER

3D VIEWER INSTRUCTIONS

While thumbing through this book, you may have noticed that many of the pictures are double. This is because they are intended to be seen in three dimensions with the help of the viewer.

Remove the page and paste it to a piece of thin cardboard. Cut out the pieces and assemble them according to the directions. When you are done, the two parts of the viewer should slide in and out freely.

To use the viewer, start by finding a place in front of a window where you will have a diffuse, shadowless light. Put the viewer down on the page with the divider separating the two pictures. On looking into the viewer, you will see two overlapping images. Allow your eyes to drift out of focus, and the two images will move together. Try to make them fuse into a single image. Put a finger on the divider tab and move your head and the rest of the viewer slowly back while concentrating on a prominent feature such as the crossing of two struts. When your eyes are at normal reading distance, you should see a single clear three dimensional image. With practice, you can run your eyes over it without losing the three dimensional effect, as though it were an actual object in front of you. Look out the window from time to

104

time at some distant object to rest your eyes.

You may notice an unaccustomed tugging in your eye muscles. This is because you are trying to gain voluntary control over what is normally an involuntary process. Normally your eyes angle slightly inward when focusing on a nearby object. When focusing on a distant object, the angle of convergence is so small, your lines of sight are practically parallel. With the viewer you are trying to combine close-up focus with parallel (distant) eye angle. It will take some practice. If you find that using the viewer causes eyestrain or headaches, stop until you get the advice of an eye doctor. If you can't get the viewer to work right away, don't despair. Put it away and try again another day. It's like whistling—some people learn the knack more quickly than others.

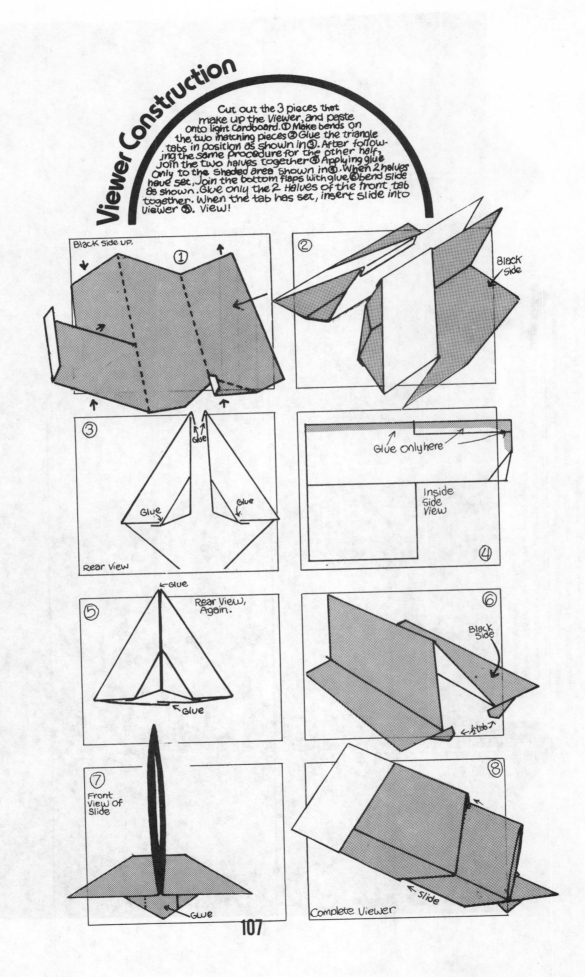

Viewer Construction

Cut out the 3 pieces that make up the Viewer, and paste onto light Cardboard. ① Make bends on the two matching pieces ② Glue the triangle tabs in position as shown in ③. After following the same procedure for the other half, Join the two halves together ④ Applying glue only to the Shaded area shown in ④. When 2 halves have set, Join the bottom flaps with glue ⑤ bend Slide as shown. Glue only the 2 Halves of the front tab together. When the tab has set, insert Slide into Viewer ⑧. View!

① Black Side up.

② Black Side

③ Glue — Glue — Glue — Rear View

④ Glue Only here — Inside Side View

⑤ Glue — Rear View, Again. — Glue

⑥ Black Side — ½ tab

⑦ Front View of Slide — Glue

⑧ Complete Viewer — Slide

107